DISCOVER
NORTH
AMERICA

Reader's
Digest

PUBLISHED BY THE READER'S DIGEST ASSOCIATION LIMITED

LONDON   NEW YORK   MONTREAL   SYDNEY

DISCOVER NORTH AMERICA

Translated and edited by Toucan Books Limited, London
for Reader's Digest, London

Translated and adapted from the French
by Andrew Kerr-Jarrett

For Reader's Digest
Series Editor: Christine Noble
Editorial Assistant: Caroline Boucher

Reader's Digest General Books
Editorial Director: Cortina Butler
Art Director: Nick Clark

First English language edition Copyright © 1999
The Reader's Digest Association Limited
11 Westferry Circus, Canary Wharf, London E14 4HE
www.readersdigest.co.uk

Reprinted with amendments 2000

Copyright © 1999
Reader's Digest Association Far East Limited
Philippines copyright © 1999
Reader's Digest Association Far East Limited
All rights reserved

ISBN 0 276 42442 5

Discover the World: NORTH AMERICA
was created and produced by Hubert Deveaux & Co, Paris
for Selection Reader's Digest S.A., Paris, and first published
in 1998 as *Regards sur le Monde: L'AMERIQUE DU NORD*

©1998 Selection Reader's Digest, S.A.
212 boulevard Saint-Germain, 75007, Paris

CONTENTS

INTRODUCING
NORTH AMERICA

From the jagged, man-made contours of the Manhattan skyline in the east to the snow-capped peaks rising above Vancouver in the west, from the icy wastes of Alaska and the Canadian tundra in the north to the steamy Gulf of Mexico and the swamplands of the south, from the pancake-flat expanses of the Great Plains to the rugged drama of the Rockies – the United States and Canada share a continent nearly twice the size of Europe and a history of European settlement.

Images of a continent

Space and diversity are the hallmarks of North America. Embracing the concrete canyons of New York, Chicago and Toronto as well as small Midwestern towns and villages set in the vast prairie grainlands, the continent rejoices in variety – of scenery, of climate, of people. Space, and the opportunities it offered to make a new life, is what drew people to the continent in the first place. They started with North America's earliest human colonisers who crossed from Siberia to Alaska some time between 30 000 and 11 000 years ago. Much later came the waves of European migration which broke over the continent from the east following Columbus's epoch-making transatlantic voyage in 1492.

For many Americans, the constantly shifting frontier was one of the defining experiences of their culture. Marking its westward progress are natural barriers, and as each one was crossed, new areas were opened up for settlement. Jamestown, England's first successful colony, lay near the northern end of the coastal plain that fringes the Atlantic seaboard, stretching from Cape Cod in the north, southwards to Florida, then west along the Gulf coast into Mexico. Rising less than 200 miles (320 km) west of the original Jamestown colony is the first major barrier, marking the landward edge of the coastal plain: the Appalachian Mountains slant diagonally for about 1500 miles (2400 km), from Alabama in the south to New England and Newfoundland in the north.

West of the Appalachians lie the great expanses of North America's interior lowlands. Underpinning these is a platform of ancient rock which for 600 million years has lain undisturbed by major mountain-building activity. In the north this platform lies naked, exposed and heavily scoured by ice age glaciers; it is known to geologists as the Canadian Shield. The permanently frozen wastes of Arctic tundra compose the northernmost swathes of the Canadian Shield. Farther south spread huge coniferous forests dotted with innumerable lakes. The Great Lakes of North America – Superior, Michigan, Huron, Erie and Ontario – fill huge valleys gouged out and expanded by advancing and retreating glaciers during the ice ages.

South and west of the lakes, the landscape changes, with sedimentary rocks such as sandstone and limestone covering the underlying shield. Here, the interior lowlands are shaped like a huge saucer. At the centre of the saucer is the upper Mississippi basin where the Ohio, Missouri and Mississippi rivers converge from the east, west and north respectively. To the west lie the Great Plains, once open prairies where the wild buffalo ranged, now North America's wheatbowl, rising to more arid cattle country farther west.

Then comes the great barrier of the Rockies. Beyond the Rockies lies a vast region of plateaus and desert basins, which rises on its far side to yet more mountain ranges emerging almost directly from North America's Pacific shore. This region, cradled between the Rockies and the coastal mountains, includes the deserts of Arizona, Nevada and southern California. To the west, the Pacific coast ranges include California's Sierra Nevada and the Cascade Range, stretching from northern California into the Canadian province of British Columbia. In the north, these mountains are clothed with forests, which feed a thriving timber industry. In California their valleys shelter fruit orchards and vineyards. Together with the Rockies and the Andes of South America, they are part of the great cordillera that runs along the entire western edge of the Americas, from Tierra del Fuego in the south to Alaska in the north.

Image of immensity Physically, the continent of North America comprises not just Canada and the United States, but also Mexico and the countries of Central America. The colours on this satellite photograph reflect the density of vegetation, from the reddish hues of the mountain tops and Arctic tundra, to the rich greens of the forested north-east and Mississippi Delta, to the icy wastes of Canada's far north and its island neighbour, Greenland.

Wilderness in Acadia Mount Desert Island off the coast of Maine. Cobblestone beaches, evergreen forests and granite cliffs are among the attractions of Acadia National Park, which covers much of the island. Early European visitors included the Frenchman Antoine de la Mothe Cadillac, founder of Detroit, after whom the island's highest peak, Cadillac Mountain, was named. Inset, right: Moosehead Lake, Maine. Lying more than 1000 ft (300 m) above sea level, the island-dotted lake, the largest in New England, is a favourite haunt of weekenders and holidaymakers.

Island sentinels The Magdalene Islands – Îles de la Madeleine to their French-speaking inhabitants – lie in the Gulf of St Lawrence, north of Prince Edward Island. Long, thin sandbanks link the six main islands, whose red sandstone cliffs rise dramatically from the beaches that skirt them. In March each year, with the Gulf of St Lawrence partially frozen over, the Madelinots used to take to the ice to hunt seal. Since that has become politically controversial, they have had to rely on their other main industry – fishing.

Mist over the Clinch River Mist fills the valley of the Clinch River, which snakes through the Appalachian Mountains in Virginia and Tennessee. In spring rhododendrons (right), originally introduced from Asia, spatter the mountainsides with colour.

The river road to the West *Dawn rises over a bend in the Missouri. In 1804-5, the army officers Meriwether Lewis and William Clark became the first explorers to follow the river from its junction with the Mississippi to its source in the Rockies. Today, a complex system of dams and reservoirs regulates the flow of the 2466 mile (3969 km) river.*

Cattle country *In South Dakota the prairies of the Midwest rise gradually to meet the foothills of the Rockies. South Dakota is one of the most sparsely populated US states and most people live from agriculture, including cattle ranching. Several Indian reservations, including the Cheyenne River reservation, lie within the state.*

The mighty buffalo *As many as 60 million buffalo, or American bison (Bison bison), roamed the Great Plains when the Europeans arrived in North America. For the Plains Indians, buffalo provided the meat they ate, the leather for their clothing and tents, and the tendon strings for their bows. By 1900 it had been slaughtered to near extinction by white hunters and was saved only by action from conservationists. Today there are some 200 000 buffalo in managed herds.*

Springtime among the glaciers *The white flowers of beargrass (Xerophylum tenax) stud a valley in Glacier National Park, Montana. Each plant has a stalk up to 5 ft (1.5 m) tall and blossoms only once every five to seven years. Since 1932 Glacier National Park and the adjoining Waterton Lakes National Park in Canada have been administered as one. Glaciers carved out the region's lakes and remain on many of the mountain peaks.*

11

Lapping waters of the Olympic
Large boulders and sea stacks dot the 57 mile (92 km) stretch of Pacific coast that lies within Olympic National Park in Washington State. Inland, the Olympic peninsula rises to the 7966 ft (2428 m) peak of Mount Olympus, named in 1788 by English sea captain John Meares after the home of the gods in classical Greek mythology. 'If that be not the home where dwell the Gods,' he wrote, 'it is beautiful enough to be, and I therefore call it Mount Olympus.'

Denali splendour A female moose (Alces alces) in characteristic pose, its feet in water, feeding on the aquatic plants that make up a large part of its diet. Covering more than 7400 sq miles (19 000 km²) of southern Alaska, Denali National Park encompasses lakes, glaciers, tundra and North America's highest peak, Mount McKinley (20 320 ft/6194 m).

Primeval forest *Mosses shroud the tree trunks and drip from the branches in the Olympic peninsula's rare temperate rain forest. The air is thick with moisture, due to fogs and rain-heavy clouds rolling in off the Pacific. Creatures that make their home here include Roosevelt elk (Cervus elaphus), a subspecies of the North American elk or moose, and 10 in (25 cm) long yellow slugs known as banana slugs (Ariolimax columbianus), which live for up to six years.*

At home in the tundra *The arctic fox (Alopex lagopus) lives in the Arctic and tundra regions of North America, Europe and Asia. In winter its fur is white; in summer some foxes turn a cream colour, some a greyish blue. The blue fur was once much sought after as a fur to wear.*

Rock and beach *Haystack Rock at Cannon Beach, Oregon, rises 235 ft (72 m) from the waters that lap its base. It is a favourite nesting spot for sea birds, including the tufted puffin. The 9 mile (15 km) strand of Cannon Beach is one of Oregon's most popular seaside destinations.*

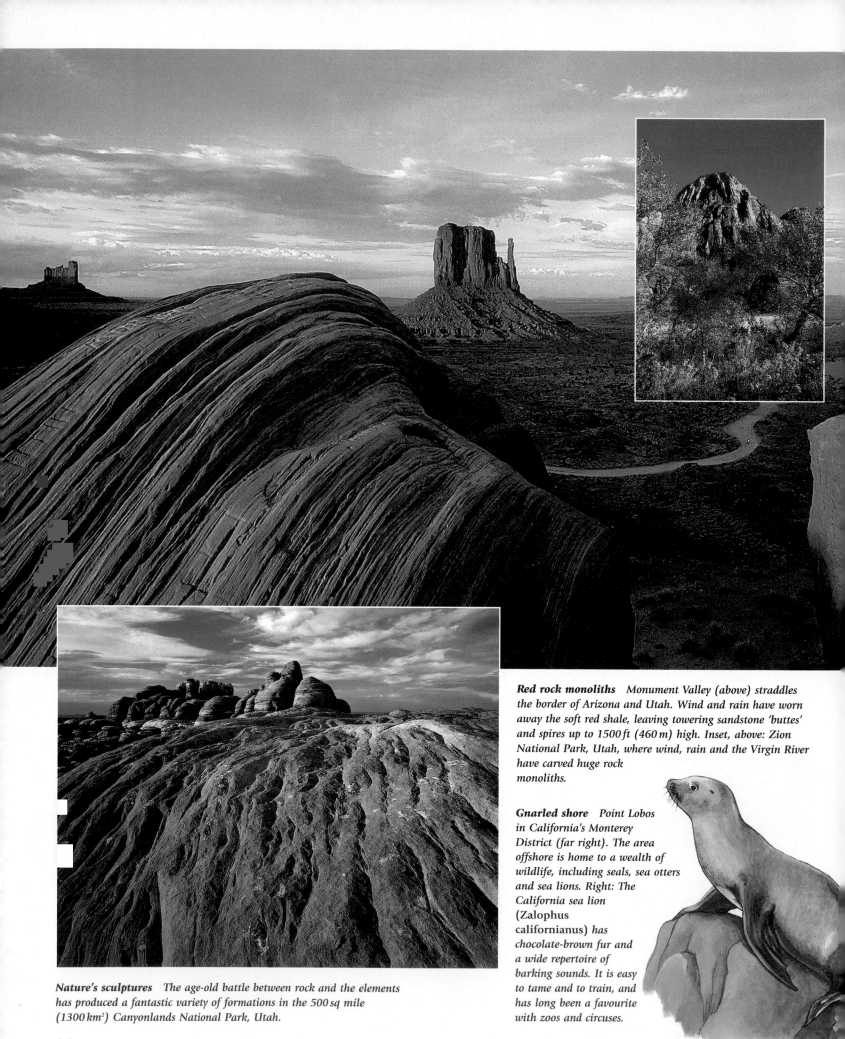

Red rock monoliths Monument Valley (above) straddles the border of Arizona and Utah. Wind and rain have worn away the soft red shale, leaving towering sandstone 'buttes' and spires up to 1500 ft (460 m) high. Inset, above: Zion National Park, Utah, where wind, rain and the Virgin River have carved huge rock monoliths.

Gnarled shore Point Lobos in California's Monterey District (far right). The area offshore is home to a wealth of wildlife, including seals, sea otters and sea lions. Right: The California sea lion (Zalophus californianus) has chocolate-brown fur and a wide repertoire of barking sounds. It is easy to tame and to train, and has long been a favourite with zoos and circuses.

Nature's sculptures The age-old battle between rock and the elements has produced a fantastic variety of formations in the 500 sq mile (1300 km²) Canyonlands National Park, Utah.

A brief history

L'Anse aux Meadows lies at the northern tip of Newfoundland. Here, in the 1960s, the Norwegian archaeologist Anne Stine Ingstad and her husband Helge Ingstad found the remains of three Viking long-houses dating from around AD 1000. They were proof that the Norse sagas, first written down in the 12th century, were records of actual events – the earliest known Europeans to reach the Americas were Norsemen, 500 years before Columbus. Leif Eriksson, their leader, was blown off course on a sea journey from Norway to Greenland and reached North America, which he named Vinland.

Life in Vinland
At L'Anse aux Meadows the first Viking settlement in North America has been reconstructed.

Conquistador Juan Ponce de León is believed to have sailed with Columbus in 1492. He took Puerto Rico for Spain in 1508, and in 1513 became the first European to reach Florida.

River meeting A 19th-century French artist, Théodore Gudin, painted this romanticised view of Jacques Cartier's first encounter with the St Lawrence River in 1534.

The early explorers

The first European outposts in North America survived no more than a few years. The next Europeans to land were led by an Italian in the service of King Henry VII of England. In May 1497, Giovanni Caboto, better known as John Cabot, set sail from Bristol in the *Matthew,* and on June 24, less than five years after Columbus made his first landfall in the Caribbean, stepped ashore on Cape Breton Island in modern Nova Scotia. Cabot sailed up the coast as far as the northern tip of Newfoundland before heading home.

Four years later a Portuguese mariner, Gaspar Corte Real, explored the coasts of Labrador and Newfoundland. Like Columbus before them, both Cabot and Corte Real had hoped to find a route west across the Atlantic to the rich trading markets of China and India, and thought they had reached a corner of Asia.

In Europe, news of the lands beyond the ocean sparked curiosity and envy, and a spate of similar quests followed. In 1513 the Spaniard Juan Ponce de León explored the Florida coast. In due course Spanish settlements and garrisons were established on the sites of Santa Barbara, Los Angeles and San Francisco. In 1524 the Florentine Giovanni da Verrazano, sailing in the service of King Francis I of France, reached the North American coast at what is now Cape Fear in North Carolina and followed it as far north as Nova Scotia. The Breton Jacques Cartier dreamed, like many others, of finding a sea route to Asia. Setting sail from Saint-Malo in 1534, he explored the Gulf of St Lawrence. He returned the next year and sailed up the St Lawrence River as far as modern Quebec and then went by land as far as an island at the confluence of the Ottawa and St Lawrence rivers where Montreal now stands. A third expedition in 1541 took Cartier once more to Quebec. In the south-west, meanwhile, Francisco Vázquez de Coronado set out in 1540 from the colony of New Spain (now Mexico) on a two-year expedition that would take him into what is now New Mexico, Texas and Kansas. One of his lieutenants was the first European to see the Grand Canyon. All this time, information was filtering back to Europe, and a new map of the world began to emerge.

Traders and colonists

By 1600, Europeans controlled most of the Atlantic coastline, the Gulf of Mexico and the Pacific coast from Mexico as far as northern California. Europe itself was in turmoil, riven by wars of religion. In this climate, more and more people opted to seek their fortunes or a new life safe from religious persecution on the far side of the Atlantic. At the same time, rivalry among the powers grew sharper as each sought its share of the spoils. The

AMERICA SEPTENTRIONALIS.

other riches: fish, furs and land to colonise. But it was not, of course, unoccupied land, and relations with the American Indians varied. The French, more interested in trade than land, invited tribal chiefs to Montreal and distributed gifts as tokens of friendship. English settlers generally negotiated agreements with the local Indian nations about what land they would occupy. The land rights of the Indians were usually enshrined in the agreements, though these were often breached. The life of Matoaka, better known as Pocahontas, daughter of a powerful American Indian leader, reflects some of the ups and downs of this relationship. The story of how she saved the life of one of the founders of the Jamestown colony, Captain John Smith, is now widely regarded as myth. But it is true that in 1612, during a time of hostilities between the settlers and the Indians, she was taken hostage by the English and one of the settlers, John Rolfe, fell in love with her. They married, and this ushered in a period of peace. In 1616 Matoaka and her husband went to London, where they were received amid great interest at the court of James I. Tragically, on the eve of her return home, Matoaka caught smallpox and died.

Amerigo and America A detail from a French atlas of 1631. A German geographer, Martin Waldseemüller, had coined the name America in his Introduction to Cosmography, published in 1507. The name came from the Italian explorer of Guyana, Amerigo Vespucci.

Voyages of Discovery:
— Erik the Red, c.985
--- Leif Eriksson, c.1000
— Columbus, 1492-93
▪▪▪▪ Cabot, 1497
— Corte Real, 1500
•••• da Verrazano, 1524
— Cartier, 1534 and 1535
— Francis Drake, 1577-80

The principal exploration routes (right)

first English attempt at a permanent colony – Sir Walter Raleigh's settlement at Roanoke Island off the coast of North Carolina – had vanished without trace by 1590, but a new and successful attempt was made at Jamestown, founded in 1607. The next year the Frenchman Samuel de Champlain settled a group of colonists at Quebec, and soon French fur traders and Jesuit missionaries led by Indian guides were penetrating far into the interior. The Mayflower Pilgrims arrived at Cape Cod in 1620, and

the Dutch founded New Amsterdam (today's New York) in 1626. By the 1670s, English explorers were crossing the Appalachian Mountains. In 1682 the Frenchman Robert de La Salle, starting in Canada, made an epic journey down the Mississippi river to its mouth, where he founded the colony of Louisiana.

In place of the treasures of Asia – spices, gold and precious stones – the Europeans in North America discovered

River navigator English explorer Henry Hudson meets chiefs of the Mohican nation in 1609. Commissioned by the Dutch East India Company to find a 'north-east passage' to Asia, Hudson sailed into New York Bay and then 150 miles (240 km) up the river that now bears his name.

Crossing from Siberia

The human story of North America started in Alaska during the ice ages. Around 28 000 years ago, with much of the world's oceans locked up as ice, a land bridge linked Siberia in Asia to America's far north-western thumb. The ancestors of today's American Indians started to cross from Asia into Alaska, where glaciers covered what is now Canada and prevented them from moving farther inland. By about 12 000 years ago, however, the glaciers were beginning to melt. Sea once more filled the Bering Strait, but to the east and south the way lay clear into the rest of the Americas. By the time of Christ, small communities were thinly scattered across much of North America.

A mosaic of peoples

By the time Columbus first crossed the Atlantic in 1492, North America's human population was a mosaic of great diversity. There were some 240 different tribal groups, speaking more than 500 different languages. In the Eastern woodlands there were three main groups – tribes speaking languages in the Iroquois family, the Algonquin family and the Sioux family. Bands a few hundred strong occupied particular territories, building wigwams or long houses of tree bark and making clothes from animal skins. By the time the Europeans arrived, a handful of tribal confederacies was beginning to emerge, the most famous of which would be the Iroquois League.

The Europeans changed everything. Even where there was little direct contact, the coming of the horse affected the way that many American Indians lived. Although indigenous horses had once roamed the continent, these had

died out some 10 000 years ago. The Spanish reintroduced horses in the 16th century, and some escaped to the wild, where they thrived and spread. Many of the Plains tribes had turned to farming for their livelihood, but with fast, nimble-footed horses to carry them, several went back to a nomadic life based on buffalo hunting. The living was so good that tribes from elsewhere, such as the Cheyenne and Blackfoot from the north-east, moved down to the Plains. The horse also proved its worth in warfare – in intertribal raids and against the Europeans.

The white man's road

Though the horse brought benefits, other European imports brought disaster on the Indians – above all, the concept of private property which was almost totally alien to Indian culture. Some tribes sought an accommodation with the newcomers. In the southern Appalachians, the Cherokee, an Iroquois-speaking nation, traded with English settlers in the Carolinas from about 1630, and sided with the British in their wars against the French and Spanish. This alliance was confirmed in a series of treaties signed during the 18th century with the British and later the new United States authorities. In spite of these treaties, the

Dance and ritual Women perform a ritual dance (far left). Totem poles were special to the North-west nations (left).

Hunting buffalo The writer and artist George Catlin was fascinated by American Indian life. He travelled extensively in the early 1830s, making sketches and paintings like this one. His Letters and Notes on the Manners, Customs, and Condition of the North American Indians was published in 1841.

lands assigned to the Cherokee were whittled away by white settlers, leading to frontier wars and the emigration of many bands to the West.

In 1828 a new leader, the mixed-race John Ross, took over among the Eastern Cherokee. He recognised the need to adapt or die, to 'take the white man's road'. In 1825 he had helped to establish a Cherokee capital at New Echota, Georgia, and later promulgated a Cherokee constitution based on that of the United States. But in 1828 Andrew Jackson was elected president and gave his backing to the Indian Removal Act, which proposed removing all American Indians to west of the Mississippi. At the same time the state of Georgia confiscated Cherokee lands and started dividing them up among white settlers. John Ross took the fight to the US courts – and won. In 1831 and again in 1832 the US Supreme Court ruled in favour of the Cherokee, but Jackson refused to enforce the decisions. In despair the Cherokee signed a treaty in 1835 by which they gave up their homeland in return for $5 million and 7 million acres (2.8 million ha) in Oklahoma.

The Indian Wars

As it turned out, the Indians were not safe even west of the Mississippi. When gold was found in California in 1848, the overland routes from the East to the Pacific suddenly became important. Wagon trains passed across the Great Plains bringing white settlers, and once more the lands and livelihood of the American Indians were under threat. The resulting Indian Wars lasted on and off for three decades, and were bitterly fought. By the end of 1890, however, the struggle was over, and for long years to come, the demoralising life of the reservation was the fate that lay in store for North America's native inhabitants.

Today's American Indians

At the beginning of the 20th century, the American Indian population of the USA stood at 300 000. On the brink of the 21st century, they number more than 2 million, more than half of whom live on or near federal Indian reservations. These are held in trust by the federal government, which has a Bureau of Indian Affairs, for the different Indian nations. Within the reservations local government lies in the hands of elected tribal councils, which represent the tribe in their dealings with the federal and state authorities.

Blackfoot
Crow
Cheyenne
Sioux
Navajo
Apache
Osage
Cherokee

■ Principal reservations

Custer's last stand On June 25, 1876, Sitting Bull led a combined Sioux and Cheyenne force in a stunning defeat of General George Custer's 7th Cavalry at the Battle of the Little Bighorn. A contingent led by another ferocious opponent of the white men, Crazy Horse, also took part.

Geronimo Apache chief Geronimo led a struggle against federal troops and settlers in south-east Arizona and New Mexico for ten years. Forced to surrender in 1886, he subsequently became a farmer in Oklahoma.

19

The French colonists

Fur provided the wealth of France's North American possessions. By 1650 the colony of New France had three main settlements along the St Lawrence River – Quebec, Trois Rivières and Montreal – and a chain of military forts and trading posts was established along the St Lawrence Valley, through the region of the Great Lakes and down into the Mississippi basin. The French colonists' dependence on Indian fur trappers and traders meant that they had to stay friendly with the local nations, in particular the Algonquin and Huron tribes, with whom they formed an alliance against the pro-British Iroquois League. Although it was never as rich or as populous as the English colonies, New France had a population that grew steadily from 200 residents in 1642 to 2500 in 1663 and 8500 in 1676. By the start of the 18th century local industries began to emerge, notably shipbuilding and iron-founding.

By the mid 18th century the French seemed to be in a stronger position to control North America as a whole than the richer British colonies on the east coast. Their

England's first American colonies

On May 14, 1607, a band of 105 settlers sent by the Virginia Company of London disembarked at the marshy site that would become known as Jamestown. They traded with the local American Indians for corn (maize), and learned how to plant tobacco, which ensured the colony's survival.

On November 21, 1620, the *Mayflower* dropped anchor off Cape Cod. Of the 102 settlers on board, 35 were members of an extreme Puritan sect. The other 67 were there to protect the interests of the London merchants who were financing the venture. The following autumn, having successfully reaped their first harvest, the settlers celebrated with a feast of turkey, corn and pumpkin – the foods that had kept them alive. The Thanksgiving holiday is still celebrated on the last Thursday in November.

On September 3, 1609, Henry Hudson, an English navigator sailing in the service of the Dutch, found a harbour at the mouth of the river that was named after him. The Dutch established the colony of New Netherland, which included Long Island and the Hudson Valley. In 1626 they bought Manhattan Island from the local American Indians, and by 1653 New Amsterdam had become a town of 800 people. In 1664 they lost it to the English. Renamed New York, it continued to thrive.

Profit from barter
This 19th-century illustration (above) shows a French fur trapper bartering with Indian hunters. In an age with no central heating, fur clothing was a valuable commodity.
Left: The first Thanksgiving took place in 1621.
Bottom: An 18th-century engraving of a tobacco plant in flower.

How France and Spain lost North America

Bit by bit the French lost ground, first to the British and then the Americans. In 1713 France ceded Newfoundland and Nova Scotia to Britain. In 1763 they lost Canada. In 1803 Napoleon sold Louisiana to the United States for $15 million. In 1819 Spain followed the French example and sold Florida for $5 million.

chain of forts boxed in the British to the north and much of the west; to the south their colony of Louisiana controlled the mouth of the Mississippi as well as much of the Mississippi basin. The one gap was the Ohio valley, and to plug this an expedition marched into the valley in 1749 to claim it for France.

The British hastily founded an Ohio Company to put in a claim of their own, and later sent an expedition led by the young George Washington. He was bested by the French in a clash that helped to trigger the French and Indian War (1754–63), which spelt the end of France's empire in

North America. In 1759 General James Wolfe won a surprise victory over the Marquis de Montcalm. Quebec fell, and so did Montreal the following year. Under the Treaty of Paris in 1763, New France and its French-speaking colonists became British.

Founding fathers

Britain had won a resounding victory, but with the French threat gone, the 13 British colonies – New York, Rhode Island, New Hampshire, Massachusetts, Connecticut, New Jersey, Pennsylvania, Delaware, Maryland, Virginia, North Carolina, South Carolina and Georgia – no longer felt much need of the mother country's military protection. The chief weakness of the British colonies was their disunity, which reflected the varied circumstances under which they had been founded – some by people seeking the freedom to pursue their particular brand of Christianity, some by settlers and London-based capitalists wanting a profitable return on their investment, and some by wealthy individual proprietors who were granted vast tracts of land by the Crown, where they could pursue a variety of philanthropic, religious or commercial schemes.

The religious motive was strongest in New England, where the Pilgrim Fathers founded their Plymouth colony in 1620 and, ten years later, another group of Puritans led by John Winthrop established the Massachusetts Bay colony. In the so-called Middle Colonies, religion also played its part in the founding of Maryland and Pennsylvania. In 1632

King Charles I granted the Catholic Lord Baltimore a tract of land beside the Chesapeake Bay, and half a century later Charles II granted another tract of land to the Quaker William Penn. In the South, the Carolinas were colonised by groups of proprietors from the 1660s onwards. Georgia's founding father was a philanthropic former army officer and MP, James Oglethorpe, whose intention was to settle imprisoned debtors there, so that they could create new lives.

In the space of 150 years, the ventures started by groups of religious refugees, wealthy proprietors, debtors and fortune-hunters prospered beyond measure. The ports and cities buzzed with commercial life and there were thriving colleges of education. A growing sense of success brought with it a growing assertiveness, which would soon make itself felt in a determination to win outright independence from the mother country.

The Salem witch trials

When two young girls in Salem, Massachusetts, fell ill in January 1692 the doctor diagnosed a case of witchcraft. Soon other girls started to fall into strange convulsive fits in which they 'cried out' names, believed to be those of the people who had bewitched them. In 17th-century New England witchcraft was punishable by death. A special court was set up and Bridget Bishop, the first to be tried and found guilty on the grounds that her name had been 'cried out', was hanged on June 10. In all, 14 women and five men were executed, before public reaction forced Governor William Phipps to disband the court in October.

A tea party and intolerable acts

Seeking to recoup some of the costs of maintaining military forces to defend North America, the British Parliament tried to impose various taxes on the colonists. The Tea Act of 1773 was designed to help the troubled British East India Company by encouraging it to dump unsold tea from India in the American colonies. American merchants suddenly found their profits threatened, and to make matters worse, the passing of the Tea Act coincided with a period of economic and financial crisis in the colonies. Anger and exasperation boiled over, and in Boston a group of citizens

Heroic moments   *A modern depiction of the Boston Tea Party in 1773 (above).*
Below: George Washington crosses the Delaware River on Christmas Day, 1776. This painting by the German-born artist Emanuel Leutze has become one of the best-loved images of the American Revolution.

A life in bondage

Slavery arrived early in the American colonies. A Dutch ship brought Virginia its first consignment of slaves from Africa in 1619, just over ten years after the colony was founded. For a long time, the numbers of slaves remained fairly modest – just over 250 000 by 1750. A century later, however, there were over 4 million slaves in the Southern states. The growth of the cotton plantations from the 1790s onwards brought a corresponding rise in the slave population. Among the slaves, 75 per cent were agricultural labourers and 25 per cent worked in industries such as mining or as domestic servants. Generally speaking, the servants were the best off and might even be granted their freedom, or earn enough to buy it.

disguised themselves as American Indians, clambered on board ships carrying the controversial tea and hurled it into the harbour – the so-called Boston Tea Party. In retaliation the Westminster Parliament passed a series of Acts – dubbed the 'Intolerable Acts' by the Americans – closing the port of Boston.

In September 1774 delegates from 12 colonies met in Philadelphia to decide upon resistance to Britain. The following April the first shots of the American Revolutionary War (the War of Independence) were fired when local militia clashed with British troops at Lexington and Concord in Massachusetts. On July 4, 1776, the Declaration of Independence,

1763 Territories :
- English
- Spanish
- French
- Russian

Alaska

Pacific Ocean

Hudson Bay

CANADA

St Lawrence

Miquelon St Pierre

NEW SPAIN

Mississippi

Atlantic Ocean

drawn up by Thomas Jefferson with the help of Benjamin Franklin and John Adams, was issued. American troops were fighting for a cause they believed in, and they received crucial help from France and, to a lesser extent, Spain and The Netherlands. The final blow for the British came on October 19, 1781, when troops under Lord Cornwallis besieged at Yorktown, Virginia, were obliged to surrender. In the Treaty of Paris in 1783, Britain experienced one of the most humiliating reverses in its history when it acknowledged the independence of the 13 former colonies.

notions of citizenship and its rights that inspired generations of political fighters from the French Revolution onwards.

George Washington, hero of the war for independence, was elected first president of the United States in 1788. The new nation expanded steadily to the west. Kentucky became a state in its own right in 1792, Tennessee in 1796 and Ohio in 1803. By 1821, these had been joined by Indiana, Illinois, Missouri,

Moment of history
This painting by Gerome Ferris shows Franklin, Adams and Jefferson signing the Declaration of Independence (above). The British surrender at Yorktown, painted by the French artist Louis-Nicolas van Blarenberghe (left).

Forging the Constitution

In 1787 a constitution was approved at a convention in Philadelphia. Carefully balancing the powers of the states with those of the federal government, it was based on the principle that the three branches of government – executive, legislative and judicial – should be kept separate in order to prevent any one branch becoming too powerful. There was to be a powerful federal Congress, where states were represented according to size of population in the lower house, but equally in the upper house or Senate. The power of the president was defined and limited. There was to be an independent judiciary, and later amendments incorporated a Bill of Rights to safeguard the freedom of individual citizens. One of the most influential documents ever published, the Constitution enshrined

Maine, Mississippi and Alabama. By mid century Texas and California had been annexed from Mexico. In the North-west, the 49th parallel had been established as the frontier with British-ruled Canada.

The population was also expanding – the 1830s and 1840s saw a huge influx of European immigrants, 2.5 million in all, mostly from Ireland and Germany. By 1850 the population had passed the 23 million mark. Visitors from Europe were often amazed by the democratic manners of this new society – the lack of deference towards wealth and rank, the freedoms enjoyed by women, the ease with which a person of ability could rise from poverty to riches and respect. But, of course, inequalities did exist, and most glaringly the inequality between the slaves and the free. By the mid 18th century this was the burning issue.

The Missouri Compromise

For most of the republic's history, a balance had existed between the slave states of the South and the free states of the North, where slavery was not permitted. Then slave-owning Missouri applied for full statehood, threatening to upset the balance. Senators from the North protested vigorously until, finally, a deal was struck. According to the Missouri Compromise, Maine, previously part of Massachusetts, would join the Union as a free state to counterbalance Missouri. Territory lying to the north of latitude 36° 30' would be free; that to the south would be slave-owning. This worked for a time, but increasingly there were those who were not willing to tolerate slavery anywhere in the Union. In 1854 the Kansas-Nebraska Act passed through Congress, helping to mobilise Northern antislavery feeling. Effectively tearing up the Missouri Compromise, this allowed new states in the expanding West to choose for themselves whether they would permit slavery or not.

Chinatown During the Gold Rush of 1849, tens of thousands of Chinese emigrated to California, especially San Francisco, where they soon formed a tight-knit community. This provoked a reaction among white workers, who felt they were being deprived of jobs by the immigrants.

Map labels:

CIVIL WAR 1861-65

- ⎯⎯ border between North and South
- ▢ Union States (North)
- ▨ Confederate States (South)
- ✮ major battle

WISCONSIN · Lake Michigan · MICHIGAN · Lake Erie · PENNSYLVANIA · New York
IOWA · MICHIGAN · N.J.
INDIANA · OHIO · *Gettysburg* · MARYLAND · DEL..
ILLINOIS · Cincinnati · WEST VIRG. · *Antietam* · Washington
MISSOURI · *Lexington* · VIRGINIA · *Richmond*
KANSAS · KENTUCKY · *Appomattox* 9 Apr. 1865 · *Petersburg*
· Memphis · Knoxville · NORTH CAROLINA · *Durham* 26 Apr. 1865
INDIAN TERR. · ARKANSAS · TENNESSEE · *Chattanooga* · SOUTH CAROLINA · Fort Sumter
Shiloh · ALABAMA · *Atlanta* · GEORGIA · Charleston
MISSISSIPPI · Montgomery · Savannah
TEXAS · *Vicksburg* · LOUISIANA · Jacksonville
New Orleans · FLORIDA
Gulf of Mexico

Breaking with the Union

In November 1860 Abraham Lincoln won the presidential election for the Republican Party, which had been formed six years earlier by a group of politicians united on two things: a belief that the interests of the Union as a whole should prevail over those of individual states, and opposition to slavery. South Carolina immediately decided to secede and quit the Union. By March 1861, Georgia, Alabama, Louisiana, Florida, Mississippi and Texas had followed South Carolina's example. By June, they had been joined by North Carolina, Virginia, Arkansas and Tennessee. The breakaway Confederate States of America had its own capital at Richmond, Virginia, its own president, Jefferson Davis, and its own currency, taxes, flag and army.

In Lincoln, however, the South faced an opponent of granite resolution. He was prepared to countenance slavery

Turning point An engraving of the Battle of Gettysburg (above). The Union victory at Gettysburg marked the end of General Lee's attempt to invade the North.

where it was already a fact of life, but the break-up of the Union – never. When the Confederacy demanded that federal troops be withdrawn from Fort Sumter in Charleston, South Carolina, Lincoln decided to make a stand. He told the commander of the fort, Major Robert Anderson, to hold fast, and despatched ships to bring supplies to the besieged garrison. On April 12,

'Let us have peace' Generals Grant (left) and Lee shaking hands during the Confederate surrender at Appomattox (above). Right: Abraham Lincoln with senators in 1863.

1861, however, before the ships had arrived, the Confederates opened fire on the fort. 'Then, and thereby,' Lincoln later told Congress, 'the assailants of the Government began the conflict of arms.'

War and reconstruction

The Civil War lasted for four years. By now the number of states had risen to 34, and the war pitted the 23 Union states of the North and West against the 11 Confederate states of the South. The Union had the advantage of numbers, greater industrial muscle and a better railroad network. The Confederates, on the other hand, were fighting for a way of life and had some of the finest commanders, above all General Robert E. Lee, to lead and inspire them. In the end, although the Southerners fought bravely, the Union armies ground them down. The Confederate defeat at the Battle of Gettysburg in July 1863 was a crucial turning point; from then on the Southerners were on the defensive. The conflict ended on April 9, 1865. General

The Ku Klux Klan

Defeat in the Civil War was bitter for many in the South. They deeply resented the emancipation of the slaves and the granting of equal rights to blacks. In 1866, former Confederate general Nathan Bedford Forrest set up the Ku Klux Klan, a secret society dedicated to the cause of white supremacy. It waged a campaign of terror against blacks. Southern blacks who stood up for their new-won rights had their homes and crops burned; many were tarred and feathered, flogged or lynched. By 1869 the violence had escalated to the point where Forrest felt obliged to disband the organisation. But the terror continued, until in 1871 Congress passed the Ku Klux Klan Act giving the federal authorities powers to bring the terrorists to heel.

The Ku Klux Klan was reborn in 1915. By then it was anti-Semitic, anti-Catholic and anticommunist as well as antiblack. Its membership peaked at over 4 million in the 1920s, then waned during the Depression of the 1930s. The Civil Rights campaigns of the 1950s and 60s provoked a Ku Klux Klan backlash. The Klan still exists, though it is nothing like as strong as it once was.

Ulysses S. Grant, the Union commander-in-chief, received Lee's surrender at Appomattox Court House in Virginia. Within a week Lincoln was dead, shot by a Confederate sympathiser.

The war cost more than 600 000 lives, and left the South crushed. Federal troops occupied the defeated states, while military governors oversaw the restoration of governments loyal to Washington; the Southern economy, much of it based on slave labour, was in tatters. In 1867 Congress passed the Reconstruction Act by which the South was under federal military occupation. The Act enshrined black civil and political rights, but many of these were whittled away in the following decades. Largely, the old white elites remained in control. Bruised and wounded, the South was condemned to be the United States' poorest, most backward region for decades to come.

Our manifest destiny

At one time, the balance of power within the Union lay between the North and South; by the 1870s the West had become the chief counterweight to the rich industrial states of the North-east. A key to the opening of the West was President Thomas Jefferson's Louisiana Purchase of 1803, which brought a vast belt of Midwestern territory under US rule. Also in 1803 Jefferson commissioned two army officers, Meriwether Lewis and William Clark, to find a land route to the Pacific. During a two-year expedition, they tracked the Missouri to its source, crossed the Rockies and followed the Columbia river as far as the Pacific before returning overland to St Louis. They were the first of a succession of explorers and scientists who set out during the 19th century to catalogue the natural wonders of the West.

In 1845 journalist John O'Sullivan gave expression to a growing sentiment when he wrote of the United States' 'manifest destiny to overspread the continent allotted by Providence for the free development of our yearly multiplying millions'. Gold gave westward expansion an added impetus after it was discovered in California's Sierra Nevada in 1848. A series of gold and silver strikes all across the West attracted thousands of prospectors, creating boom towns that mushroomed almost overnight and then disappeared as suddenly as they had emerged. Settlers in their wagons risked the hardships of the Oregon Trail across the Rockies in their search for a new life as small farmers. After the Civil War high beef prices encouraged enterprising Texans to start herding the cattle that roamed their plains; the age of the cowboy and the yearly cattle drive to railheads such as Dodge City, Kansas, was born. And all the time the railroad network was expanding across the continent: the first transcontinental link was completed on May 10, 1869, when the Union Pacific and Central Pacific lines met at Promontory Point, Utah. The Civil War had brought catastrophe, but in

Gold rush Bodie, in California's Sierra Nevada, boomed in the 1870s and 80s when gold was found nearby. Inset: The image of pioneer settlers with their wagons would imprint itself firmly on the American imagination.

the decades that followed it the opening of the West and the growing industrial might of the North laid the foundations for the United States' world-embracing economic supremacy in the century ahead: the American Century.

The Civil Rights movement

Despite measures such as the Civil Rights Act of 1875, segregation of blacks and whites in schools, on buses and in parks and other public amenities had long been a fact of Southern life. During and after the Second World War there was a stirring of active resistance. Then came the spark that set a mass movement alight. In 1955, in Montgomery, Alabama, a 41-year-old black seamstress, Mrs Rosa Parks, sat down in the white section of a bus and refused to budge. She was arrested and ordered to pay a fine. Outraged black leaders, including the young Martin Luther King, who had just arrived in Montgomery as minister of one of its churches, organised a boycott of the bus line, which eventually backed down and desegregated its facilities.

King, influenced by the ideas of Gandhi, steered the movement towards nonviolent resistance. Using peaceful boycotts and sit-ins, its members obliged transport companies all across the South to desegregate. This was followed by desegregation in libraries, university canteens, department stores, cinemas and supermarkets. Spurred on by the Civil Rights March on Washington in August 1963, Congress finally passed measures that forbade discrimination in public amenities, that penalised segregated schools and ensured black voting rights.

THE PLACE
AND ITS
PEOPLE

Manhattan's soaring skyscrapers rise like emblems of the American spirit. Thrusting heavenwards, they stand like sentinels guarding the gateway to the immense continent that lies beyond – the farms, villages, towns and cities set amid an infinite variety of plains, valleys, forests, deserts and snowy mountains. Here generations of immigrants and their offspring have carved out new lives for themselves. Finally, having conquered the Wild West and the farthest limits of their continent, the North Americans set about exporting their civilisation, a culture of success, turned resolutely towards the future.

CHAPTER 1
THE MAJESTY OF NATURE

The landscapes of the United States and Canada impress by their immensity as well as their beauty. In two vast countries, each the size of a continent, the sheer scale of a scene is often a key element in its drama. For travellers, distances seem to lose all meaning as they follow the long black ribbon of road, mile after mile, hour after hour, day after day, through plains and mountains, deserts and forests. From the giant sequoias of Yosemite to the dramatic reliefs of the Grand Canyon, from the cactuses of the Mojave Desert to the mangrove trees of the Everglades, the scale, splendour and variety of nature in North America is astonishing. And if nature has been bountiful – in resources as well as scenic riches – many Americans and Canadians have been doing their best to protect that heritage.

The awe-inspiring landscape of Bryce Canyon, Utah.

The national parks

Some have the majestic beauty of mountain landscapes; others encompass stark and awe-inspiring deserts. Some have hot springs or impressive waterfalls; others boast rare gems of plant or animal life. All the national parks are there to conserve and protect irreplaceable wildernesses which had an almost sacred character for the American Indians who once roamed in them freely.

Ice age glaciers carved out Yosemite Valley, set high in California's Sierra Nevada mountain range. About 3 million years ago the valley was a canyon, gouged out by the Merced River. Then glaciers invaded it, making it wider and deeper, and scraping out the 'hanging' side valleys from which a profusion of waterfalls now tumble down the granite valley walls. By 10 000 years ago Yosemite Valley had acquired more or less its present shape, about 7 miles (11 km) long and 1 mile (1.6 km) across at its widest point. The waterfalls include the Yosemite Falls, the tallest in North America, cascading 2425 ft (739 m) from top to bottom. Another set of falls is the Bridalveil Falls, known as Pohono, 'spirit of the puffing wind', in the local American Indian tongue. Strong winds often blow here, catching the tumbling cascade and blowing it from side to side in a movement that resembles a bride's white veil caught in a breeze and that has given the falls their English name.

Yellowstone buffalo   *The rolling Hayden Valley in Yellowstone National Park is home to roaming buffalo. Once hunted almost to extinction here, the buffalo are now protected.*

Limestone cascade   *The strange terraces of Yellowstone's Mammoth Hot Springs were formed over millions of years, as mineral-rich hot water welled up from far beneath the Earth's crust, depositing as much as 2 tons of limestone every day.*

Sunlight and snow   *The Yosemite Valley in winter (above). The setting sun gives a golden glow to the tops of the valley's granite sides. In the valley bottom, snowcapped boulders dot the course of the Merced River. Right: A giant sequoia in Yosemite's Mariposa Grove. These massive redwood trees can live for 3000 years.*

Among the national parks Yosemite holds a pioneering place. Its original inhabitants were a tribe of the Miwok Indian nation, the Ahwahneechee; there were no Europeans until the California gold rush of 1849 brought thousands of prospectors to the Sierra Nevada. They invaded Indian lands and the Indians fought back, attacking the prospectors' camps and equipment. In March 1851 state troops sent to protect the miners stumbled into Yosemite Valley and within five years it had become a tourist attraction. On June 30, 1864, in the thick of the Civil War, President Lincoln signed a grant that set aside Yosemite Valley and the nearby Mariposa Grove of giant sequoias to be 'held for public use, resort, and recreation … inalienable for all time.' It was the first such decree and is regarded as the seed from which today's system of state and national parks grew.

John Muir: campaigner for nature

John Muir (1838-1914) was the voice of forest conservation in the United States. His campaign for a federal policy of forest conservation, to keep certain special forests safe from commercial exploitation, started in the 1870s and bore fruit in 1890 when the Sequoia and Yosemite national parks were established.

The return of the wolf

By the mid 1930s wolves had been hunted to extinction in Yellowstone Park. In March 1995 they were reintroduced when three groups of grey or timber wolves (*Canis lupus*) were brought from Canada. Wolves have also been released in the mountains of central Idaho as part of a programme run by the US Fish and Wildlife Service. The programme has its opponents, however, especially among the ranchers of Wyoming, fearful for their livestock. In December 1997, they won an important victory when a federal judge ruled that the reintroduction programme was illegal and that the released wolves should be removed. In a complicated ruling, he said that the reintroduction programme breached the very Act – the 1973 Endangered Species Act – it was designed to fulfil. Under this Act, native wolves are protected, but the reintroduced ones are not. If reintroduced wolves attacked livestock, they could be shot, but native ones could not. No action was taken to put the judge's ruling into effect, pending an appeal, but the case highlighted some of the knotty problems involved in conserving wildlife.

hot spring is Grand Prismatic – the rings of yellow and orange around the deep blue centre give the pool a rainbow-like or prismatic look. Elsewhere are the astonishing limestone terraces of Mammoth Hot Springs and the 24 mile (39 km) Grand Canyon of the Yellowstone River, where the water tumbles furiously between golden-yellow cliffs.

So astonishing are Yellowstone's 10 000 geothermal features that when the first Europeans explored the region in the early 19th century, nobody would believe their accounts. In 1871 Dr Ferdinand Hayden of the US Geological Survey mounted an expedition, taking with him a well-known artist, Thomas Moran, and a photographer, William Henry Jackson, to provide visual proof. The following year Congress voted to make Yellowstone a national park, the first national park in the world to be officially designated as such. Nowadays, it attracts more than 3 million visitors each year, drawn not just by the geysers and hot springs, but also by the wide range of wildlife.

Undercliff dwellings
The Anasazi cliff dwellings in the Canyon de Chelly, Arizona, are dwarfed by the rockface above them (left). Above: A hunting scene in an Anasazi rock drawing in the Canyon de Chelly.

Yellowstone's geothermal wonderland

Nowhere on Earth has a richer display of geothermal activity than Yellowstone National Park. Extending over 2.2 million heavily forested acres (nearly 1 million ha), chiefly in Wyoming, it is a wonderland of exotic natural phenomena. Old Faithful geyser erupts every 79 minutes on average, spouting thousands of gallons of steaming hot water into the air. Steamboat geyser is less reliable, but shoots higher – up to 400 ft (120 m). The largest

Cliff dwellings in Mesa Verde

In 1888 two cowboys discovered one of Colorado's most remarkable monuments. In the Mesa Verde they found a deserted city tucked under an immense overhanging sandstone cliff. Since 1906 Mesa Verde has been a national park containing 600 cliff dwellings of differing sizes. Similar structures are scattered across the surrounding region, including Arizona's Canyon de Chelly. Scholars believe that the inhabitants of Mesa Verde were ancestors of the modern Pueblo Indians of New Mexico and Arizona. Sometimes known as the Anasazi people, or as the Ancestral Puebloans, they reached a peak of prosperity between about 1100 and 1300.

A day in the life of a park ranger

Terry Green is a Yellowstone park ranger. Among the 3 million people who visit the park each year, some come as day-trippers while others stay for a few days' hiking, camping each night. It is the job of Green and his fellow rangers to make sure that none of them comes to any harm. If people get into trouble he has to be there as soon as possible, ready to perform first aid or call out the emergency services. In addition, he must be equipped to answer all manner of questions about the park's ecology and wildlife. He is also there to protect the park itself. Rangers make sure that visitors comply with the park's safety codes, and they have the power to arrest and evict anyone who violates park laws.

National bird   *The bald eagle* (Haliaeetus leucocephalus) *has been the official national bird of the United States since 1782.*

The Grand Canyon

Erosion created one of the most astounding of the world's natural wonders. Carved out over the last 5-6 million years by wind, water, heat and cold, the Grand Canyon of the Colorado River snakes its way for 277 miles (446 km) across the deserts of northern Arizona.

A t its deepest, the Grand Canyon slices down well over a mile (1.6 km) from the rim to the river below. In places it is 18 miles (29 km) wide; at Grand Canyon Village, where most visitors come, it is 10 miles (16 km) from rim to rim as the crow flies. Getting from one rim to the other involves a 215 mile (346 km) drive around the Canyon by road, or a two to three-day hike down one side and up the other. Descending the canyon is like going back through geological time. Steadily over the millennia, the gorge has been ground down through layer after layer of soft rock – grey and white limestone, red and white sandstone, dark red oxidised limestone, green clay, dark brown

Canyon majesty   Few of the world's rivers flow through a more majestic setting than the Colorado River, as it winds and twists through the Grand Canyon. Before the Glen Canyon Dam was built upstream, the river carried half a million tons of sand downstream each day.

Sunlight and water   *The colossal Lake Powell, to the north-east of the Grand Canyon, was created by building the Glen Canyon Dam, which holds back the waters of the Colorado and San Juan rivers.*

gneiss. Although the canyon itself is a youngster in geological terms, the rocks at the bottom date from nearly 2 billion years ago and are among the oldest exposed rocks on the planet.

In 1919 President 'Teddy' Roosevelt persuaded Congress to declare the Grand Canyon region a national park. Grand Canyon Village stands on the South Rim, where the landscape is a parched brown desert with cacti, agave and yucca plants growing among occasional stands of firs, pines and junipers. The North Rim is on average 1000 ft (300 m) higher, and is colder, wetter and wilder. The park as a whole is home to some 70 species of mammal, 250 species of bird and 25 species of reptile. They include lynx, mountain lions, bears, deer, eagles, vultures, squirrels, spiders, scorpions, iguanas and rattlesnakes.

A holy place

For the Hopi Indians, who have lived in the area for more than 1000 years, the Grand Canyon is a holy place – especially the Sipapu, a hole in the rock near the confluence of the Colorado and Little Colorado rivers to the east of Grand Canyon Village. Out of bounds to visitors, this is the place where, according to the Hopis, they and all animals emerged into this world from an older world that lay beneath it. The mythological theme has continued in the naming of many of the canyon's geological features – the Wotan Throne, the Vishnu Temple and the Shiva Temple. The names are the legacy of Clarence Dutton, a student of comparative religion, who in 1881 wrote a report on the Grand Canyon for the US Geological Survey.

The promoters of the Grand Canyon

F red Harvey's name is inescapable at the Grand Canyon, because the company he founded has the concession for all eating houses and hotels within the National Park on the South Rim. In 1878 Harvey began a partnership with the Atchison, Topeka and Santa Fe Railway, which gave him the right to operate along its routes. Harvey Houses were noted for their excellent food, cleanliness and service. Harvey died in 1901, the year the railway reached the Grand Canyon, putting it firmly on the tourist map.

Ghost towns

Prospector Ed Schieffelin received scant encouragement when he set out for the Dragoon Mountains of Arizona. He was told that all he would find there would be his own tombstone. But in 1877 Schieffelin struck silver and named his camp Tombstone. By 1880 the silver rush had made Tombstone a boom town. In 1881 rivalry between two families, the Earps and the Clantons, came to a head in the famous gun battle at the OK Corral. Then the silver mines flooded and Tombstone died as suddenly as it had come alive. By 1890 it was becoming a 'ghost town' – one of many that scatter parts of Arizona and Nevada.

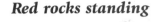

Abstract art *Sunlight brings out the beauty of the rockface.*

The Petrified Forest

Some 225 million years ago, in the age of the dinosaurs, forests covered what is now the Arizona desert. Occasional floods swept through them, dumping mud over the conifer-like trees and burying them. Over the millennia, water containing minerals seeped into the buried wood and turned it into stone. More time passed and movements in the Earth's

crust forced the fossilised wood to the surface – exposing stone trunks that are four times as hard as granite, and shaded astonishing hues of red or blue with bands of yellow, black and white, some containing crystals of clear quartz and purple amethyst. In this way the Petrified Forest of north-eastern Arizona was formed.

Red rocks standing

Lying to the north of the Grand Canyon, on the edge of the Paunsaugunt Plateau in southern Utah, Bryce Canyon stands like a city of stone in a vast amphitheatre, with hundreds of sandstone pillars, domes and spires reaching to the sky. Local Paiute Indians called it 'the red rocks standing like men in the canyon shaped like a basin'. Its more prosaic name comes from Ebenezer Bryce, a Scotsman who settled here in the 1870s. Different combinations of rainfall, light, temperature and soil composition create a multitude of different habitats. Dwarf forests of piñon pines and junipers cover the lower slopes. Higher up, they give way to ponderosa pines, and higher still to Douglas firs, aspens and spruces. In the highest, most windswept spots on the southern edge, ancient bristlecone pines grow – some of which are believed to be as much as 1600 years old.

'Red rocks standing like men' *Frosts and snowmelt were among the forces that created the extraordinary rock pinnacles of Bryce Canyon (left).*

Swampy shores to mountain peaks

In the south-east lie the Florida Everglades, one of the world's richest wetlands. In the north-west, crater lakes and snowcapped peaks create the drama of the Cascade Range. America's national parks encompass a truly continental diversity of scenery and wildlife.

Maze of waterways *In the 18th century the Everglades became a refuge for American Indians driven out of the Carolinas and Georgia. Today, the humidity and mosquitoes make it an inhospitable place for humans.*

The Florida Everglades are unique. Nowhere else in the world has their special mix of prairies, mangrove and cypress swamps, subtropical jungle and offshore reefs and keys. Bounded to the north by the freshwater expanse of Lake Okeechobee, they embrace most of the southern tip of Florida – the Everglades National Park covers only a seventh of the entire region. From alligators to egrets, manatees to panthers, the wetlands are home to a profusion of wildlife, including 350 species of bird, 50 or more species of reptile and 18 species of amphibian. When life is at its most intense, in late summer, the whole watery environment seems to hum, buzz, croak and gurgle with the exuberance of it all.

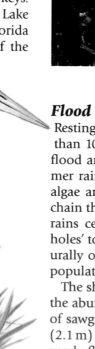

Elegant fisher *The great blue heron (Ardea herodias) is one of the magnificent birds of North America's wetlands. It feeds on fish, frogs and insects.*

Flood and drought

Resting on a bed of limestone, the Everglades are never more than 10 ft (3 m) above sea level, and an annual alternation of flood and drought underpins the way of life. During the summer rainy season water rises in the waterways and blooms of algae and plankton grow everywhere – the bottom of a food chain that extends up to mammals and large reptiles. When the rains cease and the waters recede, the alligators make 'gator holes' to see them through the dry winter. These, and other, naturally occurring, ponds become oases where the entire animal population come to drink their fill.

The sheer variety of the Everglades' environment accounts for the abundance of wildlife. Much of the region is a huge flat sea of sawgrass (*Cladium jamaicense*), whose stems grow up to 7 ft (2.1 m) tall with long saw-tooth-edged leaves; it relies upon the yearly flooding during the rainy season for healthy growth.

Mangrove forests   *Along the Everglades' Gulf of Mexico shore mangroves provide a home for a wealth of fish, sea turtles and water birds. Between the aerial roots the American alligator* (Alligator mississippiensis) *stalks its prey.*

Endangered habitat

In the 1830s the wildlife artist John James Audubon painted the birds of the Everglades and it became fashionable for women to wear white egret feathers and pink roseate spoonbill ones in their hats. By the turn of the century, thousands of the birds were being shot to supply this frivolous market. Nowadays the threat comes from a different source. The ecosystem used to rely on the annual overflowing of Lake Okeechobee, which flooded the entire wetland with its fresh water. Now canals divert the lake's water for domestic and agricultural use and dams prevent such flooding. As a result, excessive amounts of seawater are invading the Everglades, upsetting their ecological balance.

Volcanic drama in the Cascades

Rising high above the other summits of the Cascade Range, the volcanic peak of Mount Rainier is one of Washington State's best-known landmarks. Radiating from it are 25 major glaciers, including Emmons Glacier, the largest in the United States outside Alaska. In summer the alpine meadows of the Mount Rainier National Park are a carpet of wild flowers. Farther south, marking a section of the state boundary between Washington and Oregon, the Columbia River has gouged out a spectacular 75 mile (120 km) gorge through the Cascade Range. The river itself is scarcely higher than sea level, but the basalt cliffs rise 4000 ft (1200 m) on either side.

Crater Lake, in south-eastern Oregon, is the result of a massive volcanic explosion some 7700 years ago. Lava flows sealed the bottom of the caldera, allowing rainwater and melting snows to accumulate in what is now the deepest lake in the United States. Rimmed with snow for half the year, Crater Lake and its surrounding area have been a national park since 1902.

The heart of the Appalachians
Straddling the border of Tennessee and North Carolina in the southern Appalachians, the Great Smoky Mountains National Park is home to 27 species of salamander alone. The park has more than 1500 species of flowering plant, 200 species of bird, 50 species of mammal and 50 species of fish. There are also more than 2000 types of mushroom, including three that glow at night. The wealth and diversity of the wildlife led UNESCO to designate the park a World Heritage Site in 1983.

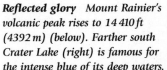

Reflected glory   *Mount Rainier's volcanic peak rises to 14 410 ft (4392 m) (below). Farther south Crater Lake (right) is famous for the intense blue of its deep waters.*

Canada's wild beauty

When French explorer Jacques Cartier sailed up the St Lawrence River in 1535, American Indians told him the way to 'kanata' – the settlement on the site of what is now Quebec City. Cartier used the word Canada to refer to the domains of the local chief.

From North America's easternmost point, Cape Spear on the Atlantic-facing shore of Newfoundland, to the frontier with Alaska in the west, Canada spans 88° of longitude, a 3540 mile (5700 km) arc of the Earth's surface. From south to north, it stretches from the Canadian-owned rock called Middle Island in Lake Erie, to Cape Columbia at the northernmost tip of Ellesmere Island, just 470 miles (756 km) from the North Pole.

Splendid isolation *Almost hidden by dense forest, a lakeside dwelling offers a peaceful retreat in the Canadian wilderness.*

Ice fork *Kluane National Park in the St Elias Mountains has the world's most extensive ice fields beyond the polar ice caps, as well as Mount Logan, Canada's highest peak.*

A mosaic

Canada can be described as a mosaic of both landscapes and peoples. In the east, the Maritime Provinces and Newfoundland were among the first parts of the country to be settled by Europeans. Now a relative backwater and badly hit in many places by the decline of the Canadian fisheries, these eastern regions rely heavily on tourism to sustain their economies. A leisurely charm clings to the towns and villages that sprinkle the numerous bays and coves of their shorelines. Inland, forests of oak, chestnut, beech, elm and Canada's national emblem, the maple, cover many of the mountains and valley sides, creating a rich harmony of colours in autumn.

Tucked away just south of Newfoundland are France's last possessions in North America, the eight small islands of Saint Pierre and Miquelon, settled in the 17th century by Basque and Breton fishermen. Farther west, the island of Anticosti stands in the mouth of the St Lawrence estuary, a notorious hazard for shipping. Between Anticosti and the north shore of the Gulf of St Lawrence, the Mingan Archipelago National Park encloses a sprinkling of 40-odd limestone islands, where natural mono-liths tower skywards from meadows that blaze in summer with

Canada's New Scotland

Facing out into the North Atlantic along its eastern side, and linked to the rest of Canada by the 17 mile (27 km) wide Chignecto Isthmus on its opposite, north-western shore, Nova Scotia has always made its living from the sea. One of its most famous sons was Captain Joshua Slocum, who sailed solo round the world in 1895-8.

Nova Scotia's first European settlement in 1605 was Port Royal – now Annapolis Royal – on the Bay of Fundy. This was the first French colony in North America, and can claim to be Canada's founding settlement. Later, in 1621, King James VI of Scotland (James I of England) granted the Scotsman William Alexander the right to establish a colony called New Scotland, or Nova Scotia; the French named the region Acadie (Acadia), from the Greek *Arcadia*. British and French rivalry resulted in the expulsion of the Acadians in 1755. The French-built fortress of Louisbourg on Cape Breton Island, separated from the rest of Nova Scotia by the Strait of Canso, is a relic of those days.

Seashore colour *Pretty villages dot the Nova Scotia coastline. The land here is poor and traditionally families eked out a living by being both farmers and fishermen.*

Whales in the St Lawrence

A fjord carved out by glaciers marks the mouth of the River Saguenay where it flows into the St Lawrence estuary. Cliffs as high as 1500 ft (460 m) rise on either side. Beneath them, the mingling of fresh and salt waters, strong tidal races and a powerful undercurrent bring nutrient-rich water to the surface to create a marine feasting ground, now protected as the Saguenay Marine Park. Five species of whale – the blue, minke, humpback, finback and beluga – feed on the rich soup of tiny krill. Sea mammals feed alongside them, including porpoises and harp seals.

Unfortunately for the whales and other water creatures, this is also one of the world's busiest shipping lanes – some 6000 ocean-going vessels pass up and down the St Lawrence each year. Pollution from shipping and industry is a particular threat to the beluga whales, and some experts fear that they are in danger of extinction. Scientists have found high levels of toxic substances in the whales' tissues and believe that this is a result of pollution in the river water. At the start of the century there were around 10 000 belugas in the St Lawrence, but now there are only about 500.

wild flowers. On the far side of the gulf, Labrador, the mainland section of Newfoundland, and the wild northern part of Quebec province stretch on and on to the shores of the Arctic and beyond – a dense blanket of coniferous forest in the south, turning to scrubby tundra in the far north.

Up the St Lawrence

From the days of Jacques Cartier, the St Lawrence has been the principal route into the heart of Canada. Here, on the banks of the mighty river, the French established their chief settlements, which have grown into the predominantly French-speaking cities of Quebec, Trois-Rivières and Montreal. Inland from the Atlantic, the St Lawrence's waters remain brackish until the sector just downstream of Quebec; the river remains tidal until it reaches Trois-Rivières. In winter, thick layers of ice form, keeping icebreakers busy as they maintain open navigable channels. Upstream of Montreal as far as the Great Lakes, the flow of the river becomes wilder, interrupted by a series of rapids, bypassed for river traffic by the man-made St Lawrence Seaway. The lowlands around the southern Great Lakes and St Lawrence are the most densely populated part of Canada. Yet even here nature asserts its grandeur, as the Niagara River, flowing between lakes Erie and Ontario, thunders over the Niagara Falls.

Jutting out into Lake Erie, the tiny Point Pelee National Park encloses an astonishing wealth of wildlife. There are marshes where turtles and muskrats live, and swamp forests that provide a home for wood ducks, great horned owls and the rare prothonotary warbler. Hop trees

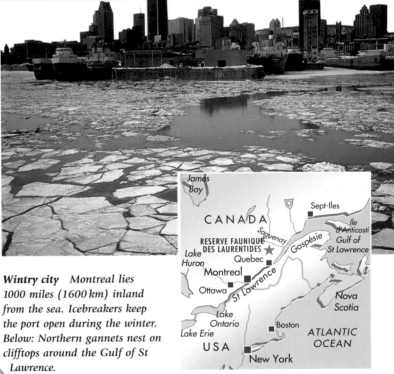

Wintry city   Montreal lies 1000 miles (1600 km) inland from the sea. Icebreakers keep the port open during the winter. Below: Northern gannets nest on clifftops around the Gulf of St Lawrence.

An adult gannet and its young

grow on the beaches that fringe the peninsula. Inland are more open spaces where in season butterfly weed opens out into brilliant orange flowers. Birds that nest here include yellow-breasted chats, white-eyed and red-eyed vireos and yellow-billed cuckoos. And above all, Point Pelee is famous for its butterflies.

Banff in the Rockies
Banff National Park encompasses 2600 sq miles (6700 km²) of the Canadian Rockies. Glacial lakes fill many valleys (right). In summer the park's alpine meadows are a blaze of wild flowers.

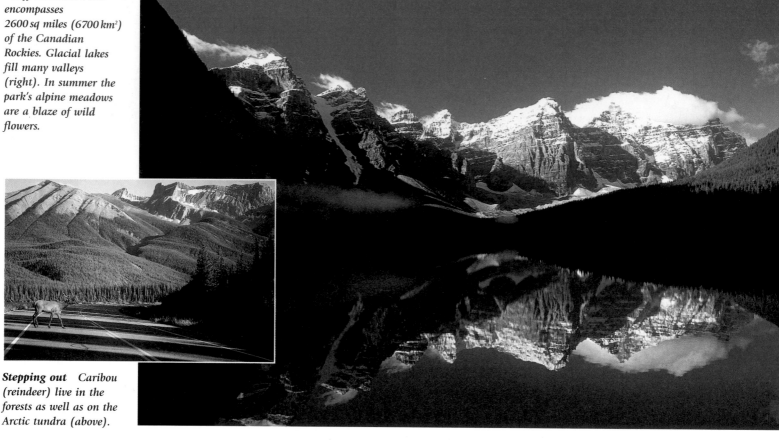

Stepping out Caribou (reindeer) live in the forests as well as on the Arctic tundra (above).

Over the plains

North of the Great Lakes, Ontario province stretches to the low-lying marshy country around the vast expanse of Hudson Bay. To the west of Ontario, the plains of Manitoba, Saskatchewan and Alberta roll on until they reach the huge barrier of the Rockies. Nowadays, the plains are mostly given over to crop-growing, but in southern Saskatchewan two units of Grasslands National Park preserve patches of the original prairie grasslands, home of the black-tailed prairie dogs.

Antlered glory The male caribou grows massive antlers, which he sheds each spring.

British Columbia is rich in copper, gold, silver and coal, and popular with tourists because of its mild coastal climate and beautiful scenery. The first British colony was established on Vancouver Island in 1849; regular overland links with the eastern provinces came only in 1885 with the completion of the Canadian Pacific Railroad. To the north, the savagely beautiful Yukon Territory was the scene of a famous gold rush in 1896; gold, silver, lead and zinc are still mined in the Yukon.

The Gaspé Peninsula

The Chic-Choc Mountains, a northern outcrop of the great Appalachian chain, form the high backbone of Quebec's Gaspé Peninsula. Forested mountains with numerous streams tumbling down their sides rise to Mount Jacques Cartier, 4160 ft (1268 m) above sea level. Fishing settlements, which are popular with tourists, dot the rocky shoreline. At the tip of the peninsula, Forillon National Park encloses sand dunes, salt marshes and cliffs, where the Appalachian system tumbles directly into the sea. Moose and black bears roam the park's forests; sea birds nest in their thousands on its shores. Offshore from the town of Percé lies the massive hulk of Rocher Percé (below), with thousands of northern gannets, which breed on nearby Bonaventure Island, wheeling through the skies overhead. The cliffs at Miguasha, overlooking Chaleur Bay, are internationally famous among geologists for their fossils of 360 million-year-old plants and animals.

Down by the bayous

The Mississippi – 'Father of Waters' in the Algonquin Indian language – loops the last few hundred miles of its course to the sea. Along the Louisiana coast, swampy waterways known as bayous crisscross in a mysterious watery maze.

Waterworld
Reflections in the still waters of a bayou.

The river no longer dominates the life of the region as it once did. In the mid 19th century the Mississippi was the single most important highway in the United States. Paddlesteamers plied up and down it, bearing mail, passengers and goods; plantations had their own private wharfs where cotton and other crops were loaded to be carried downriver to the docks of New Orleans. Nowadays, boats take tourists on nostalgic river cruises.

Although the Mississippi is no longer the transcontinental artery that it once was, it still flows on, each day depositing 2 million tons of sediment in the vast, shifting delta, or sweeping it out into the Gulf of Mexico. The river and its delta remain a defining presence in the region.

Planter country

Around the Louisiana state capital of Baton Rouge, fields of rice, cotton and sugar cane grow in the fertile mud deposited by the river before it reaches the sea. This is 'plantation country,' where stately mansions, the pride of the pre-Civil War South, still stand amid immaculate grounds. On the river's right bank, Pointe Coupée parish is the heart of French plantation country, settled in the early and mid 18th century by French Creoles.

East and West Feliciana parishes on the east bank are English plantation country, which was settled later, after the Louisiana Purchase in the early 19th century. Farther west, Cajun country

Welcome from Acadia

The word Cajun is a corruption of Acadian. The original Acadia was a French colony established early in the 17th century in the region of modern Nova Scotia. By the mid 18th century it was under British rule, and the authorities demanded that the colonists swear allegiance to the British Crown and renounce their Roman Catholic faith. Many of the Acadians refused, choosing deportation and exile instead. Thus began

long years of wandering until eventually they found a welcome in French Louisiana, and settled as farmers and fishermen in the Mississippi Delta and the bayous.

is a different world again. The French-speakers who settled here in the late 18th century were more easygoing than those in plantation country. Abbeville, on the banks of Vermilion Bayou, Lafayette, Breaux Bridge, Lake Charles – each community has its boisterous annual festival. Out in the swamps and bayous, swathes of Spanish moss dangle from cypress trees whose roots and lower trunks are permanently submerged. Egrets and herons wing their way through the sky; alligators prowl the waters beneath. The riches of this environment – rice, fish and crayfish – are basic ingredients of the famous Cajun cuisine. Beyond the bayous, dotting the Gulf of Mexico, are the oil wells and platforms that fuel modern Louisiana's prosperity.

Cajun, Creole and Zydeco

The roots of Cajun music lie in the songs that the Acadians' ancestors brought with them from France. By the late 19th century the traditional homemade fiddle had been joined by a German import, the accordion. Similar traditions among south-western Lousiana's French-speaking rural blacks gave rise to Creole music. In the 1940s Creole came under the influence of blues and jazz, and yet another sound was born – Zydeco, which owes its syncopated rhythms to the washboard, a corrugated metal board

Plantation splendour   *Oak Alley was built for the planter Alexander Roman in the 1830s.*

CHAPTER 2

LIVING WITH EXTREMES

To live in North America is to live with extremes, which can also often spell danger. In the south and east, the threat comes from hurricanes. Along the West Coast, it comes from earthquakes and volcanoes. In the Midwest, in spite of modern flood-control schemes, the waters of the Mississippi and its tributaries still periodically run out of control, inundating vast areas, destroying homes and livelihoods. Every summer fires sweep through the forests that cover 37 per cent of the United States. In Canada and the northern USA harsh winters bring snow and ice; farther north still lie the barren areas of the tundra with permanently frozen subsoil, while beyond that, zones of everlasting snow and ice spread across Canada's Arctic islands towards the North Pole. In contrast, the deserts of the American south-west include some of the hottest places on Earth.

A car comes to rest on top of a house, blown there by a tornado at Kissimmee, Florida.

Deserts of the South-west

The sky is a startling blue, with just a few wisps of cloud breaking its intensity. The sun shines hard, bright, and remorseless. The road stretches on and on, a ribbon of tarmac extending to the far horizon, dotted here and there with cars and the camper vans of tourists. The desert regions of the South-west, with their savage grandeur and many national parks, draw millions of visitors each year.

Lying in the rain shadow of the Pacific coast mountain ranges, and bounded to the east by the great wall of the Rockies, the deserts and arid wildernesses of the American South-west include some of the most starkly dramatic scenery in the world. In places, wind, water and the alternations of heat and cold have worn away at ancient mountain ranges to create extraordinary sculpted landscapes such as those enclosed by Arches National Park in Utah. In Monument Valley and the Canyon de Chelly, remnants of the mountains survive as towering buttes and mesas. Colours range from the white gypsum dunes of White Sands, New Mexico, to the sombre volcanic hues of Nevada's Black Rock Desert. In Arizona, the sandstones, shales and marls of the Painted Desert create a rainbow-like effect with bands of white, blue, purple, yellow and red.

Dry wood and tumbleweed
This scene of arid desolation (right) is in Monument Valley. The dense growths of tumbleweed break off when they wither, and are blown hither and yon across the desert, spreading seeds as they go.

Delicate arch *Among the sandstone arches of Arches National Park, Utah, this one was once known, rather indelicately, as Old Maid's Bloomers.*

Crystal clarity *In the clear dry air of Death Valley distances are telescoped, so that the bare rocks of the surrounding mountains can be picked out in sharp detail. Top: Mesas, with flat tops and sheer sides, rise sharply from the plain in Monument Valley.*

Hottest, driest, lowest

Death Valley slices 140 miles (225 km) from north to south in south-eastern California, with a span of 5-15 miles (8-24 km) across. Sand dunes cover the valley floor, which sinks in one place to 282 ft (86 m) below sea level – the lowest point in the Western Hemisphere. On either side rise deeply scored bare-rock mountains, with tiny pockets of vegetation growing in the cracks between the rocks. With temperatures that soar in summer to 50°C (122°F) and higher, this mountain-locked sea of sand is the hottest and driest place in North America. When rains do fall the valley bursts briefly and dramatically into life with a shimmering carpet of richly coloured wild flowers.

Western setting

The landscape of Monument Valley, cutting across the border of Utah and Arizona, was made familiar by one man in particular: the Hollywood film director John Ford. The dramatic scenery of sandstone towers, mesas and buttes made it a perfect backdrop for a succession of Westerns, ranging from *Stagecoach* (1939) to *She Wore a Yellow Ribbon* (1949) and *Cheyenne Autumn* (1964). Monument Valley has been part of the Navajo Indian Reservation since 1884. Its chief trading post, Goulding, was established in 1924, only 15 years before the making of *Stagecoach*.

The desert in bloom *California poppies and other flowers create a carpet of colour in the Mojave Desert, southern California (above). The rain required to make desert plants spring into life falls only a few times every century. Inset: Las Vegas in its desert setting.*

Joshua tree Growing as tall as 40ft (12m), the Joshua tree spreads its branches out in all directions. It is, in fact, a giant yucca plant, Yucca brevifolia. Some are thought to be 700 years old or more.

In the Mojave

To the south, the Mojave Desert spreads out over rugged terrain that encompasses mountains as well as gravel basins and salt flats. Joshua trees and the aromatic evergreen creosote bush (*Larrea tridentata*) provide sparse and scrubby vegetation. In the south-east the Mojave blends into the Sonoran Desert; to the north-east it merges with the vast expanse of the Great Basin Desert, which embraces most of Nevada and includes the fast-growing city of Las Vegas and large parts of western Utah.

Desert animals

Conditions could hardly be more extreme, yet there are animals that call the deserts of the South-west home. One is the roadrunner or chaparral cock (*Geococcyx californianus*), which is a poor flyer and prefers to run across the open desert or along roads – hence its name. Lizards and snakes form a major part of its diet. Antelope squirrels (*Ammospermophilus interpres* and *A. leucurus*) are ground-dwellers, and can often be seen perched on the tops of boulders. Even on the hottest days they forage busily, from time to time withdrawing into burrows to cool off. Unlike other squirrels, they do not hibernate. The bobcat (*Lynx rufus*) feeds on birds and rodents of the desert. The nocturnal cacomistle (*Bassariscus astutus*), has a long bushy tail ringed black and white – hence its other name, the ring-tailed cat. The largest lizard is the 20in (50cm) Gila monster (*Heloderma suspectum*). Black and pink bands or blotches mark its skin. It feeds at night on birds, eggs and a few small mammals. The Gila's bite is rarely dangerous to humans – unlike that of the various species of rattlesnake that live in the deserts. The rattle that gives the snakes their name consists of up to ten horny segments that are shaken to warn off possible predators. A rattlesnake bite should not be fatal so long as the victim receives medical treatment promptly.

43

The Far North: life at the limits

The Arctic regions of the United States and Canada are truly extreme, yet even here humans, animals and plants – including species of buttercup, poppy and dandelion – have adapted to the climate.

Stately carriage *Occasionally polar bears leave their ice floes to investigate villages. The villagers chase them away with sprays of cayenne pepper.*

The Americans bought Alaska from the Russians in 1867, and their investment in this rugged territory, one-third of it within the Arctic Circle, has been amply justified. In scenic splendour alone, Alaska is unparalleled and much of it is held in national and state parks. These include Denali National Park with North America's highest peak, Mount McKinley, and the volcanic drama of the Valley of Ten Thousand Smokes. Gold was struck within five years of the purchase, and 100 years later vast oil reserves were found inland from Prudhoe Bay. By 1977 the Trans-Alaska Pipeline was pumping the oil to the south coast port of Valdez. From being a frozen backwater, Alaska has become vital to the entire US economy.

Land of the Inuit

Oil and gold are also exploited in Canada's Northwest Territories. For most of the year, these northern regions lie covered in snow and ice, but for a few brief weeks during the Arctic summer the tundra springs miraculously into life and flowers blossom. In 1999 the native people of the Arctic, the Inuit, took possession of a semi-autonomous home called Nunavut in the eastern part of the Northwest Territories. It includes Baffin Island and most of the Arctic Islands. Many Inuits hope that the creation of Nunavut will enable them to preserve their traditional ways and customs, while interacting positively with the modern world.

The way they lived

Older Inuits remember a nomadic way of life and a culture that was vital to their sense of identity. Their movements were dictated by the seasons. In autumn, the families and their dog teams moved inland to the regions where the caribou roamed. Caribou meat, frozen and

cached, saw them through the winter, while the skins provided clothing. During the short days and long nights of winter there was little hunting or fishing, and families were confined for days to their snowhouses or igloos.

By March and April, the days were growing longer, and it was time to go hunting once more. Dogs sniffed out the holes in the ice where seals come up to breathe. Seals provided meat, and also fat to burn in carved-out, soapstone lamps. In June birds' eggs provided a welcome change of diet, and by then the ice was melting on rivers and lakes. Fish were plentiful and so were migratory birds, including ducks and geese; much of the fish was dried and cached. Then autumn came, families moved inland and the cycle started all over again.

Snow pilots: keeping people in touch

In the Northwest Territories pilots fulfil many important roles. They deliver the mail and often the milk. If a household appliance breaks down, a pilot will probably bring in the person to repair it. If people want to go shopping in the territorial capital, Yellowknife, they will probably fly there in one of the Twin

Otters, Beavers and Dash-8s that ply the air routes between the different settlements. In a region lying so close to the magnetic pole, officially designated an 'area of compass unreliability', the pilots have to be skilled navigators. They rely on instinct, experience and, nowadays, GPS satellite navigation aids.

Ancient skills combined with modern conveniences are symbolic of many aspects of life in the Northwest Territories. Many people maintain a number of their ancient customs, but live in modern bungalows, get around on snowmobiles and keep in touch with the world via satellite television and the Internet.

All iced up *In upstate New York trees and cables dripped with icicles during the ice storms of January 1998.*

Surviving winter snow and ice

Most winters in Canada and the northern US states are severe. Every Quebecer can recall blizzards, each of which seemed worse than the last, with cars buried under thick snowdrifts and snowmobiles buzzing through the hearts of their towns and cities.

When snow falls in Montreal and the surrounding area in November or December, it generally stays for up to four months. At Sherbrooke, some 80 miles (130 km) due east of Montreal, the average temperature in January is −9°C (16°F). Farther south, in New England and New York State, snow is a regular but less lasting visitor. Most winters have their snowstorms or blizzards, but the snow is unlikely to stay on the ground for more than a few days. The storms can, nonetheless, be impressive. The great blizzard of 1888 engulfed a huge area from Maine in the north to Washington DC in the south, Pittsburgh in the west to New York City in the east. In New York, people were stranded in offices and elevated trains. Along the coast 200 ships were sunk or damaged; in all, 400 people lost their lives.

Just under 100 years later, the blizzard of 1996 covered much of the eastern seaboard. Over 20 in (50 cm) fell on New York's Central Park, the third highest snowfall recorded there. People struggled with the conditions, but they also got into a festival atmosphere – as normal life ground to a

Coat of ice *The very low temperatures in Quebec in January 1998 paralysed towns and villages.*

halt people relaxed and even began to enjoy themselves. But after the blizzard came a rapid thaw and heavy rains. Snowmelt and rain caused some of the worst flooding in years, forcing more than 200 000 people from their homes. It was another record-breaker, but at least improved weather forecasting meant that it cost fewer lives than in 1888: an estimated 187 people died as a result of the storm, which caused $3 billion worth of damage.

The murderous cold

The harshness of Quebec winters was described by the author Louis Hémon in his best-selling tale of French-Canadian pioneer life, *Maria Chapdelaine*, published in 1915: 'Outside, the neighbouring forest, and even the fields won from it, were an alien unfriendly world ... sometimes this world was strangely beautiful in its frozen immobility, with a sky of flawless blue and a brilliant sun that sparkled on the snow; but the immaculateness of the blue and the white alike was pitiless and gave hint of the murderous cold.'

Ice storm brings chaos to Quebec

In January 1998 warm moist air from the south met a low blanket of freezing air over southern Quebec and created the worst ice storm ever recorded. Downpours of rain from the warm air fell through the cold air, then froze on impact with solid objects – trees, roads, roofs and parked cars. Layers of ice 6 in (150 mm) thick turned the streets of Montreal into a skating rink, and some 15 000 of the city's trees were damaged by the weight of the ice. In the country, farm animals froze to death.

Most devastatingly, the power system almost ceased to function as the weight of ice on pylons and power lines brought them crashing to the ground. With no electricity Montreal's water filtration and pumping system stopped working for a period, threatening the city's supply of drinking water. The power cuts hit Quebecers particularly hard as electricity is normally cheap in the province, and many people rely on it for heating, hot water and cooking as well as for light. Outside temperatures plunged to −15°C (5°F) and lower. Those who had alternative sources of power were encouraged to take in their less fortunate neighbours, while thousands took refuge in the emergency shelters.

In Canada's largest peacetime military operation, police and troops were deployed on the streets to maintain law and order, prevent looting and help the utility workers. Aid poured in, meanwhile, from other parts of North America, including truckloads of firewood from northern Quebec and cots from Virginia. At the beginning of February 150 000 people in the 'blackout triangle' south of Montreal were still without power. At least 20 people had died as a result of the storms. Estimates put the cost of the damage as high as US$1.5 billion.

Lashed by winds

Hurricane, tornado, storm – there are many words to describe the violent winds that sweep across the tropical regions along the Gulf of Mexico and the Atlantic coast, leaving in their wake a trail of havoc and destruction. Though satellites are now capable of tracking the eye of a hurricane, the extent of scientific interference stops there. There is nothing anyone can do but wait for the storm to blow itself out.

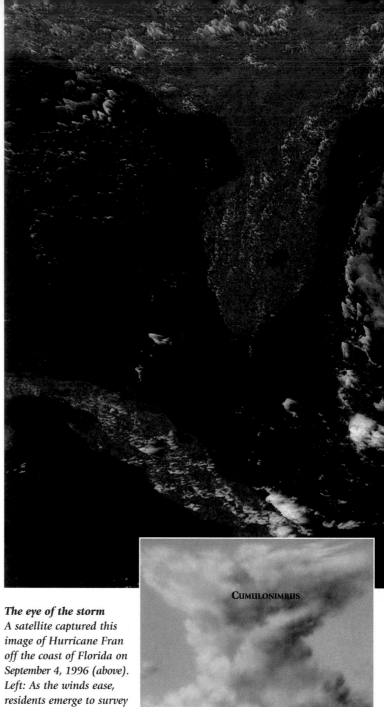

The month of February is too early to worry about the first tornadoes of the season – but El Niño, a warm Pacific Ocean current, decided otherwise. In February 1998, tornado-spawning storms, attributed to the worldwide disruption of weather patterns caused by El Niño, struck Louisiana, Florida and the Bahamas and killed 32 people. One lucky survivor was 18-month-old Jonathan Waldick. The baby was asleep in his cot when a 'twister' lifted him and his mattress into the air and deposited them in a fallen oak tree. The mattress had wrapped itself around the child, protecting him from building debris that fell on top of him. He survived with no more than a few scratches.

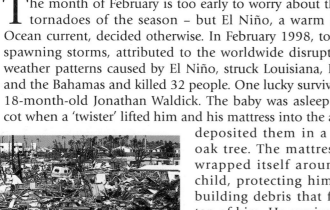

Mayhem in Miami In 1992 Hurricane Andrew caused more than $20 billion worth of damage, making it the most expensive natural disaster in US history.

The eye of the storm
A satellite captured this image of Hurricane Fran off the coast of Florida on September 4, 1996 (above). Left: As the winds ease, residents emerge to survey the damage. Right: A tornado starts when a funnel of rotating cloud forms beneath a thundercloud.

CUMULONIMBUS

Cold air   Warm air

Spirals of destruction

Technically, hurricanes are revolving storms that originate over tropical oceans and have sustained winds of at least 73 mph (117 km/h). They start as small areas of warm moist air spiralling upwards from the ocean surface. In the Atlantic, Caribbean and Gulf of Mexico, the hurricane season lasts from the beginning of June to the end of November. This is when the sea's surface is warm enough – 26°C (79°F) or more – for the initial upward spiral to be triggered. Most hurricanes that strike the east coast of the United States veer west towards the Gulf of Mexico or north up the eastern seaboard, sometimes reaching as far as New England. They rely on moisture to 'fuel' them, and so hurricanes that turn inland rapidly lose their strength.

the space of an hour, it killed 27 people and destroyed 133 homes. On May 3, 1999, as many as 76 tornadoes swept through the states of Oklahoma and Kansas, killing at least 43 people and injuring hundreds. One of them cut a swathe, 19 miles (31 km) long and ¹/₂ mile (0.8 km) wide, through the southern suburbs of Oklahoma City, levelling 1500 homes.

After the storm
Hurricane winds are strong enough to toss boats, cars and planes around as if they were no more than toys.

Cloud of destruction A tornado over the Great Plains. Below: Some of the worst hurricanes of recent decades.

Hurricanes are one of the inescapable hazards of life along the coasts of the South-east, and they have regularly left their mark. One smashed into a French fleet off the coast of Florida in 1565, destroying and dispersing the ships and putting paid to a French bid to take control of the eastern seaboard. Another, in 1609, helped to inspire Shakespeare's *The Tempest*. A fleet carrying English settlers to Virginia hit a hurricane near Bermuda. Many of the ships ran aground on the islands, where the survivors took shelter until rescued. Back in England, their tales of the storm and shipwreck found an echo in Shakespeare's play, first performed in 1611. One of the most deadly hurricanes ever hit the port and seaside resort of Galveston, Texas, on September 8, 1900. Poor forecasting meant that the tempest took the people of the city completely by surprise. Galveston lost around 15 per cent of its population and 6000 died on the nearby mainland.

Terror in a twister

Hurricanes wreak havoc, but for concentrated violence few things can match a tornado. Rotating funnels of cloud that form under thunderclouds, typically at the end of a hot summer afternoon, tornadoes often blaze a trail of destruction through the plains of Canada and the United States. Wind speeds within the funnel are believed to reach 300 mph (480 km/h) or more. One twister ravaged Edmonton, Alberta, on July 31, 1987. In

ALICIA	PAULINE	ANDREW	HUGO	AGNES
August 83 Texas	*October 97* Gulf of Mexico	*August 92* Florida and Louisiana	*September 89* South-east USA	*June 72* Florida and New York
Wind speed: 127 mph (204 km/h)	Wind speed: 132 mph (212 km/h)	Wind speed: 145 mph (233 km/h)	Wind speed: 145 mph (233 km/h)	Wind speed: 89 mph (143 km/h)

47

Spring of devastation

The Mississippi and its tributaries meander their way across the plains of the Midwest, creating a superb network of waterways – for most of the time. When the rivers break their banks, however, they deal death and destruction. Nowadays, flood-control systems seek to regulate their flow, but heavier than usual rains upstream or an unexpected snowmelt can still bring catastrophe.

Waterway *Flooded roads near Fargo in 1997.*

The 19th-century writer Mark Twain understood the Mississippi well, and its overwhelming power when unleashed. He knew that officials, engineers and their schemes 'cannot curve it or confine it, cannot say to it go here or go there and make it obey, cannot save a shore which it has sentenced, cannot bar its path with an obstruction which it will not tear down, dance over or laugh at.'

Flooded out *North Dakota homeowner Howard Hoof stands by his letterbox during the great flood of 1993.*

■ Disaster area (July-August 1993)

NORTH DAKOTA
MINNESOTA
SOUTH DAKOTA
WISCONSIN
Mississippi
NEBRASKA
IOWA
Missouri
Platte
ILLINOIS
St Louis
KANSAS
MISSOURI
Arkansas

Today, despite a comprehensive system of dykes and levees to contain the flow of the great river and its tributaries – the Ohio, Illinois, Missouri and Arkansas rivers – that truth still holds. Normally, the rivers meander in large, lazy-seeming loops across the plains of the Midwest, dropping the alluvial mud that makes such rich farming land. But it does not take much to tip the balance and change their character altogether. In 1993, heavy rains fell from January through to July. The result was massive flooding from mid June to early August, which turned the upper Mississippi basin into a vast inland sea covering some 141 000 sq miles (365 000 km²) in nine states. At least 50 people died in the 'great flood of 1993', and damage was put at $1 billion. Four years later, the Ohio burst its banks and created havoc, notably in Cincinnati where the water rose 12 ft (nearly 4 m) above its usual level. Thirty-five people died in the flooding.

'I saw a house pass by'

A year earlier, in July 1996, southern Quebec province suffered similar devastation when torrential rains made rivers, lakes and reservoirs overflow in the Saguenay valley. The floodwaters swept through towns and villages, destroying houses and office blocks. Around 16 000 people were evacuated; 488 homes were destroyed and at least 1000 flooded. Worst hit were the cities of La Baie, Jonquière and Chicoutimi. One eyewitness reported: 'I heard a noise, I looked outside, and I saw a house pass by.'

Thaw-time floods *An unusually heavy snowmelt in the Rockies caused rivers to burst their banks in April 1997.*

Flames of fear

Since 1871, when fire destroyed most of Chicago, Americans have been particularly aware of this hazard. Every year fires rage through the forests that still cover huge areas of the continent – a danger to humans and animals but an essential part of the natural ecosystem.

The perils posed by fire are deeply ingrained in the American consciousness. Historic events such as the conflagration that reduced 4 sq miles (10 km²) of Chicago to charred ruins in October 1871 have never been forgotten. The Chicago fire, which came at the end of a long spell of dry weather, raged for two days, consuming predominantly wooden buildings and pavements; it left 90 000 people homeless and some 300 dead.

Every summer, wildfires lick through vast acreages of North America's forests and threaten nearby residential areas. Sometimes they are ignited by lightning, sometimes by people, either through carelessness or, in the case of arson, deliberately. In 1991 a wildfire destroyed 3300 homes in Oakland, California, and caused damage worth $1.5 billion. Americans are well aware of how quickly fires spread and they appreciate both the skills of the firefighters and the new products that have been developed to help them – such as Phos-Chek, an environmentally safe chemical mix laid on the ground to create a barrier.

Life-giving fire

Yet experts are increasingly aware that there is another way of viewing fire. Over the millennia, wildfires have played an essential role in shaping environments as different as the pine forests of the West, the prairies of the Midwest and the Florida Everglades. 'Prescribed burns' (controlled fires) are now a tool in managing the environment in national and state parks and other reserves. The saw grasses of the Everglades and the prairie grasses of the plains, for example, grow from points near the base of the plant. This enables them to survive wildfires when other plants cannot. Without regular fires, other scrubby plants crowd out the grasses. In forests, low-intensity wildfires clear out the undergrowth, allowing new generations of saplings to grow up healthily. Paradoxically, they are also the

best guarantee against the truly destructive conflagrations that do occasionally occur, reducing forests to ashy wildernesses. Without the undergrowth, wildfires cannot build up the immense heat of these infernos.

Fighting the flames   A California firefighter silhouetted against a blaze. Below: The insignia that appears on the trucks and helicopters of the Los Angeles Fire Department.

Heroic firefighters

Around the start of the 20th century US municipalities set up their first professional fire departments. Firefighters' lives are full of drama – dashing into the flames, breaking down locked doors from the outside, carrying an unconscious person down several flights of stairs, keeping control of a hose that pumps out a colossal 2000 gallons (9000 litres) of water a minute – these are all part of the job. Many recruits drop out in the first few years, but once that threshold has been crossed, job satisfaction is high and most firefighters stay in the service for the rest of their working lives.

California: waiting for the 'Big One'

Living over one of the great fault lines in the Earth's crust, few Californians have any illusions about the dangers this presents. Yet they continue to live there, developing techniques for bracing buildings against earthquakes, and hoping they will survive when the 'Big One' strikes.

The earth shook under San Francisco at around 5.00 am on April 18, 1906, and in the ensuing mayhem and destruction some 3000 people died in central California, including 700 in San Francisco itself. The earthquake, measuring 8.3 on the Richter scale, had its epicentre around 50 miles (80 km) to the north-west of San Francisco. Fires raged in the city for three days, completing the work of devastation started during the 30 seconds of the tremor.

One survivor wrote: 'I felt that the fallen city could never rise again – people would be too fearful of living in a place which had been wracked by earthquake and consumed by fire.' In fact, of course, he was wrong: San Francisco promptly rebuilt itself. California bestrides a network of faults in the Earth's

San Andreas Fault

The San Andreas Fault is the line where two of the tectonic plates that make up the Earth's crust meet. Relative to each other, the eastern Pacific plate and the North American plate are edging their way at an average rate of 2 in (5 cm) a year in opposite directions. In reality, the movement occurs in fits and starts, due to friction between the plates, and it is this that causes earthquakes. During the 1906 earthquake the Pacific plate jerked an astonishing 21 ft (6.4 m) to the north-west.

The San Andreas Fault stretches for 700 miles (1100 km).

crust, of which the San Andreas Fault is the most famous. Yet it is a place where people want to live. Danger seems to add to the zest of living there – contributing, perhaps, to the Californians' characteristic enthusiasm for living for the moment.

Quake-proof building

Californians are not entirely reckless, however. An increasing number of federal, state and city directives have imposed or encouraged earthquake-resistant measures in buildings. Architects and engineers now have to incorporate certain basic

San Francisco, 1906 The 1906 earthquake almost completely destroyed the city. Martial law was declared, with the army called in to help the police maintain law and order and prevent looting. Firefighters dynamited whole buildings in an attempt to prevent the flames from spreading. Damage was estimated at $200 million.

All fall down *Houses in San Francisco that took a tumble in the earthquake of 1989. The earthquake measured 7.1 on the Richter scale, which goes from 0 to 10.*

features, such as metal 'braces' designed to absorb lateral (sideways) forces during an earthquake and transmit them down into the ground, rather than up into the rest of the building. At the same time, huge strides have been made in the more advanced aspects of earthquake-resistant design. These include the technique of 'base isolation' – a building constructed in this way has 'bearing pads' inserted between the building and its foundations. Often these consist of layers of rubber with steel plates sandwiched between them and a lead plug or core. In the vertical direction, the pads are rigid and strong, but they are flexible in the horizontal direction. If an earthquake strikes, the bearing pads bear the brunt of the vibrations rather than the building above.

Some proof of the effectiveness of these measures came in October 1989 when San Francisco was hit by its worst earthquake – 7.1 on the Richter scale – since the 1906 disaster. An entire section of the Oakland Bay Bridge collapsed. Pieces fell off the Interstate 208 freeway; the Embarcadero Freeway along the waterfront was severely damaged. Fires broke out in many places, and because of broken water mains, people had to form human chains to keep firefighters supplied with buckets of water – just like in 1906. The Opera House was among a number of public buildings damaged. In all, 63 people in the central Californian region died as a result of the earthquake; more than 3700 were injured and more than 12 000 were left homeless.

Yet what was also remarkable was the number of buildings that survived the shaking they had received, in particular many of the skyscrapers that had been going up in San Francisco's financial district since the late 1960s.

No through road *A collapsed flyover after the 1994 Los Angeles earthquake. It measured 6.8 on the Richter scale and displaced some 20 000 people.*

Fire from the Earth

When Mount St Helens erupted just after 8 am on May 18, 1980, it blew 1300 ft (400 m) off the top of the mountain, triggering what was probably the largest landslide in recorded history. Uncorked in this way, a blast of rock, ash and hot gas burst into the air, devastating an area of about 150 sq miles (390 km²). Up to 6 miles (10 km) to the north, the power of the blast stripped the trees from the hillsides. A column of ash rose more than 12 miles (19 km) into the atmosphere and was blown eastwards by the wind, blotting out daylight for 125 miles (200 km) – within two weeks, some of it had drifted right around the Earth.

As elsewhere along the Pacific Ocean's Ring of Fire, the volcanoes of North America's Pacific North-west have formed where two plates of the Earth's crust meet. The Juan de Fuca oceanic plate is pushing beneath the North American continental plate, and as it does so it partially melts some of the rock in the plate above; this rises towards the surface in volcanoes. Mount St Helens' neighbours include Mount Hood to the south, which last erupted in the 1860s, and Mount Rainier to the north. With its heavy topping of glacial ice and snow, Mount Rainier – rising to 14 409 ft (4392 m) above sea level – is considered particularly dangerous, partly because its slopes are weak and badly eroded, partly because it lies close to a number of urban centres, including the city of Seattle. Less dangerous are the volcanoes of the United States' other volcanic zone, the Hawaiian islands. Here, Kilauea has been erupting since 1983, releasing a steady flow of magma.

From forest to firewood *White-hot lava and ash expelled during the Mount St Helens eruption flattened all in its path.*

Flying over trouble *An aircraft dwarfed as it flies over the crater of Mount St Helens during the 1980 eruption.*

CHAPTER 3

THE RICHES OF A CONTINENT

The sea, the forests, the grass plains and the Earth itself with its mineral bounty, all yield up their riches. Lumbermen ply their trade in the immense forests of Canada. Cattle graze in the Midwest and West, where cowboys still round them up on horseback. Oil in Alaska, gold in the Yukon, coal in Nova Scotia – despite extremes of climate, companies exploit the mineral riches that help to fuel North America's mighty industrial machine. Modern technology has transformed agriculture – and also provoked an organic movement with weekly farmers' markets where growers sell direct to the people. In California and elsewhere winemakers create world-class vintages. The wealth of North America lies in the combination of abundant natural resources with dynamic, resourceful people, still imbued with the pioneer spirit of their forebears.

The cranberry harvest at Nantucket, Massachusetts.

The Chicago markets: capitalism in the raw

Capitalism created Chicago; capitalism sustains it. Strategically placed by the Great Lakes, the 'Windy City' became the hub of a growing rail network and marketplace for the agricultural riches of the Midwest.

They trade in just about everything in Chicago – and in huge quantities. Corn, wheat, soya beans, rice, eggs, pork bellies and vegetable oil are just some of the foodstuffs quoted on the exchanges. Commodities include silver bars, leather, gold, platinum and wood; then there is the trade in world currencies. Orders to buy and sell come in from all the world's great financial centres. Few of the goods traded actually make their way to the city. Instead, 'futures contracts' – a Chicago invention – bind the parties entering into them to buy or sell a fixed amount of a commodity on a specified date in the future. 'Options' are a refinement on that, giving the holder the right, though not the obligation, to buy or sell a futures contract.

Dealing frenzy Traders in one of the eight 'pits' of the Chicago Board of Trade's new trading hall, opened in 1997. This state-of-the-art facility accommodates 8000 frantic traders and their colleagues. Left: George Washington stares out from a dollar bill. The third largest city in the USA and a leading financial centre, Chicago is also home to one of the 12 Federal Reserve Banks of the Federal Reserve System.

A history of growth

Chicago's three financial markets – the Stock Exchange, the Board of Trade and the Mercantile Exchange – are a mighty power in the world of international finance. Roughly halfway between the east and west coasts, and close to the fertile plains of the Midwest, the city grew up through trade and has continued to thrive from it. Its spectacular rise began in the 1830s after the Erie Canal was completed, linking Buffalo on Lake Erie with Albany on the Hudson River. Until then the main route westward from the Atlantic seaboard had been along the Ohio valley. Now, this was shifted northward, up the Hudson valley, along the new canal and through the Great Lakes. From being little more than a collection of wooden huts and cottages around a fort, built on swampy ground where the Chicago River flows into Lake Michigan, Chicago grew into a city of 30 000 people by 1850. By 1880 it had 500 000 inhabitants.

Futures contracts

As the wheatbowl of the Midwest expanded during the 1840s, at certain times of year supply greatly exceeded demand, leading to large price fluctuations. In 1848, the Chicago Board of Trade (CBOT) was founded, and within a few years dealers were experimenting with a new way of trading that helped to smooth out the fluctuations. Instead of buying and selling the grain itself, they bought and sold contracts to deliver a specified amount of grain to a specified location on a specified date – the grain might not even have been planted. Futures contracts are now used in all the world's financial centres to trade not just in grain and crops, but also in commodities such as government bonds and metals.

Stock market latest   A street seller touting the Chicago Sunday Times' financial supplement, Final Markets. In the business district, most people take a keen interest in the markets.

Traders, brokers, runners and locals

Eight o'clock strikes, and seeming pandemonium breaks out on the floor of the Chicago Board of Trade. In the octagonal 'pits', where different commodities are traded, figures in brightly coloured jackets adorned with the logos of their brokerage firms shout and gesticulate wildly to one another. Message-bearers known as 'runners' scuttle from telephone booths to the brokers standing on the edges of each pit, bringing them orders from their clients. Another frantic day is starting in the world's leading futures market.

Behind the apparent chaos is the well-oiled machinery of a system that has evolved to cope with every likely emergency. The pits themselves are carefully designed in descending tiers to allow traders in different parts of them to see each other and pass on hand signals – an entire language by which traders can communicate with one another actross the heads of the crowd.

Each 'pie slice' of the octagon is dedicated to a particular month; traders dealing in futures due for delivery that month congregate in that slice. Brokers acting on behalf of corporate or individual clients stand around the edges of the pit; 'locals' who trade on their own behalf stand in the centre.

Winners and losers

Today, Chicago's Board of Trade and the 'Merc' are the two biggest futures and options exchanges in the world. Some 70 per cent of all futures contracts, whether for agricultural produce, metals, currencies, or even in some cases the value of a stock index, are traded in Chicago, and a jolt in the markets is often enough to send jitters circulating through world financial centres. At the same time, the atmosphere in the markets can often feel like that of a casino. Futures and options were originally devised to help to smooth the price fluctuations of certain basic commodities. The system worked, but the risks are still there, and while some people gambling on the exchanges make big profits, there is always the chance of emerging a loser.

Built on agriculture's bounty   The Art Deco front of the Board of Trade, completed in 1930. The figures on either side of the clock represent the twin pillars of the board's prosperity: wheat and corn (maize).

The Midwest: 'Heartland of America'

Across the vast grain fields roads are arrow straight, punctuated by occasional settlements with huge barns that store the precious harvest. The fertile heart of North America spreads out around the Great Lakes and the upper Mississippi, Missouri and Ohio rivers.

The winters are bitterly cold in the Midwest, with icy winds and frequent snowstorms; the summers are baking hot, with occasional tornadoes striking a trail of concentrated destruction across the plains. Making up for a climate of continental extremes is the fertility of the soil, which the farmers of the region exploit with an ever more sophisticated armoury of high-tech machines and chemicals. They are farming the so-called 'Heartland of America', covering a dozen states from Ohio in the east to Nebraska in the west, Minnesota in the north to Kansas in the south. The population live in small communities dotted across the vast flat expanse. Even in an electronic age they still hold dear the county gazette or local

Barley galore *Harvested barley being poured into a truck in Montana. Barley is used as an animal feed, especially for pigs. Malted barley – grain that has been allowed to sprout – is used to make beer and whisky.*

Techno-farming

Science and technology have transformed the business of farming in the Midwest. Bigger, better, newer machinery; strains of wheat, barley, maize and soya that have been specially bred and selected for their productivity; new high-yield

newspaper, mostly reporting the doings of other local farmers and their families. And, like all Americans, they make trips to the shopping mall, though it might take a 50 mile (80 km) drive to reach there.

Small town life

The towns themselves tend to follow a similar pattern. Laid out on a grid plan, they have a central business district where the local shopkeepers, lawyers, doctors and accountants have their premises in two or three-storey brick buildings. Outside the centre, the town-dwellers' homes mostly stand back from the street in large lots. A diverse array of churches belonging to different denominations reflects the varied ancestry of the inhabitants of the Midwest plains. Those of British Protestant stock still usually predominate, but in the Upper Midwest especially there are large numbers of Germans and Scandinavians, as well as Poles, Ukrainians and other Slavs. Lutherans, Catholics, Moravians, Baptists, Methodists and members of the Episcopal (Anglican) Church, all help to fill the pews.

Traditional country fairs

Summertime is fair time in rural North America. People come from their farms, ranches and communities and gather to inspect the latest in agricultural machinery, snap up any enticing offers from suppliers, enter their livestock in various competitions, feast on homemade delicacies or just swap news and gossip. The first fairs were held in the early 19th century to spread new ideas from Europe's agricultural revolution. By the 1830s they were becoming showcases for American inventions such as the McCormick reaper and Deere's steel plough.

Nowadays, the fairs continue their educational role through youth organisations such as the 4-H clubs and Future Farmers of America (FFA). Established in the early 20th century, these groups encourage young people to learn about plant identification, soil composition and other aspects of nature study.

On the cob *Grilled or barbecued corn is a standard treat at fairs.*

Farming belts *The Great Plains are the continent's grain basket, where three-fifths of its winter and spring wheat are grown. Soya beans, cattle, dairy foods and pigs are also produced. Fruit, vegetables and peanuts are the major crops of the south-east.*

☐ Wheat
■ Corn, soya
■ Dairy farming
■ Cotton
■ Rice, sugar cane, citrus fruit
▨ Market gardening, fruit

Giants in action Combine harvesters sweep across the summer wheat fields (left) like the tanks of an advancing army. High-tech irrigation systems (above) help the grain to grow in dry regions. Wheat is the United States' third-largest crop.

hybrid species; superefficient pesticides and fertilisers – all these are tools in a multibillion dollar agribusiness that stretches from the farmer in Missouri to the wholesale tycoon in Chicago. One result of increasing mechanisation has been a steady decline in those actively employed in agriculture, while those employed in related activities have increased – for example, agricultural advisers, technicians servicing farm machinery, chemists researching in the laboratories of fertiliser manufacturers, and bankers specialising in agricultural finance.

On a smaller scale In the north-eastern states the soil and climate are best suited to dairy farming.

World number one

The United States is the world's biggest producer of soya beans, corn and wood. It ranks second in the world for wheat, cotton and pigs. It lies third for cattle, fourth for wine and fifth for potatoes. It is the biggest world exporter of corn, accounting for about 65 per cent of the global market, and of wheat, accounting for 35 per cent of the global market. The total output of US agriculture is the largest of any country in the world, even though agriculture directly employs only 2.7 per cent of the population, living and working on more than 2 million farms. In the food industry as a whole, 18 per cent of the active population are involved in producing, processing and distributing food.

MANY SMALL FARMS BECOME FEWER LARGE FARMS

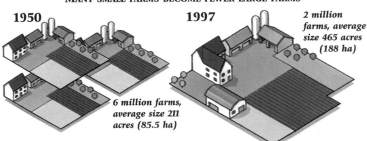

1950

1997

2 million farms, average size 465 acres (188 ha)

6 million farms, average size 211 acres (85.5 ha)

Freedom to farm

A law passed in 1996 introduced the biggest revolution in US farming for 60 years. The Federal Agriculture Improvement and Reform Act unscrambled much of the New Deal legislation, which was introduced in the 1930s to help farmers through the crisis years of the Depression but had become a straitjacket, imposing restrictions on what farmers could or could not grow. Under the 1996 Act, during an interim period from 1997 to 2002 farmers will get $30 billion in 'transition payments', but these will no longer be linked to what they grow. After 2002, the payments will cease, though loans and financial packages will be available through the US Department of Agriculture's Farm Service Agency.

The resources of the sea

The Oyster Bar at New York's Grand Central Station says it all: the bounty of North America's seas, lakes and rivers on your plate, once transported into the heart of the city by train, now more likely to go by road or air. Oysters and mussels from the Chesapeake Bay; haddock, halibut and redfish from the New England coast; sea bream, swordfish and marlin from the south-east – the seafood riches come from far and wide. Among the world's fishing nations, the United States ranks fifth, after China, Peru, Chile and Japan.

In New England they take their summer seashore picnics, known as clambakes, very seriously. First, the 'oven' has to be created. Well in advance, the picnickers make a kind of sandwich with alternate layers of rock and wood. They set fire to the wood and leave it to burn for an hour or so until the rocks are hot enough to retain their heat for a few more hours. Any unburnt wood is raked away, leaving hot coals and the hot rocks. Meanwhile, the cooks have gathered plenty of rockweed, a dark green seaweed with bubbles containing salt water. Layers of the rockweed are draped over the hot rocks, and on top of

On the rack *Walleyes (Stizostedion vitreum) are a favourite with game fishermen because of their tasty flesh. They live in the lakes and rivers of eastern North America and are fished commercially in the Great Lakes.*

them are placed racks of clams, mussels, lobsters, fish, sausages, corn, potatoes, onions and bread. The heap is then topped with a cap of canvas. Underneath the canvas, the bubbles of salt water in the rockweed burst in the heat, releasing steam that cooks the food. The whole clambake is left for up to three hours with the food steaming gently inside until the picnickers are ready to gather for their feast.

Savours of the sea

Every stretch of the North American coast has its special seafood riches. The Chesapeake Bay, slicing fjord-like into Virginia and Maryland, is famous above all for its blue crabs. The crabs are, in fact, a greenish colour on top and dirty white underneath, though the legs are blue. They are harvested when their shells are still soft, and then cooked and eaten, shells and all. More than half the fish sold in the United States comes from the Gulf of Mexico, the Pacific and the coastal waters of Alaska. Snapper, ranging in colour from red to smoky grey, is a favourite from the Gulf. From the Pacific north-west the great

France's island outposts

The last remnant of France's once extensive North American empire is a cluster of tiny islands lying off Newfoundland's southern coast. Covering just 93 sq miles (242 km²), the islands of Saint-Pierre and Miquelon were settled in the 17th century by Breton and Basque fishermen. Since 1976, they have been an overseas department of France; their 6400 inhabitants send a deputy to the National Assembly in Paris. Fishing is still their chief industry, though badly hit in recent times by the failing Newfoundland fisheries. The authorities in Paris have always taken a special interest in this last corner of France in North America – an interest that has taken the form of generous subsidies to keep the islanders' French way of life afloat.

Belonging neither to Canada nor to the USA, Saint-Pierre and Miquelon have also benefited as a base for smuggling, particularly during the Prohibition era from 1920 to 1933. Later, in the dark days of the Second World War and the German occupation of France, the islands played a small but significant part in the turning tide of resistance. In 1941 they became the first piece of French territory where General de Gaulle's Free French succeeded in ousting the Vichy authorities.

delicacy is several differing species of salmon, including chum salmon, coho salmon, chinook salmon, pink salmon and sock-eye salmon.

Salmon are anadromous fish – from a Greek word, *anadromos*, meaning 'running upwards': they live most of their lives at sea but migrate up rivers, often the same river in which they were born, in order to breed. Spring and autumn are their spawning seasons, when both game fishermen and those who fish for a living gather in the salmon-rich waters of Alaska and

Reaping the harvest Fishermen in Bristol Bay, Alaska, disentangle their catch of salmon from the nets (left). Right: Redfish (Sebastes marinus) spew out over the deck of a Maine fishing vessel. The redfish is a deep-water fish, common along the Atlantic coasts of Canada and New England. It is often used in fish fingers, though it also has an excellent flavour cooked fresh.

Cod and the Grand Banks

Newfoundland and parts of the neighbouring mainland were virtually built on cod. Since the days of explorers such as John Cabot in the 1490s, European and later local North American fishermen have braved the fogs and storms of the Grand Banks to exploit their riches. On Newfoundland, the fisheries dictated the siting of settlements and were the basis of most of its culture. Yet in 1992, to protect stocks, the Canadian government imposed a moratorium on cod fishing around the island, extending it to most of the east coast fishery the next year, and more than 40 000 people were thrown out of work.

Modern technology was to blame. From the 1950s, trawlers equipped with radar and sonar started to work the Grand Banks and the annual catch shot up from 300 000 tons in 1950 to 800 000 in the late 1960s. Then came a crash – down to about 200 000 tons a year in the late 1970s. The pressure of intensive fishing methods had proved too much.

Crowded waters The shallow waters of Bristol Bay off Alaska keep out larger vessels, leaving the riches of its salmon harvest to numerous smaller fishing boats like these.

British Columbia to reap the harvest. On the east coast, the Pacific fish's cousins, the Atlantic salmon, make their way up the rivers of Labrador, Quebec and New England, and offer similar sport. Eels, another anadromous fish, are also savoured. Their life cycle is a mirror image of the salmon's: they live most of their lives in fresh water but migrate to the Sargasso Sea in the mid Atlantic to breed.

The coastal waters of the Gulf of St Lawrence, meanwhile, have a wealth of lobsters, scallops, shrimps, crabs and sea urchins. Inland, the Great Lakes and rivers yield harvests of whitefish, smelt, trout and walleyes. In the far north of Alaska and Canada is the most northerly freshwater fish of all, the Arctic char, for centuries one of the mainstays of the Inuit diet and now much prized by anglers and food lovers.

Fish by the basket

When John Cabot returned to England in 1497 after exploring the north-east coast of North America, he reported that the fish were so abundant you could simply scoop them up in baskets. Today, huge factory ships and their attendant trawlers, some from as far afield as Russia and Spain, prowl North American waters. At the same time there has been a significant fall in the catch. Experts have put forward various explanations. In the Great Lakes and Chesapeake Bay, pollution is a serious factor, and a changing global climate may also have had an effect. Some people blame the growing numbers of seals, protected from hunting by international treaties; but the most likely cause is quite simply overfishing. Here, Canada has led the fight to try to prevent it, and in April 1992 its fisheries minister, Brian Tobin, hit world headlines when he announced the seizure of a Spanish trawler accused of violating international agreements to preserve fish stocks.

Jumping high Salmon spawn in fresh water.

The land of opportunity

Individuals and families seeking a better life gave North American society its present shape. Immigration is written into its very soul – and so is mobility, for people who crossed oceans to get to North America were also prepared to travel to find work. Americans are among the most mobile of nations, happily uprooting and following a job to the far side of the continent.

A young man from the United States' Hispanic community tells a story that thousands identify with: 'My grandparents were migrant workers. Every year when harvest-time came, they sought a work visa to go to California and Washington State. When the harvest was over, they went back home to Guatemala. My father was born when they were working in California. He became an American citizen – just like that. My parents, too, were farm workers. But my sister and I are studying at university. Lots of people think that just because my parents and their parents were migrant workers, we must lack intelligence or qualifications. Of course, my grandparents didn't have much money, but they weren't either lazy or idiots.'

Seasonal workers

Migrant workers have a key place in certain sectors of the US economy. A mobile work force, they follow the cycle of the seasons, arriving in time to pick particular fruits or vegetables, then taking to the road again when the harvest is over. Employers call on their services when they cannot get enough hands from among the local work force. As well as agriculture, other industries that make regular use of migrant workers are fishing and the timber trade, both of them seasonal.

Many of the workers are Mexicans who go back home when the work runs out. Conditions are hard, and few local American workers would put up with them. The labourers often have to toil away at monotonous tasks for 12 hours at a stretch, whatever the weather. Their temporary homes are ramshackle huts or sheds, sometimes with their families, sometimes without them. They are never in one place long enough to become integrated into local life or to keep their children in the local schools. In any case, from the age of 12, or even younger, the children are often expected to work in the fields alongside their parents, even if this breaks the labour

Harvest   *California fruit groves.*

Mass acceptance   *Above are just some of the 10 000 immigrants – more than half of them Mexican – granted US citizenship in an open-air ceremony in Texas Stadium, Dallas, on September 17, 1996.*

César Chavez: fighting for farm workers

César Chavez was born in Arizona in 1927. Of Mexican descent, his family lost their small farm in the Depression. During the Second World War Chavez served in the US Navy; after the war, he settled in California, where he became an organiser for the workers' rights group Community Service Organization (CSO). In 1962 he founded his own farm workers' union and led a strike against California grape growers; later he directed his energies into organising a nationwide boycott of California grapes. By 1970 this had persuaded most grape growers to sign contracts with his United Farm Workers (UFW).

laws. A number of organisations have tried to improve the living and working conditions for the migrant workers, but despite various pieces of legislation and the best efforts of the unions, progress has been slow.

Nation of immigrants

North America was, of course, built on immigration, both forced and voluntary. Europeans, Africans, Chinese 'coolies' who came in the late 19th century to work as labourers on the expanding railroad network – all arrived from across the seas. Even the American Indians originated many thousands of years ago as immigrants from Asia. At the start of the 20th century, the object was to assimilate immigrants into the American 'melting pot'. 'There can be no fifty-fifty Americans in this country,' asserted former President 'Teddy' Roosevelt in 1918. 'There is room here for only 100 per cent Americanism, only for those who are American and nothing else.'

In recent decades, the flow of immigration has stepped up once more, this time coming mostly from other parts of the Americas and from Asia. Combined with natural demographic

change, this has transformed many of the old notions of the melting pot. Nowadays, many Americans regard themselves as 'hyphenated' Americans – African-Americans, Italian-Americans, Irish-Americans, Polish-Americans – proud of being American, but proud also of their roots in other cultures, which are maintained through the language of the 'old country', through religion, through special newspapers and by trips abroad to see where their forebears came from. One of the fastest growing groups are Hispanics. Until recently, an estimated 1.5 million illegal immigrants came across the Mexican frontier each year. The flimsy fortifications that guard much of the border, insulating the rich world to the north from the poorer one to the south, have reduced but not stopped the flow.

Wading in   Many illegal immigrants wade through rivers, swamps and marshes to get into the United States – hence the term 'wetback', often taken as an insult. For most, it is worth the hardship. Below: Before 1890, the bulk of immigrants came from Europe, though there had also been the enforced transportation of slaves from Africa and some immigration from China. Since 1961, however, the biggest influx has been from Latin America.

Ellis Island

Between 1892 and 1943, Ellis Island in New York harbour was the gateway to America for 20 million people. Established as an immigrant reception centre in 1892, it processed an average of 5000 people a day in the year of its opening. On

April 17, 1907, an astonishing 11 747 immigrants passed through Ellis Island. For most, the process involved a medical inspection and registration formalities. Some two per cent of immigrants were turned away because they were carriers of infectious diseases, held subversive political views or had questionable morals.

Before 1890

1890-1960

1961 onwards

In the forest: the lumber industry

The forest features strongly in the stories and legends of North American pioneers. Early settlers made clearings and built log cabins; fur trappers disappeared into the forest for months on end. Nowadays, the forests are a source of wealth in many regions, providing timber for building and furniture, and pulp for paper.

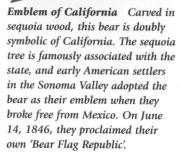

Emblem of California *Carved in sequoia wood, this bear is doubly symbolic of California. The sequoia tree is famously associated with the state, and early American settlers in the Sonoma Valley adopted the bear as their emblem when they broke free from Mexico. On June 14, 1846, they proclaimed their own 'Bear Flag Republic'.*

Lumberjacks *Alaska's timber trade (left and below) is the state's second biggest industry after oil.*

The life of the lumberjack has been transformed during the 20th century. In the early days of the lumber industry in Canada, men usually worked on farms during the summer and autumn until the last of the harvest had been gathered in. Then as the first snows fell, some headed for the forests. Frequently, they did not come home again until spring, then they came floating down the rivers on rafts of logs destined for the sawmills and pulp factories. This hard and often lonely life has changed steadily over the course of the century until, by the 1950s and 60s, the men were often better paid and better fed in the forest camps than they were at home. Today, the timber industry is a high-tech business, staffed by skilled machine operatives, mechanics, assessors and accountants.

A home in the woods

In both the east and west of North America, the forest was for a long time more an obstacle than a resource. It was something the pioneer settlers had to clear before they could start sowing the crops that would provide their livelihood. Its only positive uses were as a source of wood for building homes and outbuildings, and as fuel for heating. In itself, the forest was considerably less valuable than the skins of the animals that lived in it; for 200 years until the early 19th century, fur was the gold of the north.

It was Napoleon's continental blockade, imposed in 1806 during the Napoleonic Wars against Britain, that transformed the fortunes of the North American timber industry. By then the French had most of the continent of Europe in their hands; according to an edict issued by Napoleon, any ships from Britain or its colonies that entered a port under French control would be seized. The Royal Navy, which had long relied on timber imported from the continent of Europe to build its ships, had to turn to Britain's remaining North American colony to supply its needs. As a result, Canada's forests acquired an economic importance that they have had ever since, although nowadays they supply the requirements of the wood pulp and paper industry, as well as wood for building and for furniture.

Giants of the east and west

The Canadian forests cover an area equivalent to almost half of Europe. The ways in which they are commercially exploited depend partly on the lie of the land, partly on the kinds of tree

The axe man In south-eastern Alaska, tree trunks are bound together and transported as rafts. Timber is exported to Asia and the Pacific region.

Forest cover Forests spread over 970 000 sq miles (2.5 million km²) of the United States, and 1.6 million sq miles (4.1 million km²) of Canada.

The insect tree-strippers

Insects help to keep forests healthy by breaking down litter on the forest floor and getting rid of diseased and old trees, but in some circumstances they become serious pests. In North American forests, the spruce budworm (*Choristoneura fumiferana*) can eat its way through enormous quantities of evergreen needles and leaves. Infestations of the caterpillars strip vast areas of forest bare, often leading to the death of the trees. Between 1970 and 1985, a series of major spruce budworm infestations defoliated some 200 000 sq miles (500 000 km²) of forest in Canada and the north-eastern USA – an area roughly the size of Spain.

that grow in them. In the Pacific coastal forests of British Columbia, giant trees such as Douglas fir, western red cedar, Sitka spruce and western hemlock predominate. Most of the wood goes to the building and furniture industries. In the east, Ontario and Quebec have vast softwood forests of spruce, balsam fir and jack pine spreading as far north as the tundra. Their chief use is for making wood pulp. In the west, the towering trees are felled and their branches are logged off using chainsaws. Then they are fed into huge machines to be turned into planks. In the east, machines with immense hydraulic jaws plough through the softwood forests, stripping the branches from the trunks and placing the logs in neat piles. The axe has not quite become a museum piece, but its importance is no greater than that of a spoon in a food processing plant.

Import, export

The timber industry is less important in the US economy than in the Canadian. The United States imports more timber than it exports; what little it does export comes mostly from Maine and the north-western states and goes to Canadian timber factories. The industries on both sides of the frontier benefit from disasters such as Hurricane Andrew, which destroyed 85 000 homes when it struck Florida in August 1992.

Ready to roll These trunks, felled in Oregon, will be turned into pulp for making paper.

63

Mineral riches

North America is rich in mineral resources. In the 19th century gold triggered the spectacular gold rushes in California and the Klondike. In the 20th century oil, dubbed black gold, has been found in several regions of the United States and Canada. The United States and Canada are the world's second and third-largest producers of copper. Both countries have vast resources of coal, nickel, iron and uranium.

Ready to blow *A miner in British Columbia laying explosives. Coal, copper, iron and lead are all mined in the province.*

Petroleum riches *In 1996 Canada produced 1.8 million barrels of crude oil a day. The USA produced almost 6.5 million barrels a day.*

Expanding industry

In the United States, unlike most other countries in the world, coal mining has been steadily growing since the 1960s – as have most other types of mining. Even so, it still imports large quantities of minerals – even the ones it produces itself – because the needs of US industry are greater than the country's production. For those involved in mining, it is a much safer business today than it was in the past. Miners still die in accidents – 30 in Virginia and Kentucky since 1983 – but these figures are small compared to events such as the 1924 Benwood colliery disaster in West Virginia, which took 119 lives.

When gold was found at Sutter's Mill in California's Central Valley, in January 1848, it triggered the first great gold rush in North America. Some 80 000 eager prospectors made their way to the West Coast, many braving the sea route round Cape Horn. Four decades later, in 1886, another strike was made in US territory, in the Alaskan sector of the Yukon valley. That, and a later find across the Canadian frontier in the Klondike, set off more stampedes. For the most part, the strikes were alluvial deposits, gold dust or grains, which had to be 'panned' from river sand or rock. Dirt was placed in a pan or basin and then washed with large amounts of water until only gold, if there was any, remained. A few keen amateurs still try their luck at panning, but almost all gold is now mined from underground deposits. Gold, iron, nickel, copper, magnesium, niobium (a soft, greyish-white metallic element used in stainless steel and other alloys) and silicon – all these and more are mined in North America.

Fossil fuels

North America has ample supplies of fossil fuels for generating electricity, and in Canada the fossil resources are supplemented by the widespread use of water power. Alberta, British Columbia and the Northwest Territories also have big oil and natural gas reserves, and more have been discovered on the continental shelf off Newfoundland and Nova Scotia. Canada is counting on the supply from these offshore oilfields as a source for its future needs.

Abandoned by time

Les Forges du Saint-Maurice, near the city of Trois-Rivières in Quebec, could be described as one of North America's oldest industrial sites. It was here, in the 1730s, that a local merchant and landowner, François Poulin de Francheville, established Canada's first iron mines and foundries. Among their products were iron stoves that replaced the more traditional hearths in Canadian homes.

The foundries at Saint-Maurice, which ceased operating in 1883, are now a National Historic Site. Dawson City in the Yukon preserves memories of the Klondike gold rush in 1897-8. Thousands of prospectors poured into the Klondike region, and almost overnight Dawson City sprang from being a small trading post to a boom town where at its height 20 000 to 30 000 people lived in makeshift log buildings or tents.

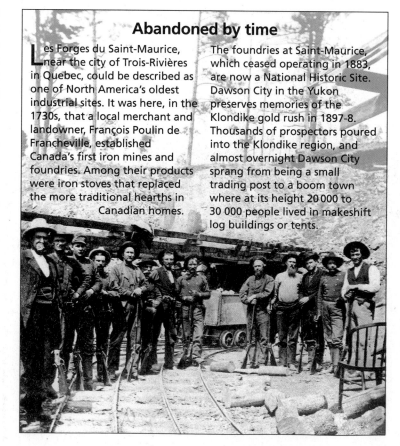

A life of danger

The rewards in mining can be good, but the risks are considerable. At 5 am on May 9, 1992, an underground blast tore through the brand-new Westray colliery, near Stellarton, Nova Scotia, and left 26 miners dead. A spark had ignited a pocket of methane gas at the coal face, triggering a massive coal dust explosion. A public inquiry uncovered a complicated story of incompetence that left few reputations intact, from the mine owners to the government officials supposed to enforce safety regulations. The wrecked mine was closed down, and the surviving workers laid off. Six years later, they were still fighting for compensation. Justice Peter Richard noted that the explosion was 'an event that, in all good common sense, ought not to have occurred. It did occur – and that is our unfortunate legacy'.

In the same month miners at the Giant gold mine in Yellowknife, Northwest Territories, went out on strike in a bitter dispute that tore the community apart. The owner, Peggy Witte, brought in replacement workers, and tragedy struck on September 18, 1992, when a bomb planted in the mine by one of the strikers exploded, killing nine men.

At the face *A worker and his drill in a Kentucky coal mine.*

Oil from sand *A plant for treating oil-impregnated sand in the Athabasca River valley in northern Alberta, Canada (below). The oil sands line a 70 mile (110 km) stretch of the river. By 1995 more than 200 000 barrels of oil a day were being extracted.*

Laying the line *Sections of pipe for the Trans-Alaska Pipeline, which was completed in 1977 (left). By the late 1990s, the pipeline was carrying over 1.4 million barrels of oil each day.*

Cowboys and rodeos

The cowboy is still very much a reality on the cattle ranches of the West and Midwest. At traditional rodeos amateurs and professionals test their skills in calf-roping, bull-riding, steer-wrestling, saddle bronco-riding and bareback bronco-riding.

In the carnival atmosphere of the rodeo, the one group of people who cannot let themselves relax are the cowboys. Riding bareback on an angry bull or an unbroken horse (a bronco), the rodeo cowboy can never forget the hair's-breadth gap that separates triumph from possibly fatal disaster. With his Stetson on his head and his leather 'chaps' (protective overleggings), the cowboy has his few fateful seconds in the corral. Winner or loser, he is an authentic survivor of a world that really did exist, though most people know it only in the version presented in Hollywood Westerns.

Out on the range *The horse is still the best way of getting around (above). Below: Bull-riding is a traditional rodeo event.*

'Daddy of 'em all'

Even today, although rodeos are a speciality of the more rural states of the West, they have an appeal that grips even the most sophisticated visitors. Each year hundreds of thousands of spectators gather for the most famous annual events. Oldest among these is the Cheyenne Frontier Days, the 'Daddy of 'em all', held every year since 1897. This six-day bonanza is staged in June in Cheyenne, Wyoming, with American Indian dancing, costume parades, transport cavalcades and all the usual fairground attractions, as well as the rodeo events. A traditional contest for cowgirls is the barrel race, a saddle (as opposed to bareback) horse race around sets of barrels. The other world-famous rodeo festival is Canada's Calgary Stampede, featuring re-enactments of battles between cowboys and American Indians. The rodeo circuit

Bull-riding *Canada's most famous rodeo is the Calgary Stampede.*

Life of a cowboy: old ways, new ways

Tom Garrison is a cowboy in Montana, the fourth-largest of the states, with one of the lowest population densities – roughly five people per sq mile (two per km²). Rolling hills cover most of the eastern part of the state, grazed by millions of cattle and sheep. The Great Plains stretch into Canada to the north, the Dakotas to the east and Idaho and Wyoming to the south. The huge barrier of the Rockies rises to the west. Settlements are few and widely scattered. The outdoors with its overarching skies and mind-boggling vastness is the environment in which most people live and work. Ranches are enormous, some covering hundreds of square miles.

For Tom Garrison, life is a mix of old and new. Working on a large ranch, he spends three-quarters of the year living in a log cabin by a creek with wooded slopes rising on either side. Beside the cabin is a corral, where he keeps his four horses when he is not out on the range, checking up on the hundreds of cattle that he is responsible for. In many ways, his life is like that of his predecessors a century ago, except for the four-wheel-drive vehicle parked outside his cabin. Thanks to that, he can drive into town along the bumpy tracks and roads in about two hours – a journey that would take a whole day on horseback. And every day he is in touch with the ranch manager on CB radio.

Bears and pumas roam the hills that surround Garrison's cabin, and at night he can sometimes hear coyotes howling at the moon. For his day-to-day work, the horse remains by far the most efficient way of getting around. Twice a year the cattle are taken from their winter pastures to their summer ones and back again, and then there is the annual round-up, when they are brought together to be counted and branded. During a drive, Garrison is in the saddle nonstop from before dawn to after dark.

Deserted ranch
A former cowboy's hut preserved in Arches National Park, Utah. Today, even the remotest hut has electricity, radio and other basic modern conveniences.

also includes many small or medium-sized events, sponsored by local chambers of commerce or other civic bodies. Youth associations and schools hold junior rodeos.

Hubbub, timing and style

Events unroll against a background uproar of bands playing, choirs singing and loudspeakers booming out snippets of country music, interspersed with expert commentaries on the cowboys' performances. Timing and style are the things to watch for. In riding events, the cowboy enters the corral already mounted on his bronco or bull, and has to stay on for at least 8 seconds. The judges award points according to the performance of the animal as well as that of the rider. In calf-roping, a mounted cowboy has to lasso a calf, then dismount and throw the animal to the ground and tie up three of its feet with a rope. The cowboy who does this fastest wins; some manage to complete the whole exercise in less than 15 seconds. In steer-wrestling, the mounted cowboy has to dive onto the bullock from his horse, grab its horns and wrestle it to the ground; this is sometimes done in under 10 seconds.

At the end of the day, with the prizes awarded, the cowboys take a rest. For the professionals among them the road then beckons. For them the rodeo season is an exhausting round, taking them to many corners of the United States and Canada and countless motel rooms.

The Texas Rangers

When, in the 1820s, the first American families settled in what was then Mexican territory, they needed protection. In August 1823, the settlers' leader, Stephen F. Austin, got permission from the Mexican government for ten volunteers to guard their frontiers against neighbouring American Indian groups and Mexican outlaws. These men were called the Texas Rangers. Fighting against the Indians, they learned many Indian ways, including superb horsemanship. By the time Texas set itself up as an independent republic in 1836, the Rangers had become a formidable force, organised into companies of 25 men each. After Texas joined the Union as a state in 1845, they were incorporated into the US Army and saw action in the Mexican War of 1856-8, where they earned a high reputation for their fighting skill and courage. When Texas seceded from the Union at the start of the Civil War, they became the state's chief military force – but were disbanded after the North's victory. They were re-formed in 1874 with two chief tasks: to help to maintain law and order within Texas and to protect settlers from the still hostile American Indians. Today, the Rangers come under the Texas Department of Public Safety. There are just over 100 of them, while 300 'special Rangers' can be appointed in an emergency. They have many of the powers as a sheriff, but their authority extends throughout Texas.

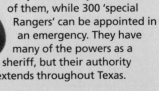

High-tech agriculture

Agriculture in California is twice as profitable as the national average: some 20 per cent of US agricultural exports come from the state. Many farms are huge, but there is another trend – small-scale fruit and vegetable growers who sell their produce in farmers' markets.

Citrus ices *What Florida citrus growers dread most are unexpected frosts that blight their ripening fruit (above). Industrial-scale farming in Florida and California coexists with smaller-scale fruit and vegetable production that supplies shops like Bread of Life (below) at Cupertino in California.*

Grapes, tomatoes, strawberries, figs, dates, citrus fruit, almonds, asparagus, lettuce, rice, sugar beet, cotton – California grows them all. In the Central Valley, the agricultural heartland, the air is thick in season with the scent of fruit blossom; a few weeks later trucks and trailers loaded with oranges, grapefruits, lemons or limes, trundle along the roads, the image of abundance. Sheltered on either side by mountains running parallel with the coastline, and watered by the Sacramento and San Joaquin rivers, the Central Valley boasts the three most productive counties in the United States – Tulare, Fresno and Kern. Other rich agricultural areas include Monterey Bay and the Salinas Valley, south of San Francisco; and near the Mexican border in the far south the Coachella and Imperial valleys, huge oases surrounded by desert.

Drip-feed watering

Irrigation is the key to this abundance, with networks of canals, dams and pumping stations. California's irrigation systems are state-of-the-art – a series of droughts has obliged farmers to make sure that as little water as possible is wasted. Open canals lose water through evaporation, so most farms now have systems that drip-feed the trees in their orchards. Sensors measure how much water each tree is losing through its leaves and a nozzle feeds it with exactly the amount of water it needs. Some 75 per cent of farms use this equipment, with a 30 per cent saving in the water they use. As 80 per cent of the region's water is used in agricultural irrigation, the saving is considerable.

Farmers and researchers have long enjoyed a close relationship through the University of California's campus at Davis in the Central Valley. Farmers drive ultra high-tech tractors and manage their costs using the latest software packages. They get advice from the Internet; some even sell their produce via the Web. They have equipment that regularly measures the condition of the soil and the results are fed into a computer, which analyses them to assess the best times to plant crops. In California, the farmer's age-old instinctive relationship with the soil and the weather has given way to this more scientific approach.

Selling it direct

Farmers' markets are booming in North America. They take place at the same time each week in empty city blocks, neighbourhood centres, even churches. Farmers bring along their produce and the customers buy direct, assured of a freshness and seasonal variety rarely available at a supermarket. For small and medium-sized farmers, the markets free them from the tyranny of the supermarket chains.

Producers growing for farmers' markets have to diversify; week after week, they need a relatively small amount of produce to sell. In California, for example, fruit growers who sell chiefly through the state's numerous farmers' markets may cultivate 100 or more varieties from species as diverse as apples, plums, peaches, pomegranates and citrus – all on 20 acres (8 ha) of land. Some of these are new varieties, but many are heirlooms, often varieties passed over by supermarkets, perhaps because their flesh is soft and bruises easily while being transported. This is not a problem for producers selling locally. As a result, the markets have sparked a new interest in nearly forgotten strains. Produce does not have to be organic, but most is.

Bread of Life
ALTERNATIVE   FOOD   STORE

West Coast wines

Until the 1960s, California wines were regarded as cheap fare for easy drinking. Since then, the wine-makers of the Napa and Sonoma valleys have established themselves as producers of world-class fine wines, even exporting to proud European wine-producing nations such as France.

Wine country *The attraction of tasting wine makes the Napa Valley (left) a popular tourist spot. Above: The chief wine-making regions, north of San Francisco.*

For many health and style-conscious Americans, wine is less and less a luxury and more a pleasure of everyday life. The United States is now firmly established as a major wine-producing nation, ranking fourth in the world after the formidable European trio of France, Italy and Spain. In 1998 it exported $425 million worth of wine, the bulk of it going to Britain, Canada and Japan.

World-class players

The most famous and widely esteemed wines are the powerful Chardonnays and Cabernet Sauvignons from California's Napa Valley – more than 90 per cent of US wine comes from California. But recent years have seen a shift in the balance, due in part to an outbreak of the damaging phylloxera louse in the 1990s. Many Napa wineries have had to replant their vines, and some have experimented with new varieties, including a number of Italian and Rhône Valley ones, such as Marsanne for white wine, and Barbera and Sangiovese for red wine.

Other regions have started to make their presence felt, notably the Napa Valley's neighbour, the Sonoma Valley, best known for its Chardonnays and Pinot Noirs. Outside California, Oregon also makes Pinot Noirs, many of them much prized by connoisseurs. Farther north, Washington State has vineyards on the slopes of the Cascade Mountains. Even Canada has entered the fray, notably with its German-style 'icewines', made in British Columbia and Ontario from grapes that are left on the vine until the first frost and then picked and crushed while still frozen. On the East Coast, vineyards on Long Island have achieved some fame for their soft fruity Merlots. Other wine-producing pockets are scattered as widely as Arizona, Georgia, Texas, Missouri, Virginia and Maryland.

The birthplace of Californian wine

Matured in oak
A Californian wine cellar.

Sonoma Valley can claim to be the birthplace of the Californian wine industry. It was here, in the 1820s, that Franciscan missionaries planted the first vines. Later, in 1857, the Hungarian-born adventurer Count Agoston Haraszthy founded Sonoma's thriving Buena Vista Winery. Encouraged by Governor John Downey, he toured the wine-growing regions of Europe and came back with thousands of cuttings from 300 different grape varieties. He kept some of them and sold the rest. Above all, he spent many years experimenting, planting different varieties in different places, until he had established the soil and climatic conditions in which each yielded the best results.

CHAPTER 4
THE HEART OF NORTH AMERICA

The fevered bustle of a Wall Street dealing room; the clip-clop of a horse-drawn Amish wagon; the gowns and mortarboards of ranks of university students on graduation day – the North American continent presents a kaleidoscopic variety of images. In the south, cities such as Savannah and Charleston preserve the privileged elegance of pre-Civil War days, and exploit it for their survival in the present. In the north, ice hockey and snowmobile trails provide the entertainment. In the west, Las Vegas, 'Sin City', has transformed its image in recent years, becoming a place for family fun. Back east, huge events like New York's St Patrick's Day parade bring whole cities to a festive standstill each year.

Los Angeles police cadets celebrate the end of their training.

Giants of the highways

They steer their huge vehicles along the highways of North America. Their cabs are their mobile workplaces; like modern nomads they are constantly on the move, spending every night in a different motel. The truckers of North America are the men and women who keep this mightiest of consumer societies afloat, transporting and delivering, linking the four corners of the continent.

Some 3 million gleaming 18 wheel monsters thunder along the United States' highways, carrying goods to all corners of the continent. According to the ATA (American Trucking Associations), the trucking industry employs 9.5 million people nationwide. It consists of 450 000 haulage firms, which in 1996 carried 6.5 billion tons of freight, covering in the process more than 166 billion miles (267 billion km) – equivalent to travelling to the Sun and back nearly 900 times. The ATA estimates that 77 per cent of all US communities are served by trucking and by no other means of freight delivery.

Life on the road

The trucker has entered American folklore as a stereotype – a fat, boorish, solitary creature whose only contact with civilisation is the motel where he spends the night. The truth, of course, is rather different. The nature of the truckers' job means that they are undoubtedly a breed apart, with a language and slang of their own. They are individuals with a nomadic roaming spirit and a resolute independence – like that of many of the pioneers of the Wild West. Generally speaking, truckers are people with no appetite for the routine of regular office hours or the factory floor. They want to be their own bosses, heading small businesses. A CDL (commercial driver's licence) offers them this freedom. Hundreds of trucking teams consist of married couples who have managed to rake together the $100 000 they need to buy a long-haul truck and who work, travel and make their living together on the road. Even so, there are limits to their freedom. To some extent, all – even those who own their own trucks – are dependent on the big haulage firms that offer them work, tell them where they have to go and when, and fix the rates at which they will be paid.

Duel on the highways

In the smash-hit film *Jaws*, director Steven Spielberg plays on the fears so easily aroused in us by those monstrous 'killing machines' of the deep – sharks. Four years earlier, in 1971, he had used the gleaming monsters of the US highways to much the same effect. American trucks, unlike their European cousins, have a prominent 'snout' that houses the powerful motor and an enormous exhaust pipe beside the driver's cabin.

Duel, Spielberg's fourth film for television and his first for the big screen, took just 16 days to shoot. In it a travelling salesman driving peacefully along a not very busy highway becomes involved in a chase with a huge black petrol tanker. At first, the salesman, David Mann, assumes that this is little more than a game. He overtakes the truck, which then overtakes him in what seems like a playful bout of tit-for-tat. But gradually things take on a more sinister aspect. The truck seems to have a life and will of its own – the driver is never seen – and it seems to be out to destroy Mann.

The salesman's name suggests a level of allegory hinted at in the

film. The increasingly terrifying chase as Mann seeks to escape the monstrous black impersonal truck suggests another duel: the modern duel between humans and the machinery they create, which seems to have assumed a life and momentum of its own.

Truck stop   *The air shimmers above the hot tarmac (left); and the road stretches on and on. A trucker's life may seem monotonous to some, but it is also free. Left, inset: Up to 100 trucks may gather at a truck stop equipped with a garage and a diner.*

Magnificent machines   *The gleaming grills and exhaust pipes bear witness to the love and care that most truckers lavish on their precious machines. Inside will be a comfortable cabin for those who prefer not to stay in motel rooms.*

Caring and promoting

America's trucking associations are a force to be reckoned with. For the truckers they act as trade unions, providing legal and financial aid, health insurance and pension plans, and publishing special interest magazines and Web sites. Through bodies such as the American Trucking Associations (ATA) they act as a powerful pressure group on Capitol Hill and in the various state legislatures.

Promoting highway safety is another of their concerns – the number of accidents involving trucks is in fact relatively low. According to the ATA, nearly 42 000 people died on US roads in 1997. Of these deaths, only 13 per cent were accidents involving trucks. A feature of the ATA's safe driving campaign is America's Road Team, operating under the slogan 'Safety is our driving concern'. Each year 12 drivers are chosen to be Road Team Captains. Generally, they each have at least a million miles of accident-free driving behind them. They take a few days off each month to speak on local radio and TV stations, addressing high schools and business associations, and passing on safe driving tips – and improving the profile of truckers in the process.

Military might

With the ending of the Cold War, the US has had to rethink military policy. The long-range nuclear missiles built during the time of US-Soviet rivalry remain, but today the US armed forces are more likely to be involved in localised conflicts, such as the Gulf War.

'Hail to the Chief'

At the pinnacle of the US defence hierarchy stands the Commander-in-Chief, the President. At official ceremonies he alone has the right to the anthem 'Hail to the Chief'. Under him is the Department of Defense (DoD), headquartered since 1947 in the Pentagon. Conscription ceased in 1973 near the end of the Vietnam War. Since then the four branches of the US armed services have been entirely professional forces. A fifth service, the Coast Guard, is under the Department of Transportation in peacetime, but can be transferred to the DoD in time of war. Each armed service has reserve forces that can be called up in wartime, and each state has a National Guard that can be called out at any time.

The intelligence operations of the DoD include the National Security Agency, which is responsible for code-cracking and electronic eavesdropping. Other DoD agencies include the Ballistic Missile Defense Organization, which oversees research into missile technology and the acquisition of new missiles, and the Defense Advanced Research Projects Agency, whose chief task is 'to maintain US technological superiority over potential adversaries'.

In 1997, the US had some 1.4 million of its citizens under arms, and was spending 3.6 per cent of its gross domestic product (GDP) on defence. Canada had fewer than 62 000 people in its armed forces and was spending 1.5 per cent of GDP on defence.

As the sole surviving superpower, the United States has been kept busy since the end of the Cold War. Its armed forces have seen action in Iraq during the Gulf War in 1991, in Somalia in 1992, in Haiti in 1994, in Bosnia in 1995 and most recently against Serbia in the Kosovo crisis. However, the absence of a single, clearly defined enemy, as in the Cold War decades, has led successive presidents and Congress to reduce defence spending. The four branches of the armed forces – the Army, Navy, Marines and Air Force – have each seen their budget cut by a third.

Military manpower

With 491 000 active duty troops serving in ten divisions, the Army has the highest manpower of the services. The Air Force, with 370 000 men and women, has seven bombing divisions and 20 fighter divisions. The Navy has 365 000 sailors and more than 300 warships of different kinds, including 12 aircraft carriers. The 170 000 Marines pride themselves on being the toughest infantry troops in all the US armed forces, and usually the first into action. Today, 90 per cent of the United States' service personnel have some kind of further education and an appropriate qualification. Officers are trained to the rigorous standards of the military academies, notably West Point for the Army, Annapolis for the Navy and Colorado Springs for the Air Force.

Women are accepted into the armed forces, but with certain restrictions. In the Army, female troops are never included in combat units; in the Navy, they do not serve on submarines. There are a number of women fighter pilots, however, and a woman can rise to the command of a ship. Recent charges of sexual harassment have highlighted the continuing difficulties involved in integrating women into the armed forces.

Defence web

The vast office block of the Pentagon stands in Arlington, Virginia, across the Potomac river from Washington. Headquarters of the US Department of Defense and the command centre for the armed forces, the Pentagon is at the heart of a complex web of alliances and treaties of mutual assistance, of which NATO is by far the most important. Nowadays, US policy is usually to play the lead role in a multinational force rather than to go into a conflict single-handed. Nuclear deterrence is just one strategic element among a number of others. Even so, the nuclear arsenal is considerable: intercontinental missiles are still in their silos; bombers and submarines carrying nuclear weapons patrol the skies and seas.

In recent years the Pentagon has pumped research funding into ways of combating chemical and biological weapons. It has also

75

Wall of remembrance *Dedicated in November 1982, the Vietnam Veterans Memorial in Washington DC (above) soon became the federal capital's most visited monument. It is the work of the sculptor Maya Ying Lin, when she was still an architecture student. The black granite wall is inscribed with the names of 58 191 soldiers known to have died in the war. Directories help visitors to find the names of loved ones.*

GI Joe

In the 1930s the term GI was used to describe anything supplied by the US military, such as GI shoes – government issue shoes. Then it came to mean anything relating to or characteristic of the US military, such as a GI haircut. Finally, in the Second World War, it came to mean the US serviceman himself, well supplied with government issue cigarettes, corned beef – and dollars.

In 1944 the Serviceman's Readjustment Act was passed, in a move to help the US armed forces to make the transition back into civilian life, and the new law was rapidly nicknamed the GI Bill of Rights.

A year later, the movie *The Story of GI Joe* was released. This hymn of praise to the grit and valour of ordinary GIs during the Italian campaign was based on coverage by Ernie Pyle, the prize-winning war correspondent. The figure of GI Joe, the all-American serviceman hero, had entered the national mythology.

had to rise to the challenge of new technology. The ability of the Air Force to deliver computerised 'surgical strikes' against carefully pinpointed targets was proved in Iraq, both during the Gulf War in 1991 and in punitive raids in 1998. Ships are tied into a computer network that relays commands but also allows shore-based personnel to control weapons, and the Army has set up a trial 'digitalized brigade' to experiment with the use of computers on the field of battle.

True to the flag *A soldier in gleaming white carries the flag in Chicago's Independence Day parade (left). Above: Soldiers on parade at a US military base in Germany. Opposite, top: A woman Marine. Opposite, below: A trainee Marine with his drill sergeant at the US Marine Corps Recruit Depot on Parris Island, South Carolina.*

Sports spectacles

The Super Bowl, the World Series, the NBA Championship – the great North American sports events are watched by millions, live by the lucky few, on television by the rest. Successful players, such as Joe Montana and Mark McGwire, become idols for an adoring public.

Clash of the titans *Razzmatazz as the players line up before the Super Bowl (right).*

Major American football games regularly draw television audiences of 40 million people. Key contests are often played on public holidays such as New Year's Day and Thanksgiving, and become festivals in their own right, with parades of floats before the game, 'half-time shows' and female cheer leaders to spur on the enthusiasm of the supporters. Actual playing time in professional American football is 60 minutes in four quarters of 15 minutes each, but when the intervals are included the game lasts 90 minutes or more from start to finish. Professional football, which includes such well-known teams as the Denver Broncos, New York Giants, Houston Oilers, Washington Redskins and Green Bay Packers, is organised by the National Football League into two conferences, the American Conference and the National Conference. In January each year, the football season culminates in the Super Bowl, when the champions of the two conferences play each other for the League Championship.

Summer baseball

With their protective helmets and huge padded shoulders, American football players look almost as ponderous as medieval knights in armour. Baseball players present a far more sprightly appearance. Their game, which was derived in the 19th century from the English game of rounders – just as American football was derived from rugby – is North America's

Perfect form *Baseball hitter Todd Hundley playing for the New York Mets (above). Below: Basketball superstar Michael Jordan.*

favourite summer game. In the United States, it is known as 'the national pastime' and cherished players and teams from the past are still remembered and talked about with great nostalgia.

Major League baseball is divided between the American League and the National League. The winners of each league meet in the World Series at the end of the season to decide the world championship in the best of seven games. Players sometimes get into professional baseball through the minor leagues, a system of regional conferences around the country that include farm teams for the Major League franchises.

Dealing the cards

Baseball and other sports cards are big business, along with the autographs, gloves and bats of famous players. In 1990 the volume of business in baseball cards totted up to $1.5 million. Originally issued by cigarette manufacturers, baseball cards are now published by companies such as the betting firm Bowman International and bubble-gum manufacturers Topps. They are bought and sold by specialised dealers, who publish catalogues and have their own Web sites.

In 1996 Christie's in New York held a sports memorabilia sale, which included a cigarette card from 1910 showing the legendary Pittsburgh Pirates player Honus Wagner, still revered as one of the best shortstops in baseball history. The card sold for $640 500. This particular set of cards is especially rare, supposedly because Wagner disapproved of smoking and had the bulk of the issue destroyed. Among recent and contemporary players, stickers of the basketball star Michael Jordan, bought for 50¢ in 1985, have changed hands ten years later for $2000.

High days and holidays

North America's festivals reflect the diverse origins of its people. Halloween has its roots in pagan Europe, while Thanksgiving is all-American.

It is October 31, Halloween, and groups of children dressed as witches, vampires, skeletons and devils make their way along the streets, where porches are set with glowing jack-o'-lanterns and theme decorations centred on all things scary. 'Trick or treat,' they cry as they go from door to door seeking candy, rarely playing the 'trick' (a payback) if they are not given any – soaping a screen door, say, or breaking the limb of a shrub. Today Halloween is as much for adults as children, with urban streets crowded by people trying to outdo one another with their costumes.

In New York's Greenwich Village, the annual Halloween party has become one of the biggest events of the year. This ancient Celtic tradition was brought to America by Irish immigrants. Halloween, the eve of All Hallows' (All Saints') Day, forms part of a Christian festival that has its roots in a pre-Christian past.

Thanks for surviving

The fourth Thursday in November in the United States and the second Monday in October in Canada are celebrated as Thanksgiving Day, when North Americans commemorate the successful first harvest of the Pilgrim Fathers. Against the odds, and with help from friendly American Indians, the pioneer colonists had survived their first year in New England, and they held a feast to celebrate. Traditional Thanksgiving fare is based on what they are said to have eaten that day: turkey, bilberries, maize, sweet potato and pumpkin pie.

Tickertape welcome Tickertape parades have become a traditional way of greeting returning heroes.

Independence Day

Independence Day is the United States' great national holiday, commemorating the Declaration of Independence, issued on July 4, 1776. Parades march through the streets and friends and neighbours traditionally get together for barbecues. Canada (formerly Dominion) Day celebrates the formation of the Dominion of Canada on July 1, 1867.

Saint Patrick's Day parade

St Patrick's Day, March 17, is the special yearly jamboree for Irish-Americans. New York has a huge parade which includes representatives from political organisations all over the United States and Ireland. Millions of people watch the procession, which receives the blessing of the Cardinal-Archbishop of New York at St Patrick's Cathedral.

The many faces of faith

The freedom to worship as they wanted – that is what drew so many of the earliest settlers to North America in the first place. Quakers, Amish, Baptists, Catholics – they all continue to flourish, along with some American-born sects and religions such as the Mormons.

When Americans ask, 'Which church do you belong to?', they might as well ask, 'What community do you belong to?' From the extrovert effusions of a black Baptist congregation in the South to the reverent silence at a Quaker or Amish meeting, the way you worship in North America says much about who you are – not just your values and preferences, but also your roots, where your ancestors came from, which ethnic or cultural group you identify with.

Polls in 1996 showed that 85 per cent of US citizens called themselves Christians. Among them an estimated 58 per cent of the population were Protestant, including Baptists (18 per cent), Methodists (9 per cent) and Lutherans (6 per cent); 25 per cent were Roman Catholics. Jews represented just 3 per cent of the population, though they still outnumber the Jewish population of Israel and make a contribution to US economic, social and political life that is out of all proportion to their numbers. The first Muslims to reach North America were immigrants from Syria at the end of the 19th century. In the 20th century the Black Muslim movement swelled their numbers; nowadays, about 2 million Americans call themselves Muslims of one tradition or another.

Living apart   The plain homemade clothing of the Amish reflects the costume of their forebears in 17th-century rural Europe.

In Canada, according to the 1991 census, 46 per cent of the population were Catholic, 36 per cent Protestant, 1.4 per cent Eastern Orthodox Christians and 1.2 per cent Jewish.

Puritan work ethic

Religion, particularly the steadfast Protestantism of the 17th-century Puritans, played a defining role in the founding of the North American colonies. Puritans were a significant presence among the settlers who in 1607 established the first successful colony, Jamestown in Virginia. New England's Pilgrim Fathers were extreme Puritans fleeing religious persecution in old England. They founded a society shaped by a strong work ethic and strict moral discipline. They were also the source of the Wasp (White Anglo-Saxon Protestant) ascendancy that would dominate economic and political power in the United States well into the 20th century.

The Latter-day Saints

In the Church of Jesus Christ of Latter-day Saints, the United States gave birth, in 1830, to a brand-new religion in the hills of upstate New York. Its 25-year-old founder, Joseph Smith, claimed to have received a revelation

A mighty organ   The Mormon Tabernacle dominates the central Temple Square in Salt Lake City. Its splendid organ provides music for the world-famous Mormon Tabernacle Choir.

from God, in which he was told the hiding place of gold plates buried by a group of Israelites who had found their way from Jerusalem to North America about 600 years before the time of Christ. The plates were supposed to contain the writings of the prophet Mormon, and Smith claimed to have received a special gift enabling him to translate them into English. The result is the Book of Mormon, believed by Smith's followers to be a divinely inspired addition to the Bible. The Mormons were persecuted at first, chiefly because they practised polygamy, and a group of them led by Brigham Young set out west to find a place where they could live and worship in peace. In 1847 they settled in Utah, in a barren, region beside a large salt lake. Here, they built their capital, Salt Lake City, where Mormons still outnumber other religions.

The Mormons send their young people out into the world as missionaries. As they travel, they gather documents or archives relating to genealogy, including yearbooks, registers of births,

Glory on high *Gospel music is a dialogue between the preacher and his choir. Recordings of these sermons interspersed with music became popular first among black and later white listeners.*

Singing gospel

The origins of gospel music go back to the era of slavery, when the slaves were forbidden to practise their traditional African rites. These survived, however, in secret meetings, and as the slaves were converted to Christianity the rites mingled with Christian ways. In particular, the blacks took popular Christian hymns and added their own beat and vocal styles to create the 'negro spiritual'. In the 1920s, gospel music developed from these spirituals among the black Baptist churches of the South.

marriages and deaths, and census returns. The Mormons believe that it is possible to baptise people into their faith by proxy, including people who are already dead. By gathering as complete a record as possible of their ancestors, they hope to be able to save their forebears' souls by proxy baptism. Salt Lake City's Library of Family History is the largest collection of genealogical material in the world, including a huge cache of documents stored on microfilm. Among the living the Mormons have 5.9 million followers worldwide, including 3.8 million in the United States.

Life without technology

The Mormons have never hesitated to use the latest in modern technology. In marked contrast, the Amish live apart from the modern world, having deliberately opted out of the technological rat race. Their forebears were European Protestants who rejected the paths set out by both Luther and Calvin; they believed that Church and State should be kept separate and refused to let their children be baptised until they were adult. They were also devout believers in nonviolence. Persecuted in the old world, they set sail for the new towards the end of the 18th century. They founded several rural communities that are scattered over 20 states and Canada.

Today, there are about 46 000 Amish. Using neither electricity nor motor vehicles of any kind, they raise their livestock and grow their crops much as people did three centuries ago, and yet they often obtain roughly the same yield from their farms as their technologically equipped non-Amish neighbours. They build their own homes, make their own clothes and at night use candles and oil lamps.

The televangelists

'Hour of Power' *A broadcast from Schuller's Crystal Cathedral.*

Television is a favourite means of outreach among Evangelical Christians, some of whom have built up huge media and leisure empires dedicated to the spreading of the Gospel. Using nationwide cable or satellite networks, people like Pat Robertson and Robert Schuller pass on their versions of Christian teaching to millions of North Americans. Viewers are encouraged to send donations to 'further the work of the Lord' via the post, telephone or e-mail.

The stereotype of the Holy Roller preacher is one that televangelists have long contended. A few still put on a distinctly operatic show, pacing up and down and exhorting viewers to 'expel the evil that is in them', but today they are often impeccably tailored, button-down types who take a somewhat calmer approach. The degree of respectability they have gained is exemplified by Robert Schuller, who wears elegant dove-grey robes and holds forth from the soaring Crystal Cathedral, the largest glass-exterior building in the world, designed by Phillip Johnson.

Rural grace *A tiny clapperboard church in Custer County, Montana.*

Black pride *Louis Farrakhan, leader of the Nation of Islam movement, addresses his followers at a meeting.*

Fever on Wall Street

It started as a wooden wall built by the Dutch colonists to protect their settlement, and became the financial hub of the world. The Crash of 1929 spelt temporary disaster, but Wall Street recovered and its Stock Exchange was well able to survive later shocks, such as the crash of October 1987.

Share prices rise, tumble, hold steady. In the old days, their ups and downs were signalled on huge wooden boards; nowadays, electronic screens chart the market value of North America's biggest companies and the handful of foreign businesses large enough to merit a listing on the New York Stock Exchange. On Wall Street – a short, rather nondescript street at the southern end of Manhattan – the adrenalin flow is rarely other than high.

On the trading floor of the Stock Exchange, the tiniest rumour can send ripples through the marketplace. Sometimes, this results in a swelling wave of confidence. The market takes on the aspect, as it were, of a mighty bull in all its pride: it is 'bullish'. Sometimes there is a loss of confidence and the market is 'bearish'. At the forefront of all these movements are the whiz-kid traders. Backing them up is an infrastructure of investment bankers, lawyers, accountants and financial advisers, minutely analysing the latest company results for the benefit of their clients.

Making a deal Traders make frantic hand signals on the floor of the New York Stock Exchange (right and above left).

A quiet moment Taking a snack on the steps of the Stock Exchange. Although so closely identified with Wall Street, the Exchange stands at 18 Broad Street. To be listed, companies have to meet a number of requirements, including pretax earnings of at least $2.5 million.

Junk bonds

Officially, junk bonds are securities that are rated as 'below investment grade'. They are issued by companies who want to raise capital easily and quickly; often the companies are 'corporate raiders', out to expand through takeover bids against other companies. The yields from junk bonds can be high, but so are the risks.

A young Wall Street financier, Michael Milken, first promoted junk bonds in the early 1980s. He took an interest in small and medium-sized companies that were ignored by most of the big financial institutions; many of them had significant potential for growth. Of particular interest were up-and-coming businesses in the telecommunications industry, including cable and satellite broadcasting networks and companies developing the new cordless and mobile phone technology. It was a dynamic sector, and takeovers were rife.

Encouraged by Milken and others, even the big pension fund investors were gripped with junk bond fever, despite the high risks involved. The bubble burst, however, in the late 1980s, when Milken was charged with fraud. The king of junk bonds ended up with a ten-year prison sentence in 1990 and a fine of $600 million. The markets, meanwhile, continued to show an interest in junk bonds – but with more caution.

Boom and bust

The Stock Exchange was founded in 1792 by 24 New York merchants and brokers, who signed an agreement setting out the ground rules by which they would buy and sell shares in one another's companies. During the 20th century its movements have both reflected and influenced the successive crises in world affairs. In 1914 when Europe plunged into war, Wall Street shut down for nearly four months. By the end of the First World War it had emerged as a global centre of finance and investment that soon outstripped the City of London. Then, on Thursday, October 24, 1929, share prices collapsed and 13 million securities were thrown onto the market, losing on average 30 per cent of their value and ruining thousands of investors. 'Black Thursday' ushered in the Great Depression that lasted through most of the next decade. Today, technology has transformed the way Wall Street operates, but for more than a century it has used the same barometer to measure changing conditions: the Dow Jones Index, first published in 1897. This tracks the ups and downs of the market, using as its basis the average share price of 30 top US industrial companies.

The mighty media

Freedom of the press is one of the three freedoms – along with those of religion and speech – guaranteed in the First Amendment to the US Constitution. The power and occasional excesses of the modern US media are famous; less well known is its diversity.

The high-water mark of press power in the United States probably came on August 9, 1974 – the day that Richard Nixon announced his resignation from the White House. In the Watergate affair it was the press, through the revelations of investigative journalists, notably the *Washington Post*'s Bob Woodward and Carl Bernstein, that had finally prodded the US public into action. It had forced the public to question the government and bring electoral pressure to bear on it. Journalists had exercised to the full the freedom of expression so proudly proclaimed in the First Amendment to the Constitution.

Press proliferation

This freedom has always encouraged a proliferation of newspapers, magazines and journals, both local and national. Today, nearly 9000 US newspapers print a total of 65 million copies, and there are more than 11 000 magazines. And yet in recent years the biggest dailies, such as the *New York Times*, the *Washington Post* and the *Los Angeles Times*, have seen a noticeable decline in their readership. A number of possible explanations have been put forward, including the suggestion that younger readers prefer a more radical, less bland approach.

In many of the big cities, the weekly freesheets, distributed at newsstands and in diners, bars and cafés, are a huge success. One of their attractions seems to be their lively, often opinionated coverage of music and the arts, both popular and classical; at the same time, they take an iconoclastic rough-and-tumble attitude towards politics that is rarely seen in the big dailies. They have become a force to be reckoned with, and are also attracting increasing amounts of advertising. Another development has

been the Internet and World Wide Web, giving users another way to access the information they need.

Cable and satellite

In television, the expanding cable and satellite networks have fragmented the viewing patterns. Increasingly, the old networks, such as ABC, CBS and NBC, are losing audiences to channels that specialise in fields ranging from cooking to cartoons, golf to history, chat shows to religion. More than half of all viewers now prefer to watch these special channels. The big networks try to reverse the trend by churning out a diet of action shows, comedy series, soaps, sitcoms and major sporting events.

The line separating information from entertainment has become ever more tenuous. Since the end of the Cold War, international news, in particular, has been given a back seat on the major national networks. The cable channel CNN has filled

TV without the ads

Public Broadcasting Service (PBS) is the USA's sole public television network. It is non-profit-making, with around 350 member stations in different parts of the country and in the associated 'commonwealths' of Puerto Rico and Guam. Its aim is to distribute cultural, scientific and educational programmes, along with news and current affairs. About 20 per cent of its funding comes from viewer donations; the rest from corporate supporters and a small government subsidy.

this gap by broadcasting world news around the world 24 hours a day – but CNN's viewing figures fluctuate wildly, depending on how much interest current events succeed in arousing among the US public.

Take your pick *A streetside choice of newspapers in Maine (left). The editorial offices of the* Washington Post *(above), one of the nation's leading dailies. Top: A recording studio at CNN (Cable News Network), launched in Atlanta, Georgia, in June 1980.*

Schools and the ladder of learning

When the Puritans of Massachusetts set up the college they named after its chief benefactor, John Harvard, they were founding one of the world's proudest university traditions. The modern USA has both private universities, such as Harvard and Yale, and state universities.

Harvard, Yale, Princeton, Stanford, Berkeley, MIT (Massachusetts Institute of Technology) – the names alone often act as passports for graduates entering the jobs market. In the east, the Ivy League universities are long established and have worldwide fame. Canada has highly regarded English-language universities such as McGill in Montreal and the universities of Toronto and British Columbia, as well as French-language universities such as the Université de Montréal and the Université Laval in Quebec City.

The education ladder The US education system, from kindergarten through to a postgraduate master's degree (left). Below: Summertime on the campus of Montana State University, one of the country's state-funded universities. Top left: A school bus in New Orleans.

3▶6 yrs	6▶12 yrs	12▶15 yrs	15▶17 yrs	17▶21 yrs	21▶23 yrs

Master

Four-year college

Senior high school

Junior high school

Primary school

Nursery school and kindergarten

Funding education

Most Canadian universities are funded by the federal and provincial governments. Many US ones get state funding or subsidies, but several of the most famous are autonomous institutions that rely on student fees to finance their day-to-day running. For major projects to improve their facilities they have to court the sponsorship of big business. The expense of higher education in the US means that it is chiefly the children of reasonably well-off parents who can afford it.

Harvard, the grand old lady of education

The Pilgrim Fathers landed at Cape Cod in December 1620. Within 16 years the new colony had its first educational establishment, which still stands in Cambridge, Massachusetts, its principal campus spreading out along the Charles River, west of Boston. Harvard now has more than 30 000 students, and the 800 books bequeathed by the Puritan minister John Harvard have multiplied mightily. From John Adams, the second president, to John F. Kennedy, the 35th, it has been the alma mater of six US presidents, as well as countless ministers, historians, chemists, biologists and astronomers.

Graduation in blue Columbia University, New York City, has 5000 teaching staff for 18 000 students.

Democracy, American style

Checks and balances define much of the US political system. There is the delicate balance between federal government and the rights of the state governments. The Constitution itself was built on the separation of the executive, legislative and judiciary powers.

Washington scenes *The Lincoln Memorial (left) commemorates the president who freed the slaves. Far left: Hundreds of quilts in remembrance of AIDS victims line the Mall on the approach to the Capitol. Open spaces in central Washington have played host to many demonstrations. Below: The White House.*

The US president is both powerful and vulnerable. Elected for four years, he has considerable powers under the Constitution, yet can easily become a lame duck if the public loses confidence in him. Simply by virtue of his office, he is the living symbol of national unity. He has to stamp his personality on the presidency, moulding strong and effective policies on key foreign and domestic issues. To assist him, he has a cabinet consisting of the Secretary of State, responsible for foreign policy, and the other departmental secretaries. Most presidents also have a 'kitchen cabinet' of private advisers – the two may well disagree, in which case a president has to steer his own course between them.

The president holds executive power; the two houses of Congress, sitting in the Capitol, represent legislative power. The 435 members of the lower house, the House of Representatives, are elected for two-year terms. Seats are allocated according to the size of each state's population. The upper house, the Senate, has 100 members, two for each of the 50 states, elected for six-year terms; every two years, elections are held for a third of the seats.

Presidential hopefuls

The road to the White House is long, hard and costly. First, candidates have to get themselves known. Then come the primaries, state-wide ballots in which voters – party members only in some states, all registered voters in others – indicate the candidates they prefer from the two parties: Democrats and Republicans. The final selection is made at the national conventions, held in July and August. Different factions within the party wheel and deal, and the tension mounts. Eventually, a candidate is announced amidst carnival-style razzmatazz.

Power in the United States

The president has the right of veto over laws passed by Congress.

The president's veto is invalidated if the law is passed by a two-thirds majority of Congress.

POWER OF THE EXECUTIVE
The president is also commander-in-chief.
He has direct authority over the CIA.

The president nominates the federal judges.

The judiciary determines whether the acts of the executive are constitutional.

The Senate ratifies the nomination of magistrates.

POWER OF THE LEGISLATURE
House of Representatives and the Senate
Congress initiates legislation, which must be passed by both houses.

The judiciary determines whether laws are constitutional.

POWER OF THE JUDICIARY
The Supreme Court and other federal courts

Life in the suburbs

Suburban America lies near the heart of the American dream. Traditionally seen as a place of safety, comfort and with a strongly democratic sense of community, the suburb is under pressure in the late 20th century. The old community spirit is in decline, while the violence and criminality of inner cities have spilled out increasingly into the leafy retreats surrounding them.

Suburban idyll *Queen Ann, one of Seattle's most desirable suburbs.*

The daily shuttle *A suburban commuter train in Chicago. Commuting has long been part of the American way of life.*

At the start of the 20th century, people began moving out to the suburbs because they wanted a change from the bustle and anonymity of city centres and to enjoy the company of like-minded neighbours.

Over the course of the century, attitudes have changed. Those who can afford it still like to live in the suburbs, and on the face of things the suburbs themselves look much as they always have done. In many places, the classic two-storey wooden houses, with light and airy kitchens downstairs, bedrooms with en suite bathrooms upstairs and large garages at the side, still look out onto shady, tree-lined streets. And yet there is a difference – the neighbourhood ties that were once all-important have weakened. Today suburb-dwellers tend to be less public-spirited than their predecessors. For many, their home is a refuge, a place where they can get away from the stresses and strains of hectic working lives.

Suburban values

For a long time it was the women who stamped their mark on the life of suburbia – neighbours were friends and the children all went to the same schools. Nowadays that kind of intimacy is less and less common. Many suburbs are becoming less suburban; more houses are being built and the semirural atmosphere is being lost. The very problems people wanted to get away from, such as vandalism and traffic congestion, are pursuing them into the suburbs. At the same time, more families where both parents go out to work leave fewer people to do the daytime volunteer work that used to be the foundation of much of suburban life.

Planners and designers have responded in various ways, building entirely new communities that are towns in their own right. Even Disney became involved, commissioning a group of world-class architects and designers who spent ten years studying the best features of American towns. The result is Celebration, Florida, a thriving community with a population expected to reach 12 000 to 15 000 people.

The sanitised life of a compound

In some US suburbs, people take extra steps to insulate themselves against intruders of any kind. They buy homes in 'compounds', fenced-in private housing estates. They are for the most part well-to-do retired people anxious to preserve their peace and quiet, or couples without children who want a place for weekends and holidays where they can play tennis and golf and enjoy the amenities of a swimming pool – children are often frowned on by their co-owners. Compounds became popular in the 1970s. Developers acquired beaches, river bank areas and forests. The people who bought into the compounds assured the conservation of these sites – but they also made certain that they were the only ones to enjoy them. Security is a key consideration in compounds and crime levels are low. This is not surprising in communities where a strange face or car number plate may well result in a call to the local police station.

Old-time housing *Wooden houses like these were only meant to last for 30 years or so, but they have survived and now command relatively high prices: around $200 000 on average, and as much as $1 to $3 million in the smarter suburbs.*

Two Southern belles

The prosperity of the South was based on a plantation economy that depended on slavery. When the South lost the Civil War, Southern port cities such as Charleston and Savannah seemed destined to be eclipsed by the industrial cities of the North. Yet both, in their different ways, have adapted to the modern world.

Wedding day *A bride in Savannah's Lafayette Square.*

Gingerbread glory *Less elegant than the aristocratic mansions of Savannah's wealthier districts, the 'gingerbread houses' have an ornate charm of their own. During the Civil War, Savannah surrendered rather than risk destruction.*

Two of the most beautiful cities in the United States, Charleston and Savannah, have carefully retained the old-world charm of the Deep South, giving a glimpse of the society that vanished with the Civil War – rich, elegant . . . and based on slave-owning. Though its moral foundations were questionable even at the time, it is easy enough to imagine how those enjoying its privileges were prepared to fight to maintain them.

Gone with the Wind
Vivien Leigh in the film that defined people's image of the old South.

Charleston grace

Charleston was founded in 1670 on a peninsula between two river estuaries in South Carolina's marshy Low Country. It boasts one of the most strikingly beautiful seafronts of any major port in the world: The Battery – a row of antebellum (pre-Civil War) mansions, painted immaculate white, their fronts adorned with graceful Corinthian columns. They bear witness to the city's prosperity as a hub of the slave trade from the 17th to the early 19th centuries. Today, Charleston is still one of the chief seaports of the USA's southern Atlantic coast, and despite the old associations with slavery, it has turned its past to full tourist advantage. Visitors from the North wander through the old centre, where the historic wooden houses have been carefully restored by private owners, who still enjoy the high ceilings, wide porches sited to get the best breeze and walled gardens.

Where time stood still

Across the border in Georgia, Savannah is no less seductive. Founded in 1733, like Charleston it became a major port. Slaves poured in from Africa and the produce of the plantations – rice, indigo and cotton – poured out across the North Atlantic to Europe. In the 19th century the town began a steady decline after it refused to have a railroad station. Today, its isolation is part of the charm for tourists, and its 18th-century mansions, squares and public parks have won numerous conservation awards. In 1996, the city of Savannah made the news when it elected its first black mayor.

Down by the river *The waterfront in Savannah.*

Midnight in Savannah

He was supposed to be just passing through, but he became an honorary citizen, spending a great deal of time there. New York journalist John Berendt fell in love with Savannah and made it the subject of a best-selling book. An affectionate look at the city, *Midnight in the Garden of Good and Evil* was published in 1994 and turned into a film in 1997. An antiques dealer is charged with murdering his young male lover, but the book also explores the way of life of this extraordinary city, with its gracious mansions and special brand of Southern charm.

Land of the people

A vast ice sheet covers most of the interior, but Greenland's fringes are habitable and it boasts hidden riches, including deposits of lead and cryolite.

Snow and ice *Kangaatsiaq on Greenland's west coast (above). Right: Icebergs scattered across a west coast fiord. Greenland has started to promote itself as a tourist destination, offering dog-sledge tours, visits to the ice cap and glaciers, and heli-skiing.*

The people of Greenland call their country Kalaallit Nunaat, 'Land of the People'. Still nominally a part of Denmark, Kalaallit Nunaat has been self-governing since 1979, and in 1985 withdrew from the European Economic Community. It now sees itself as part of an unofficial community of Nordic regions, which includes Alaska, Siberia and the northern zones of Scandinavia.

After Australia, Kalaallit Nunaat is the biggest island in the world, roughly four times the size of France. It has a population of nearly 56 000 people, most of whom are of the same stock as the Inuit of Canada and Alaska, though with a small mingling of Danish blood. They live in communities scattered along the coast, mostly in the south-west. Their industries are fishing and a small amount of sheep-farming in the ice-free pasturelands of the far south; there are also deposits of lead and cryolite, used in refining aluminium. A fifth of the population lives in the capital, Nuuk (Godthaab in Danish), which has big processing plants for prawns, shrimps, salmon and cod. In the far north-west, the USA maintains a military base at Thule, including the world's most northerly airfield.

One of Kalaallit Nunaat's most striking sights is of calving glaciers dropping chunks of ice into the sea. The best place for this is Ilulissat (Jakobshaven) fiord on the west coast. Every day at the height of the calving 'season' in summer, around 25 million tons of ice float past the town of Ilulissat at the mouth of the fiord.

A climate of freeze and thaw

Greenland's northern tip is less than 500 miles (800 km) from the North Pole; its southern tip lies on roughly the same degree of latitude as southern Shetland or the Norwegian capital, Oslo. Along the south-western coast, warmed to some extent by the Gulf Stream, the average winter temperature is a comparatively mild –6°C (21°F), and in summer the average is 7°C (45°F). In the far north, by contrast, human activity is scarcely possible in winter outside the US airbase at Thule. The average winter temperature here is –35°C (–31°F).

Canadian unity

Resting like a giant capstone on the top of North America, Canada is rich, well ordered and diverse. The country has more than 100 ethnic groups. People with British or French backgrounds are the largest groups, but neither represents a majority of the population. Other large ethnic groups are Germans, Italians, Chinese and Ukrainians.

Boating fun *On holiday at Deer Lake, Newfoundland.*

Covering 3.8 million sq miles (10 million km²), Canada is a country almost the size of Europe. It came into being as a self-governing dominion within the British Empire in 1867, when it included Ontario, Quebec, Nova Scotia and New Brunswick. Other provinces were added piecemeal, the tenth and last being Newfoundland, which joined only in 1949. With its mixture of many peoples, its range of landscapes and climates, and its sheer size, modern Canada encompasses a huge diversity which at times seems to threaten its existence as a unified state. Yet despite the fragility, the country has survived so far, held together, above all, by the very freedoms it stands for – freedoms of religious, cultural and linguistic expression.

Taming the land

Climate accounts in part for Canada's relatively sparse population. The most densely populated region is the Windsor-to-Quebec City corridor, which lies along the lower Great Lakes and the St Lawrence River valley. This region was initially used for agriculture. In the mid 19th century, Montreal started to grow rapidly as a port. As the port grew, so did the city, and this attracted industry. In the remote north, forestry and mining are often the only industries that make towns viable; and then only if the resources are valuable enough to make exploiting them worthwhile.

Keeping in touch

Economically, Canada's vertical ties with the United States have always been as strong as, often stronger than, the horizontal ties among the different Canadian provinces. This has also been true culturally – Vancouver, for example, is a lot closer to Seattle than it is to any comparable Canadian city. Nowadays, modern telecommunications make it much easier to keep in touch across the vast breadth of the continent, from British Columbia to Newfoundland.

A more intractable problem is that of francophone (French-speaking) Quebec. French-speakers make up roughly a quarter of the population of Canada, and 85 per cent of them live in Quebec province, where '*péquiste*' (Parti Québécois) governments, with a strongly nationalist, pro-independence agenda,

Winter sports *Snowmobiling is a favourite winter pastime (above). Enthusiasts set out on treks that can last for several days. Left: Canada lost to Sweden in the ice hockey finals of the 1994 Winter Olympics at Lillehammer in Norway.*

have regularly been elected in recent decades. Another source of discord has been the sharing out of resources. For all its wealth and apparent stability, Canada is a country where the constitutional debate continues to be argued.

A national passion on ice

'*Et le but!*' ('Goal!') cries sports commentator Claude Quenneville from the TV station of Radio-Canada. Among the spectators, both in the stadium and at home watching the game on television, some leap up and down with joy, others scowl, depending on their team loyalties. Ice hockey is a national obsession, and there are not many Canadians who stay indifferent when a big game is on. Indoctrination starts young: first a pair of skates under the Christmas tree; the next year a team sweatshirt. After a few tumbles on the local ice rink, the youngster's career is off. Some parents spend years hunched at the edge of ice rinks egging on their offspring. Their yells of encouragement could scarcely be more ferocious if they were watching an NHL (National Hockey League) match.

Casino capital

Mormons founded the first settlement at Las Vegas; a gangster, 'Bugsy' Siegel, turned it into a world-famous gambling haven. Today, the place once known as 'Sin City' promotes itself as a resort for family fun.

Saucy signs *The neon glitter that is Las Vegas's trademark.*

The Vegas Vic cowboy, standing 60 ft (18 m) tall in his neon boots, makes an apt symbol for the city: almost everything in Las Vegas is big, brash, bright and based on an American stereotype. The city caters for 30 million visitors each year and has 110 000 hotel rooms. On average no room is occupied by the same person or people for more than four nights running – after a few days, all but the most addicted find themselves flagging amid the explosions of sound, light and hyped-up emotion.

Generations of hotels and casinos follow one another in quick succession, each conceived on a more grandiose scale. The most famous of them stand on The Strip, the neon-lit heart of the gambling district where casinos and nightclubs stay open 24 hours a day. The architecture of the hotels is a spectacle in itself, each trying to outdo the others in the over-the-top extravagance of its decor. The Treasure Island Hotel boasts meticulous reconstructions of pirate battles. The Luxor, shaped like a pyramid, has a replica Nile flowing through it. At the Mirage, you can watch exploding underwater volcanoes. Caesar's Palace is famous among boxing fans for hosting many world heavyweight title fights.

Having a flutter *Young or old, male or female – anyone can have a go on the slot machines or one-armed bandits.*

Counting up *A casino employee keeps a check on the banknotes in the establishment's 'soft count room'. Taking all kinds of gambling into account, the people of the United States staked $241 billion in 1989.*

Casino road *For all its emphasis on family entertainment, Las Vegas is still dedicated to gambling, and gambling can still ruin an unlucky or foolhardy player. Casinos have been known to offer free air tickets home to players who have lost all.*

Bigger, bigger, bigger

In Las Vegas, size matters. Hotels, theme parks and casinos – all aim to overwhelm the visitor by sheer scale. The same is true of the gambling. In Las Vegas anyone can become a multimillionaire by the mere placing of a lucky bet or the picking of a lucky number. The humblest fruit machine or one-armed bandit offers winnings of millions of dollars. Some of the world's highest-paid singers and other entertainers perform, meanwhile, in the numerous variety shows, and magicians stage spectacular displays of their skills, where they make elephants, not just white rabbits, vanish into thin air. Churches, too, are represented on an appropriate scale; there are 500 of them in Las Vegas. Competing with them for weddings are dozens of wedding chapels, where couples can get married at any time of the day or night.

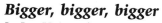

Marriage haven *Weddings are big business in Las Vegas. Up to 200 couples a week get married in the chapels.*

The Big Apple in miniature *A hotel built as a replica of New York is one of the tourist sights of Las Vegas.*

Murder and the Mafia

Nevada legalised gambling in 1931. Fourteen years later, in the last year of the Second World War, the New York-born gangster Benjamin ('Bugsy') Siegel built the Flamingo Hotel and Casino just outside what was still a relatively small town called Las Vegas. It was a casino with a five-storey bedroom block, and his target market was rich Californians. The lure was Nevada's relaxed legislation, allowing them to pop across the state line and enjoy amusements forbidden in other states. Thus was born modern Las Vegas.

From the start, crime and killing were features of the enterprise. Siegel, an associate of the gangster boss Meyer Lansky, was a former hit man who ran a number of big-time crime rackets on the West Coast, including narcotics smuggling and blackmail. His venture in Las Vegas proved his undoing. Costs for the Flamingo overran by millions of dollars; much of the money came from Lansky and other East Coast crime bosses, and a good deal of it ended up in Siegel's European bank accounts. As far as Lansky and his fellows were concerned, Siegel had overstepped the mark: he was gunned down in his girlfriend's Beverly Hills mansion on June 20, 1947. In Las Vegas, Lansky's henchmen took over the Flamingo and during the next ten years opened more hotels and casinos at a breakneck rate. Las Vegas gained its 'Sin City' reputation, and eager sinners arrived from all quarters.

Place your bets

Inside the casinos, eager gamblers can take their pick among dozens of dice, blackjack and roulette tables; ranks of coin-jangling slot machines; the pulsating lights of battalions of pinball machines. The overhead lighting is restful and subdued, drinks are on the house – everything is done to encourage visitors to play. To one side, the serious gamblers play interminable games of baccarat and poker; some may stay long enough to lose everything they have. If they win, there is plenty more to tempt them, including slot machines just about everywhere – in hotel lobbies, restaurants, even launderettes. Rumour has it that the machines at the airport offer a higher chance of winning – a bait to lure people in, or encourage them to come back again.

Lion in splendour The MGM Grand Hotel is the second largest hotel in the world. It has 5005 rooms and cost $1 billion to build.

Expanding city

Las Vegas is constantly reinventing itself. After the abortive Mormon settlement of the 1850s, the town put on its first big spurt of growth after the arrival of the railroad in 1905. The state of Nevada legalised gambling in 1931, and in 1945 Las Vegas's first casino-hotel was opened. In recent years the city has made huge efforts to clean up its reputation. It now presents itself as a family destination, a giant theme park where gambling is a key element in the local folklore. With its healthy climate and clean desert air, it has also become a centre for immigration.

For every 100 000 people who come for the gambling, 250 stay; Las Vegas welcomes roughly 75 000 new inhabitants each year. The cost of living is cheaper here than in most other parts of the United States and unemployment is low. There are no taxes, and residential accommodation is less expensive than in Phoenix, Arizona, another popular destination with a similar climate. The city is steadily reclaiming more and more land from the desert in order to build new houses; the telephone company has to print a new phone book twice every year.

The Golden State

The body beautiful, health food, sport for all – these are some of California's classic obsessions. And yet, behind the gilded façade of the beach and the perfectly tanned bodies, there lies another culture, in which people come together to promote and encourage a diverse array of alternative talents.

Baywatch *Surfing conquered California in the 1920s, popularised by figures such as Duke Kahanamoku from Hawaii. Inset, above: A lifeguard keeps watch.*

The 40 miles (60 km) between Malibu and Palos Verde are a year-round playground for the people of Los Angeles. Every beach along its shoreline caters for a different clientele: family beaches; beaches for water-sports fanatics; beaches for the young and trendy. People drive out from LA to go jogging along the sands, and then enjoy a macrobiotic sandwich with an energy-giving yoghurt drink or a freshly made fruit juice, free of even the suspicion of an additive. On some beaches you can have a massage, or a tattoo, while you sunbathe.

Beach culture

Both the symbol of, and the setting for, the most-flaunted side of Californian culture, the beach is like a temple for the 'beautiful life'. Here, the human body is tanned, built up, cared for and displayed for others to admire. The sea is there for surfing; tarmacked tracks behind the beaches offer miles of rollerblading paradise. At spots like Malibu Lagoon or Santa Monica's Palisade Park, visitors and immigrants drawn to California from the four corners of the planet mingle with native-born locals to

create a fizzing brew of people, trends and outlooks. Fashions for clothing, food, music, sport, just about everything, mingle, re-form and often generate new fashions, which then ripple back around the globe.

Civic virtue

Amidst a highly mobile, constantly shifting population, friendships tend to come and go, yet a number of core civic values often hold fast. Individualistic Californians readily sign up for causes they find worthwhile, whether cleaning up a highway or demonstrating against government policies. In October 1998 thousands of high school students marched through the streets of San Leandro chanting, 'Education, not incarceration.' Their protest was prompted by reports that state spending on higher education had declined by 3 per cent since 1990, while spending on prisons and penal policy had risen by a massive 60 per cent.

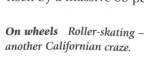

On wheels *Roller-skating – another Californian craze.*

90

Fun parks in Florida

Fairs and amusement parks are almost as old as North America's cities, but the 20th century saw an explosion of them, in one place in particular – Florida, the 'Sunshine State'. Cypress Gardens, Busch Gardens, Sea World – the selection is enormous, and crowning them all is the greatest of them all, Walt Disney World.

Political and religious ideologies apart, one of the biggest influences on the collective imagination of the 20th century may have been the farmer's son from Marceline, Missouri, who brought to the screen Mickey Mouse, Donald Duck and Snow White. Through Walt Disney, the ethos of small-town Midwestern America, which he imbibed during his formative years, has been conveyed to millions worldwide, and the process continues through the hugely popular Disney parks, starting with the original Disneyland, which opened near Los Angeles in 1955, and Walt Disney World near Orlando, Florida, which opened in 1971.

Leisure parks old and new

Cypress Gardens, founded in 1936, in Winter Haven, Florida, claims to be the ancestor of all modern amusement parks. Although far outshone today by its more spectacular offspring, it is still popular with visitors who come to admire its 8000 different plant species. Among the attractions are boat rides through the park's canals, lakes and swamps, where there are 27 species of palm, along with an occasional alligator.

Busch Gardens, established in 1959, now has two branches, one at Tampa Bay, Florida, the other at Williamsburg, Virginia. Among the attractions at Tampa Bay is a monorail, taking visitors for an air-conditioned ride over the zoo, where 3400 animals live in settings that as closely as possible reproduce their natural habitats.

Sea World opened in 1973 and now has four branches in Florida, California, Ohio and Texas. Attractions include tanks where visitors can watch moray eels, barracudas and sharks. You can also have the simulated experience of deep-sea diving in the Bermuda Triangle. The big attraction in Ohio is the Shamu Adventure, where killer whales cavort in a giant pool, splashing the delighted spectators.

Disney World

The Florida project began before Disney died in 1966. He bought some 44 sq miles (114 km²) of swamp southwest of Orlando, drained it, then set about building a park that would enshrine for generations to come the fantasy, humour and down-home values that he and his empire stood for. Disney World welcomed its first visitors on October 1, 1971, and since then has amply fulfilled its creator's vision.

Typhoon lagoon *Visitors relax and enjoy one of the many attractions at Disney World.*

Sea world *Spectators crowd around the pool to watch the sea mammals perform astonishing acrobatic feats and even sometimes eat out of their hands.*

Enter the Magic Kingdom

Disney insisted that the park should be dynamic in its approach. Its core is the Magic Kingdom, 'home' to Disney characters such as Mickey Mouse, Donald Duck, Bambi, Peter Pan and Snow White. In 1982 the Epcot (Experimental Prototype Community of Tomorrow) Center was added. This includes Future World, where visitors can experience what the world may be like in 100 years' time, and World Showcase, a potpourri of experiences that include a skyride over Paris and a tumble down Norwegian waterfalls.

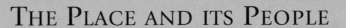

CHAPTER 5

LIFE IN THE CITY

Quebec, the only walled city north of Mexico, has the charm and grace of an old European city. On the other side of the continent, San Francisco, built on the Gold Rush, has its own much-loved elegance, with cable cars, wooden Victorian houses and the superb sweep of the Golden Gate Bridge. New York is the city that never sleeps; Los Angeles sprawls over hundreds of square miles; Chicago, the hub of the Midwest, gave the world a further symbol of North America – the skyscraper. Each of Canada's great cities has its own special character: Vancouver, booming as a gateway to Asia; Toronto, the nation's financial heart; Ottawa, the graceful political capital; Montreal, vibrant, colourful, bilingual. Down south, Miami is another bilingual city, in Spanish and English, and New Orleans mingles French, Spanish, Caribbean and African influences – a rich brew that gave the world jazz.

A gaudy city in the middle of nowhere, Las Vegas floods the desert with its lights.

Chicago, the Windy City

A city of wood became a city of steel after the great fire that ravaged its centre in 1871. Steel-framed buildings rose higher and higher as Chicago gave birth to the modern skyscraper. This great hub of commerce and transport reaches out to dominate the Midwest. In its turn, it has received wave after wave of immigrants, each group establishing its own overlapping enclaves and creating a buzzing cultural diversity.

Patchwork city

Most Chicagoans are proud of their ethnic heritage. In a city of 2.8 million inhabitants, countless cultural and linguistic enclaves interlock with one another, still bearing the marks of the immigrants who founded them. The Chinese, Germans, Ukrainians, Filipinos, Puerto Ricans, Indians, Irish and others who established themselves here have their own churches or temples, businesses, shops, foods, schools, clubs and sports groups. All have sought to reproduce in some measure the way of life of their homelands. It is estimated that some 80 distinctive ethnic groups live in Chicago in a patchwork of 175 different districts.

The biggest group of all were immigrants from the still largely rural South at the start of the century. Drawn by Chicago's economic boom, they mostly settled in the southern districts of the city. Today, nearly 40 per cent of the population is black, still mostly living in the south of the city in areas bedevilled by overcrowding, poverty and gang violence. On the other hand, there is also a sizable and ever-growing black middle class. Chicago was the first major US city to elect a black mayor.

From Chicago, ocean-going ships can reach the Atlantic via the St Lawrence Seaway; waterways leading to the Mississippi link the city to New Orleans and the Gulf of Mexico. No fewer than 27 railroad lines spread out from Chicago in different directions; it was the expanding railroads that, from the 1850s, allowed the town to develop as an industrial and commercial centre. Sandwiched between the Great Lakes and the industrial heartlands of the Midwest, Chicago's docks and wharves are constantly busy as longshoremen (dockers) load and unload cargoes of coal, steel, iron ore, oil, chemical products and the bounty of the Midwest's cereal harvest. Thousands of wholesale houses are based in Chicago, making it a key distribution centre for much of the rest of the United States. As goods have spread out from this mighty hub of activity, so successive waves of immigrants have been drawn in, seeking jobs: Irish, Poles, Czechs, Germans, East European Jews, blacks fleeing segregation and discrimination in the South, Mexicans, Italians, Greeks and many more.

Bleak beginnings

The story began in 1673, when the French explorers Jacques Marquette and Louis Jolliet established a temporary base on the swampy shores of Lake Michigan. It was a bleak spot, offering little protection from snowstorms, fogs and icy winds, and the local American Indian tribes avoided it as a place to live. Nonetheless, the area continued to be used as a stopping-off place by trappers and traders. A century after Marquette and Jolliet passed through, Jean-Baptiste Point du Sable, the black son of a Quebec merchant, built himself a log cabin in the swamp, the first properly constructed dwelling on the site of modern Chicago. Gradually, as the Americans

Local hero *Basketball star Michael Jordan led the Chicago Bulls to six NBA (National Basketball Association) victories between 1991 and 1998, as well as skippering the US national team to two Olympic gold medals. In one season alone, 1986-7, he scored 3000 points. Above: Michael Jordan's restaurant on Chicago's LaSalle Street.*

pushed their frontier farther west, the strategic location of this otherwise unappealing spot became more and more obvious. Settlers farming the prairies needed to get their harvests back to the markets of the East or, increasingly, to the opening markets farther west. Chicago grew rapidly as their market centre.

Reborn from the ashes

In 1871 a fire licked through a large part of the mostly wooden city, reducing it to ashes. Undaunted, Chicago's city fathers rebuilt the metropolis, abandoning wood as a construction material and calling on the services of a supremely talented group of architects and engineers known as the Chicago School. They transformed the modern cityscape, since it was they who invented the steel-framed skyscraper and built the first example: Chicago's 10-storey Home Insurance Building, designed by William Le Baron Jenney.

The Loop *In the chasms between skyscrapers, elevated railroad lines form a loop around Chicago's downtown area. The city developed its elevated network in the 1890s to cope with transport problems arising from its dramatic growth. This was also the decade of the World's Columbian Exhibition, held in Chicago in 1893, which first introduced many Americans to the wonders of electricity.*

Frank Lloyd Wright (1867-1959)

While central Chicago was reaching for the skies, the architect Frank Lloyd Wright, who came to work in the city in 1887, drew his inspiration from the great flat spaces of the Midwestern prairies. The use of horizontal rather than vertical space was the key to his Prairie Style, which sought to integrate a building into its natural surroundings. In his houses in the Chicago suburb of Oak Park, rooms flow into one another without the rigid box-like compartmentalisation of traditional houses. Frank Lloyd Wright is now considered to be the father of a truly American style of architecture. One of his most famous memorials is his New York masterpiece, the Guggenheim Museum: with its internal spiral walkway, he regarded the museum as a kind of ascent into the realms of art.

Moving forward Chicago moves with the times. Once dependent on agriculture, iron and coal, its economy is now based on financial services and high-tech industries.

Washington grandeur

The new nation needed a new federal capital, independent of the rivalries among the different states. In 1790 Congress carved out the 68 sq mile (176 km²) District of Columbia, lying between Maryland and Virginia, balanced between the North and the South.

City of contrasts   The morning sun sheds a warm light on the Lincoln Memorial, the obelisk of the Washington Monument and the Capitol (left). Far left: Cherry blossom and the Jefferson Memorial. Above: One of Washington's predominantly black neighbourhoods.

The president's cherry trees

In the 1806 edition of his *Life and Memorable Actions of George Washington*, clergyman 'Parson' Weems told the story of George Washington and the cherry tree. Almost certainly apocryphal, it has nonetheless entered deep into the national mythology. The tale goes that the young Washington chopped down a small cherry tree with a hatchet. When his father asked who had committed this outrage, the child stepped forward. 'I can't tell a lie, Pa; you know I can't tell a lie. I did cut it with my hatchet.'

It was George Washington who set in motion the process of establishing a brand-new federal capital for the infant United States. And it was in memory of him that its streets were planted with cherry trees.

devised a rectangular grid with diagonal avenues. Although L'Enfant was eventually sacked, the essence of his plan survived, above all in the superb sweep of The Mall. Here, the Capitol stands imposingly on its hill at one end; the more discreet charm of the White House faces it at the other end. In between are monuments to US democracy and culture. The surrounding avenues and circles, with their parks and ponds, lend grace to the whole.

| BLACKS | WHITES |
| ASIANS | AMERINDIANS | OTHERS |

Before it became the new nation's new capital, the stretch of marshy land where the rivers Anacostia and Potomac meet was called Foggy Bottom. The name appealed to George Washington when he chose the site: it seemed appropriate to the often murky world of high politics.

L'Enfant's city

It was a French architect and engineer, Pierre-Charles L'Enfant, who drew up the plans for the new city. Drawing inspiration from a number of European models, including Versailles and Sir Christopher Wren's plans (never realised) for London, he

Black Washington

Since the abolition of slavery in 1863, emancipated blacks have settled in Washington in large numbers, enjoying personal freedom at last, but living in conditions of strict social and economic segregation. Today, blacks make up around two-thirds of the capital's population.

For a long time black Americans were deprived of educational opportunities enjoyed by most whites, and as a whole have only relatively recently started to make their presence felt in the highest positions of power in the federal capital. A recent example was Colin Powell, who was chair of the Joint Chiefs of Staff during the Gulf War. He was also briefly considered as a presidential candidate.

New York scenes A game of basketball in the Bronx (left). Familiar from the movies, inner city playgrounds surrounded by high wire netting are the setting in which many young Americans have their first taste of sport. Above: The view from the Brooklyn Esplanade across the East River to the skyscrapers of Manhattan's financial district.

Houses in Brooklyn

New York, a city of extremes

There is scarcely a tongue on Earth that is not spoken somewhere in the streets, shops, bars, playgrounds, churches or temples of New York, scarcely a culture that is not somehow represented in this extraordinary metropolis – a city of extremes and infinite variety.

You are never far from water in New York. The city grew up in the age of sail on islands at the mouth of two rivers, the East and the Hudson. Nowadays, in the age of the motor car, it sometimes seizes up due to the congestion of its land-based traffic. In 1997 the population of New York's five 'boroughs' was estimated at 7.3 million people – greater New York's metropolitan area has a population of almost 20 million. Of the five boroughs, Manhattan is the most famous, where many people from other boroughs work.

The Bronx is New York's foothold on the mainland, with a population of 1.2 million in 1997. To the east, Brooklyn (with 2.3 million inhabitants) and Queens (2 million) cover the south-western tip of Long Island, making them the gateway to such supersmart Long Island colonies as the Hamptons, immortalised in F. Scott Fitzgerald's *The Great Gatsby*. Alternating slums with middle-class residential areas, the Long Island boroughs hold themselves somewhat apart from the rest of the city. To the south-west, Staten Island – officially known as Richmond – is the least crowded, most suburban of the boroughs, with a population in 1997 of just 0.4 million. It is linked to Brooklyn by the 4260 ft (1298 m) span of the Verrazano-Narrows Bridge, the world's longest suspension bridge when it was opened in 1964, though several times overtaken since then.

Many tongues

New York is a city of immigrants. Streets in Brooklyn, in particular, are a babble of different tongues and dialects. In the borough's Williamsburg district, notices are as likely to be written in Yiddish or Hebrew as in English. Brighton Beach is dominated by Russians. Haitians, Jamaicans and Hasidic Jews congregate in Crown Heights, while Bedford-Stuyvesant has the largest black community in the city.

Coney Island New York's pleasure beach at Coney Island. The Wonder Wheel, built in 1920, is still the tallest ferris wheel in the world.

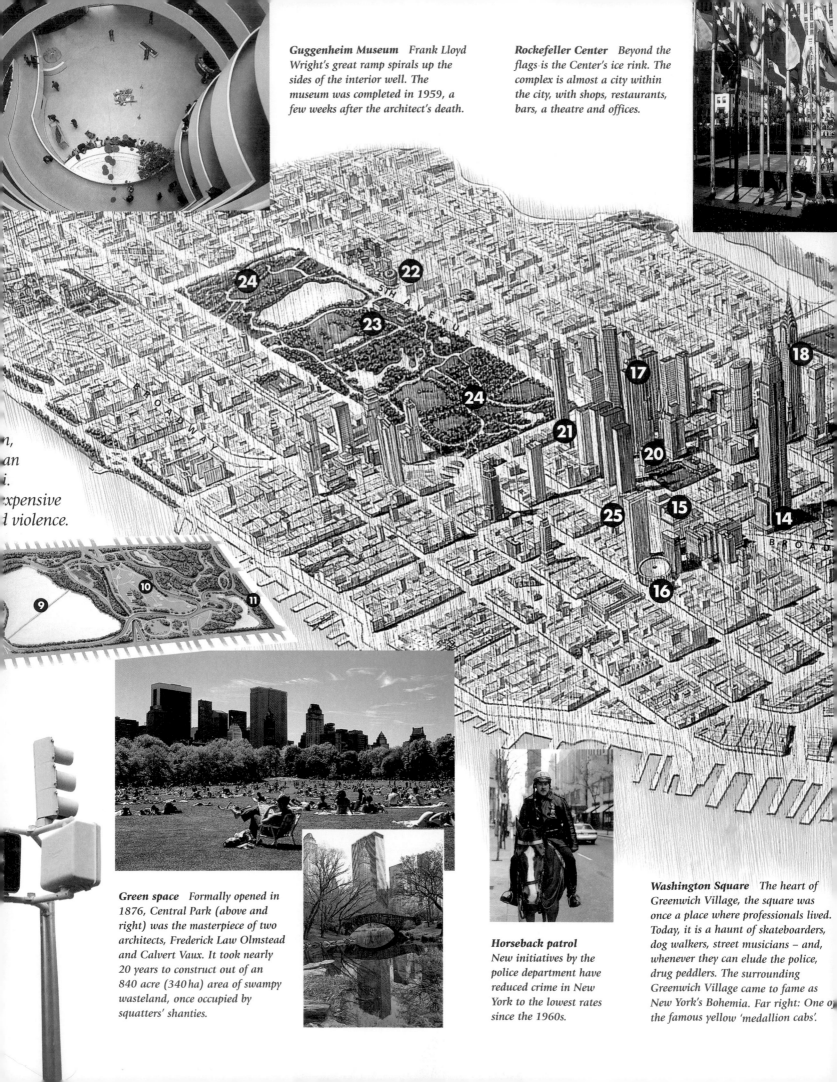

Guggenheim Museum Frank Lloyd Wright's great ramp spirals up the sides of the interior well. The museum was completed in 1959, a few weeks after the architect's death.

Rockefeller Center Beyond the flags is the Center's ice rink. The complex is almost a city within the city, with shops, restaurants, bars, a theatre and offices.

n,
an
i.
xpensive
d violence.

Green space Formally opened in 1876, Central Park (above and right) was the masterpiece of two architects, Frederick Law Olmstead and Calvert Vaux. It took nearly 20 years to construct out of an 840 acre (340 ha) area of swampy wasteland, once occupied by squatters' shanties.

Horseback patrol New initiatives by the police department have reduced crime in New York to the lowest rates since the 1960s.

Washington Square The heart of Greenwich Village, the square was once a place where professionals lived. Today, it is a haunt of skateboarders, dog walkers, street musicians – and, whenever they can elude the police, drug peddlers. The surrounding Greenwich Village came to fame as New York's Bohemia. Far right: One of the famous yellow 'medallion cabs'.

A tour of The Big Apple

A Manhattan is a vermouth and bourbon cocktail; the mix in the island after which it was named is no less heady. Manhattan island is the distillation of New York City, indeed of the entire United States. For the jazzmen in the earlier part of the 20th century, this tongue of land was the Big Apple – if you landed a good contract there, you were made. Its diversity is reflected in at least 30 distinct districts. Midtown is the corporate heart, where the biggest of big corporations have their monumental skyscrapers. In the southern tip lies Wall Street and the financial district. Little Italy is like a scene from a Scorcese movie; neighbouring Chinatown bustles with countless small restaurants. SoHo houses many of New York's most unusual boutiques and is famous for its immense lofts. Also downtown, Greenwich Village and the East Village, haunt of the Beat generatio evoke memories of Jack Kerouac and Andy Warhol. North of Midtown Manhatt spreads Central Park, venue for concerts, joggers, rollerbladers and fans of tai-ch Scattered around it are most of New York's museums. The Upper East Side has antiques shops and restaurants; beyond lies Harlem, notorious for its poverty an

1. The Pond
2. The Zoo
3. Heckscher Playground
4. Sheep Meadow
5. The Lake
6. Conservatory Water
7. Great Lawn
8. Metropolitan Museum of Art
9. Reservoir
10. North Meadow
11. Harlem Meer

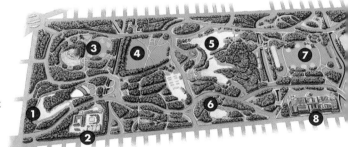

World Trade Center
The Center's twin towers are more than a quarter of a mile (400 m) high. Views from the higher floors on a clear day are spectacular: New York harbour, the city and parts of New Jersey.

Sunshine in Harlem *The elegance of its brownstones is a reminder that in the mid 19th century Harlem was a prosperous upper middle-class suburb.*

Getting around *Cycling can be quicker than driving in New York's traffic-clogged streets. At street crossings, lights instruct pedestrians 'Don't walk' or 'Walk'. Crowded sidewalks make pedestrian control almost as important as traffic control.*

Manhattan

1. Statue of Liberty The world-famous statue, created by Parisian sculptor Frédéric Auguste Bartholdi, was a gift of the French nation. President Cleveland formally dedicated the statue in 1886.

2. Madison Square Garden The huge sports complex is home to the Rangers ice hockey team and the Knicks basketball team. It also doubles as a venue for pop concerts. Beneath it is the Pennsylvania railroad station.

3. St Patrick's Cathedral When completed in 1879, this Gothic-style Catholic cathedral dominated its sector of Fifth Avenue. It still holds its own between the black-glass Olympic Tower and Saks department store.

4. Carnegie Hall Rachmaninov, Mahler, Sinatra and Garland – all have played to packed audiences in the Carnegie Hall, famed for its acoustics.

5. Harlem The Dutch settlement of Nieuw Haarlem had become a predominantly black neighbourhood by the late 19th century. Overcrowded and poverty-wracked, it was also a seedbed of talent, including figures such as Billie Holiday and Paul Robeson.

6. Chinatown The first full moon after January 19 is the Chinese New Year, when Chinatown becomes a riot of colour and firecrackers. A huge dragon makes its way along Mott Street, the district's principal thoroughfare.

New Year's Eve Times Square, where revellers gather to watch out the last seconds of the old year (above). Below: Little Italy, squeezed between Chinatown and the East Village.

Sideways wedge Completed in 1902, the 285 ft (87 m) Flatiron Building was one of New York's first steel-framed skyscrapers. Its curious shape was determined by the convergence of Broadway and Fifth Avenue.

Brooklyn Bridge Opened in 1883, the bridge was one of the engineering wonders of its day. But the work cost the lives of at least 20 workers, including its architect John Augustus Roebling.

Map of Manhattan

Hudson River
Broadway
Harlem
Upper West Side
Central Park
5th Avenue
Upper East Side
MANHATTAN
Chelsea
Greenwich Village
Soho
East Village
Broadway
East River
Little Italy
Chinatown
World Trade Center
Civic Center
Statue of Liberty
Financial District

1. Battery Park
2. New York Stock Exchange
3. Trinity Church
4. World Trade Center
5. Brooklyn Bridge
6. Manhattan Bridge
7. Chinatown
8. Lower East Side
9. Little Italy
10. SoHo and TriBeCa
11. Greenwich Village
12. Flatiron District
13. Union Square
14. Empire State Building
15. Macy's
16. Madison Square Garden Center
17. Rockefeller Center
18. Chrysler Building
19. United Nations Headquarters
20. St Patrick's Cathedral
21. MoMA (Museum of Modern Art)
22. Guggenheim Museum
23. Metropolitan Museum
24. Central Park
25. Times Square

Back view A characteristic mesh of fire escapes at the rear of buildings.

Chinese delicacies Food stalls in Chinatown. The district offers some of the best-value eating in New York.

Battery Park Taking its name from a battery of cannons, the park overlooks New York harbour.

Manhattan's skyscrapers

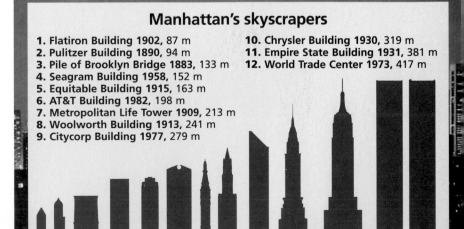

1. Flatiron Building 1902, 87 m
2. Pulitzer Building 1890, 94 m
3. Pile of Brooklyn Bridge 1883, 133 m
4. Seagram Building 1958, 152 m
5. Equitable Building 1915, 163 m
6. AT&T Building 1982, 198 m
7. Metropolitan Life Tower 1909, 213 m
8. Woolworth Building 1913, 241 m
9. Citycorp Building 1977, 279 m
10. Chrysler Building 1930, 319 m
11. Empire State Building 1931, 381 m
12. World Trade Center 1973, 417 m

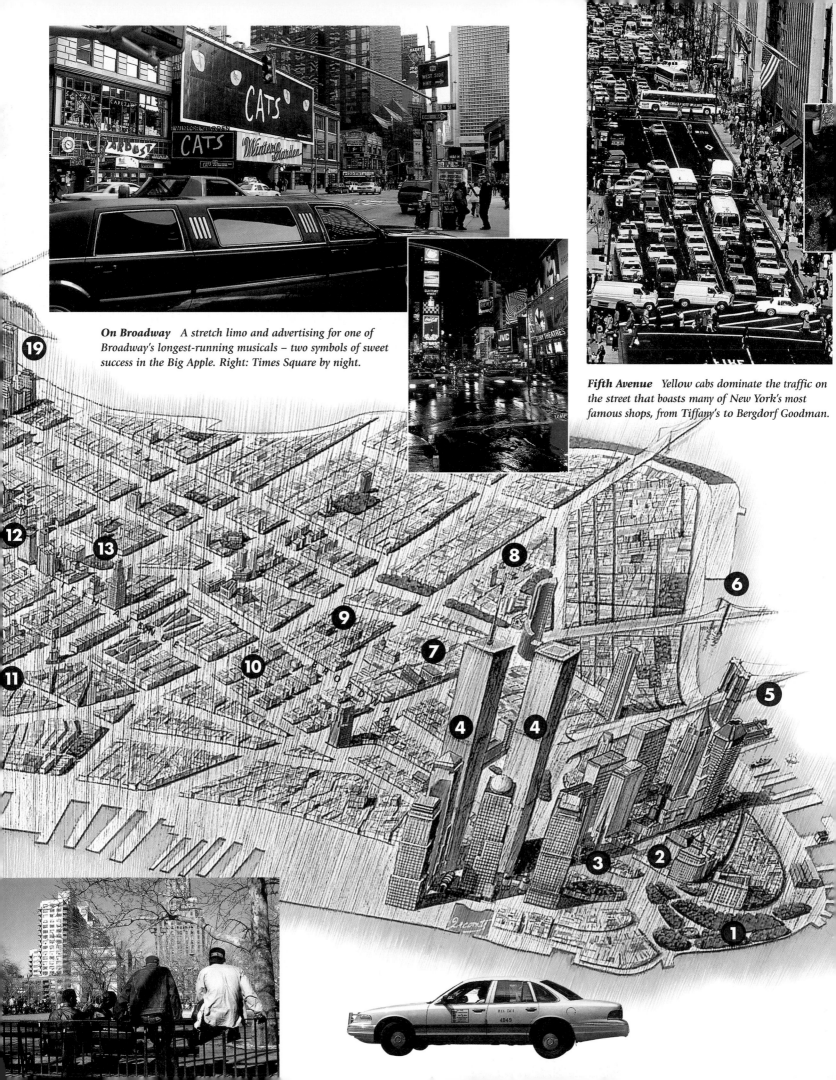

On Broadway A stretch limo and advertising for one of Broadway's longest-running musicals – two symbols of sweet success in the Big Apple. Right: Times Square by night.

Fifth Avenue Yellow cabs dominate the traffic on the street that boasts many of New York's most famous shops, from Tiffany's to Bergdorf Goodman.

Skyscraper record-breakers: climbing high

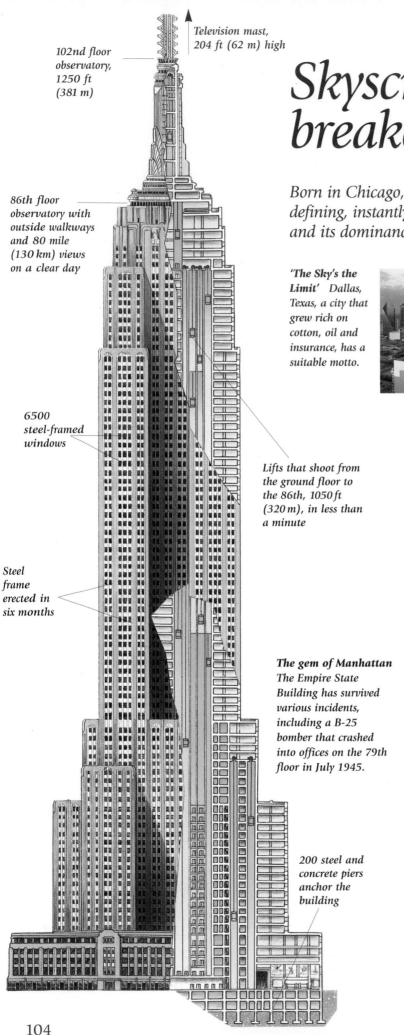

102nd floor observatory, 1250 ft (381 m)

Television mast, 204 ft (62 m) high

86th floor observatory with outside walkways and 80 mile (130 km) views on a clear day

6500 steel-framed windows

Lifts that shoot from the ground floor to the 86th, 1050 ft (320 m), in less than a minute

Steel frame erected in six months

The gem of Manhattan *The Empire State Building has survived various incidents, including a B-25 bomber that crashed into offices on the 79th floor in July 1945.*

200 steel and concrete piers anchor the building

Born in Chicago, adopted by Manhattan, skyscrapers became one of the defining, instantly recognisable symbols of North American urban culture and its dominance worldwide. They are cathedrals of a commercial age.

'The Sky's the Limit' *Dallas, Texas, a city that grew rich on cotton, oil and insurance, has a suitable motto.*

Skyscrapers would never have been feasible without an earlier invention, demonstrated by its creator, Elisha G. Otis, in May 1854. This was the safety elevator, a lift with a safety device to stop it from crashing to the ground if the cable broke. Before a small crowd at the Crystal Palace building in New York, Otis got onto the platform, which was then pulled high into the air. An assistant cut the cable and the platform held steady, secured by its safety device. Three years later, Otis's first passenger – as opposed to freight – elevator was installed in a New York department store.

Chicago's great fire in 1871 was another step along the way to the skyscraper. When the city was rebuilt, it was expanded vertically as well as horizontally. The birth of the skyscraper was the result, and with it the origins of the CBD – the steel, glass and

The Empire State Building

Some 25 000 people work in one building on the corner of Fifth Avenue and 34th Street – the Empire State Building, masterpiece of the architects Shreve, Lamb and Harmon. When completed in 1931, it was the world's tallest building, at 1250 ft (381 m) ousting the Chrysler Building, which was completed the year before. The Empire State Building reigned supreme for more than 40 years until topped in 1972-3 by the 1368 ft (417 m) World Trade Center.

The 60 000 tons of steel that made up the inner frame were assembled in six months. Ten million bricks were used to clad the 37 million cu ft (1 million m³) enclosed by the building. It swallowed up 60 miles (100 km) of piping and 3500 miles (5600 km) of telephone cables. There are 73 lifts, or 1860 steps up to the 102nd floor.

Construction started just before the Wall Street Crash; by the time it was completed, the Great Depression had set in and many of the 4000 offices were tenantless for a while. But the movie classic *King Kong* helped to solve that problem.

The Empire State Building has been a tourist attraction from the start. The first stage is an enclosed terrace on the 86th floor. Another set of lifts then climbs to an observatory on the 102nd floor, above which a TV mast pokes skyward. Skyscraper is an appropriate name for this giant, which is struck by lightning an average of twice every day. In 1956 it also became a lighthouse when four mercury arc lamps were installed, which can be seen 80 miles (130 km) away. At night the view over the shimmering lights of Midtown Manhattan and well beyond takes the breath away.

High-rise superstars The spire of the Chrysler Building (right) was assembled in secret inside the building's fire shaft and hoisted into place at the last minute – to make sure it topped a rival project, the Bank of Manhattan building. Above: The twin towers of the World Trade Center dominate the skyline at the southern end of Manhattan. Left: Chicago's 1454 ft (443 m) Sears Tower, completed in 1974, stretches skyward.

concrete 'central business district' that has become a feature of most American cities – and of modern cities worldwide.

Race for the skies

The basic structure that makes skyscrapers possible is simple. A rigid steel frame bears the weight of the building, with 'curtain' walls effectively hanging from it. Because the walls are not load-bearing, they can be made of lightweight materials such as glass. The first skyscrapers included Chicago's 180 ft (55 m) Home Insurance Building, completed in 1885, and its 200 ft (61 m) Reliance Building, completed in 1895. The idea soon caught on in New York, where space on Manhattan was at even more of a premium. Here, architects and engineers were ever more ambitious as they reached for the skies. The 285 ft (87 m) Flatiron Building was completed in 1902; more than twice as tall were the 700 ft (213 m) Metropolitan Life

Mighty monster King Kong at the top of the Empire State Building in the 1933 movie.

Insurance Tower, completed in 1909, and the 792 ft (241 m) Woolworth Building, completed in 1913.

Rivalry to construct taller buildings reflected New York's growing importance as a world financial centre. The 1046 ft (319 m) Chrysler Building was completed in 1930, and then the 1250 ft (381 m) Empire State Building was christened the following year. The latter, a supremely graceful, much-loved structure, remained the world's tallest building for 40 years, until it was topped in 1972 and 1973 by the 1368 ft (417 m) and 1362 ft (415 m) towers of the World Trade Center near the southern end of Manhattan. The World Trade Center was no sooner completed than the record for the tallest building returned to Chicago with its 1454 ft (443 m) Sears Tower, finished in 1974 – which was eclipsed in 1976 by the CN Tower in Toronto. And so the challenge goes on.

Los Angeles, an American dream

The United States' second-largest city, Los Angeles is an endless sprawl of tarmac and concrete, where wealth contrasts with grinding deprivation.

Shopping de luxe *Expensive boutiques in Santa Monica, a seaside resort.*

The greater Los Angeles area covers some 4000 sq miles (10 000 km²), bigger than the English counties of Norfolk and Suffolk put together. Spread out between the coast and the San Gabriel Mountains, it encloses 86 'towns', including Long Beach, Beverly Hills, Hollywood, Pasadena, Watts and Bel Air. The total metropolitan area has a population of more than 15.3 million people, putting it slightly ahead of Florida, the fourth most populous state in the Union. The city 'proper' has 3.6 million inhabitants.

Seen from a plane, Los Angeles is a vast tangled web of highways with no real centre. Between the wars, the critic and wit H.L. Mencken described the city as '19 suburbs in search of a metropolis', and it remains true that each town or suburb is its own more or less self-contained centre. Contrasts are often startling. Simply by following the 21 miles (34 km) of Sunset Boulevard, you pass through areas of grinding poverty and ostentatious wealth. Violence is never far from the surface somewhere or other in the city; and with 3000 gun shops, the murder rate is high.

Waiting, watching *Blacks and Hispanics make up more than 52 per cent of the city's population.*

Living side by side

Yet rich and poor Angelinos do usually manage to coexist. Even in the most rundown black ghetto of Watts or the poorest Hispanic barrio, a luxury limousine with smoked glass sits patiently in the inevitable traffic jam alongside an antiquated Dodge lovingly souped up with all the flashy accoutrements of the current fashion. While crime rates are higher in the poorest neighbourhoods, violence on a large scale has erupted only when controversies bring emotions to a boil.

Freeway city *Roughly 500 miles (800 km) of highways crisscross Los Angeles. Right: One of the bronze stars on Hollywood Boulevard that commemorate the stars of the screen.*

Shameless riches

In Beverly Hills, the place to be seen is Rodeo Drive, the most prestigious shopping street on the West Coast, where all the great names of European and North American luxury have outlets. You can have a haircut for $300, buy a dress for $5000 or a watch for $18 000. You may even be offered champagne as you make your choice. You may have booked an appointment beforehand to make sure that the shop staff are ready and waiting. By the time you hand over your credit card, the bill may tot up to $30 000 or more. A visit to the shops is frequently worth it for the interior decor alone: Gucci, for example, spent $10 million renovating its store on Rodeo Drive. Not even Beverly Hills, however, was immune to the recession of the early 1990s. In 1990 profits sank so low that a number of shops had to close. But business picked up again in mid decade. Shops started opening up again, and profits soared to unprecedented highs.

Beyond Rodeo Drive, Beverly Hills is a suburb of comfortable detached houses. It is not unlike a number of other suburbs on the edges of US cities – except that houses are likely to have dozens of bathrooms, servants and a handful of Rolls-Royces or Ferraris in their garages.

The 42 hills of San Francisco

For many people, San Francisco is their favourite US city. It is a city built on a human scale, and communities from the four corners of the Earth have taken root on the sides of its steep hills.

Skyscrapers rise behind a row of 'painted ladies', the city's characteristic Victorian wooden town houses, painted an array of warm colours. The skyline creates a jagged profile of highs and lows; at ground level long streets slice, straight as a die, up the many hills and down the other side. San Francisco is quite unlike any other North American city, in part due to its

Victorian charm   San Francisco is proud of the 19th-century wooden houses in residential neighbourhoods that were spared by the earthquake and fire of 1906. There are more than 13 000 such homes, ranging from the confusingly named Queen Anne Victorian to Italianate Victorian. Above: One of the unmistakable towers of the Golden Gate Bridge rising out of a typical West Coast fog; behind it are the skyscrapers of the financial district and the San Francisco-Oakland Bay Bridge.

position. Situated at the tip of a peninsula, with San Francisco Bay on one side and the Pacific on the other, it is almost completely surrounded by water and has not been able to spread out like so many other US cities. It is also one of the busiest ports in the USA, in constant contact with other parts of the Pacific, notably Japan, China and Australia, and open to all kinds of cultural currents.

Showcase for diversity

The moment you start to explore, you become aware of the exceptional variety of San Francisco's inhabitants. Virtually every group that has ever settled in North America is represented here. North Beach is the heart of the city's Italian community, while the Mission district is Hispanic. Nihonmachi, Japan Town, was destroyed as a residential community after the attack on Pearl Harbor in the Second World War; even so, it survives as a commercial area with Japanese businesses, restaurants and shops. The famous Chinatown continues to thrive as home to one of the largest Chinese communities outside Asia.

Hispanics and Asians represent nearly half the population. With communities of Hong Kong Chinese, Japanese, Koreans, Vietnamese, Filipinos, Mexicans and other Latin Americans, as well as Russian Jews, Sicilians and Scots, San Francisco is a shop window for the ethnic and cultural diversity of North American life. It is a melting pot that integrates the communities, but also allows them to flourish as distinctive groups. For newly arrived immigrants this has had the advantage of offering them a sheltered base among their own people, where they can find their feet in the strange new setting.

Hallidie's cable cars

Many a horse suffered from San Francisco's 42 hills. Hundreds of them died every year, worn out from heaving loads up the steep slopes. Then a Scottish-born wire cable manufacturer, Andrew Hallidie, had the idea of equipping the city with special cable-car trams. The first trams went into service in 1873, and they still run, giving the city a faintly old-world air, although there is nothing quaint about their importance in the city's transport network. The trams became so strongly identified with the city that when the authorities proposed replacing them with modern buses in 1947, there was an outcry. The people of San Francisco made sure that the project came to nothing.

The 30 trams crisscrossing the city are established as a feature of the landscape. To heave Hallidie's original cable cars up hills with a 21 per cent incline at 9 mph (15 km/h), they had mechanisms similar to those of ski lifts. Each car was attached to a cable running between the rails and kept moving by a steam-driven shaft. Today, the trams are electrically powered.

Bridges of all shapes and sizes

From the Brooklyn Bridge on the East Coast to the Golden Gate on the West, North America's bridges include some mighty feats of engineering, but many are in need of repair.

Many of the United States' bridges are vulnerable giants, far from indestructible. According to data published by the Federal Highway Administration in 1997, more than 30 per cent of the nation's bridges were in need of extensive repairs or were in other ways deficient – for example, they needed to be widened or strengthened to cope with increased traffic flows. In recent decades, no fewer than 120 bridges have collapsed, due, in part at least, to restrictions on federal and state maintenance budgets. The worst disaster was in 1967 when the Silver Bridge across the Ohio River collapsed suddenly, hurling 46 people to their deaths. In 1983, three people died when a section of a bridge across the Mianus River in Greenwich, Connecticut, crumbled and fell. After heavy rains in 1987, a highway bridge near Amsterdam, New York State, tumbled into the swollen waters below, plunging ten people to their deaths.

In 1995 a similar incident occurred near Coalinga, California, causing five deaths.

In 1997 experts estimated that 200 000 bridges need replacing or repairing in the next two decades. On the Capital Beltway that carries traffic around Washington DC, the Woodrow Wilson drawbridge urgently needs to be replaced: the estimated cost for rebuilding this one bridge alone is $1.6 billion. A number of bridges on major highways have been closed to heavy trucks and buses, which have to be diverted along special routes. Funds have now been set aside for a programme of renewal.

Country span *A wooden covered bridge in Vermont (left). Top: Construction work on New York's Brooklyn Bridge.*

The Golden Gate

When it was opened in 1937, San Francisco's Golden Gate Bridge was the world's longest suspension bridge, and it has remained one of America's best-known bridges ever since. It crosses the Golden Gate Strait at the mouth of San Francisco Bay. According to Joseph Baermann Strauss, the engineer who built the bridge, it took 20 years and '200 million

Crossing the strait *During building, Strauss insisted on safety nets beneath the bridge.*

words' to convince the authorities of its feasibility. They were particularly sceptical about the height involved: 217 ft (66 m) in order to allow ocean-going ships to pass through the strait.

It took four years and four months to build the 4200 ft (1280 m) bridge. On May 27, 1937, the day before it was opened to vehicles, 200 000 pedestrians walked across the new marvel. Each of its steel piers is as heavy as a battleship; they were made by a Pennsylvania firm, Bethlehem Steel. Huge quantities of concrete were needed to provide a secure base for the piers in the deep waters of the strait. Around 80 000 miles (129 000 km) of cable were used to suspend the roadway. Its trademark colour, International Orange, was specially chosen to blend in with the setting.

Image of the South *A river steamer and a cantilever bridge across the Mississippi near Natchez.*

Hispanic Miami

Tourism is Miami's lifeblood – it is the sunshine capital of the USA, where young people play and older people spend their retirement. It is also one of the world's biggest Spanish-speaking cities, its population swelled by refugees from Cuba.

Little Havana   *In Miami's Cuban district you are much more likely to hear Spanish spoken around you than English.*

In 1896 the railroad reached an area of swamps, populated by Seminole Indians, panthers and alligators – and Miami was born. Within a few years it had become a booming tourist resort, thanks largely to the energies of Henry Flagler, who built luxury hotels and dredged the harbour. Miami today has urban sprawl that spreads around Biscayne Bay near Florida's south-eastern tip, and a population of 380 000 people. Its sister resort Miami Beach lies on an island 3 miles (5 km) offshore, connected to the mainland city by causeways.

Key West, the end of America

Cayo Hueso, 'bone islet', lies roughly 100 miles (160 km) from Cuba, and about the same distance from Florida. The world's longest overwater road, the Overseas Highway of US1, links the island to the mainland, jumping from islet to islet in a succession of 42 bridges. Key West's indigenous inhabitants, who refer to themselves as Conches, are descended from a colourful mix of Bahamian, Cuban and New England seafarers. Nowadays, the island is a popular centre for fishing, diving and snorkelling, drawing visitors from all over the world.

Duval Street is a favourite spot for hanging out, with many of the best restaurants and bars.

Mallory Square at the western end is the scene of a daily ritual, the Sunset Celebration, when hundreds of people come to watch the sun sink in multihued glory beneath the horizon. Key West's year is punctuated by a succession of festivals and regattas. Ernest Hemingway was one of its most famous residents.

Hemingway's home from 1931.

Tourists and immigrants

'Sun and fun' is the most appropriate slogan for Miami. All year round, tourists throng popular shoreline districts such as Coconut Grove. Some visitors admire the period architecture of South Beach's Art Deco district or Coral Gables, one of the first housing developments put up in the 1920s.

Florida as a whole, and Miami in particular, is popular with retired people, drawn by its year-round sun; Miami has the highest proportion of retired people of any US city.

There is also a huge population of immigrants, almost all of whom hail from the Caribbean region, and in particular Cuba and Haiti. Today, more than half of the city's inhabitants are Hispanic. Local radio and TV stations are more likely to broadcast in Spanish than in English. Districts such as Little Havana are more Cuban than American. Eighth Street has become Calle Ocho, where men sit outside the bars and cafés playing dominoes, and Cuban food is served in street stalls.

Art Deco   *The Marlin Hotel and Bar on Miami Beach's Collins Avenue.*

Vancouver, gateway to the Orient

Vancouver started life as an obscure sawmill town, but started to boom after it became the western terminus of the Canadian Pacific Railway in 1886. Much of its prosperity today rests on its links with Asia and its growing status as the Hong Kong of the West.

Facing the future *Vancouver's waterfront (above and right). The port and business districts lie along Burrard Inlet and False Creek.*

Canada's third largest city, Vancouver is situated on Burrard Inlet, one of the world's finest harbours, and sprawls across British Columbia's lower mainland to the Fraser River Delta. The snow-capped peaks of Coast Mountains provide a spectacular backdrop for this dynamic metropolis. Beyond the coastal peaks lie the Columbia and Rocky Mountains, which run north to south across the province. At the British Columbia-Alberta border, the Rockies subside abruptly to foothills and prairies.

Boom town

The first settlement was called Granville, until in 1886 the railroad arrived and it was classified as a city. For this event, it changed its name in honour of George Vancouver, an English explorer who first set foot there in 1792. In 1986, 100 years after its inauguration as a city, Vancouver hosted the world fair Expo 86, confirming its 'boom' status as one of North America's fastest-growing metropolises. Vancouver has nearly half of British Columbia's population of 3.9 million people living in its metropolitan area, including communities of Chinese, Iranian, Lebanese and European origins.

Hong Kong's home from home

The skyscrapers of Vancouver Bay, great cliffs of steel and glass, are symbolic of the city's ambition to be at the economic forefront. In particular, they express determination to exploit the city's position as a commercial linchpin between Asia and North America. Expo 86 was a key stage in this development, leaving Vancouver with an improved transport infrastructure that was developed for the occasion.

One person who spotted the opportunities was a Hong Kong billionaire, Li Ka-shing, who bought the 210 acre (85 ha) world fair site to redevelop it in an ambitious real estate venture:

Concord Pacific has 3.2 million sq ft (300 000 m²) of office and shop space and 8500 apartments.

In the build-up to the return of Hong Kong by Britain to China in 1997, many Hong Kong Chinese wanted to leave. Canadian immigration policy was generous in this regard. Every year during the 1990s, 10 000 to 25 000 Hong Kong Chinese arrived in Vancouver. Soon its Chinese community became the biggest along the West Coast, ousting San Francisco's Chinatown from top place. Numbering nearly 350 000 people, it accounted for 20 per cent of the city's population.

Canada Place *Built as the Canada Pavilion at Vancouver's Expo 86, the complex houses shops, a theatre, a conference centre and a hotel.*

Toronto and Ottawa

Ottawa, the federal capital, holds the political reins; Toronto holds the economic and commercial ones. The two cities stand in marked contrast to each other.

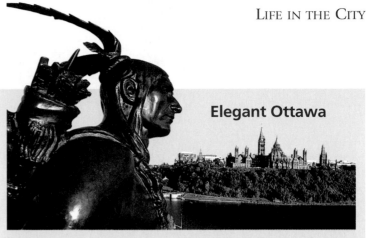

Elegant Ottawa

Built as a telecommunications transmission station, the CN Tower has become an emblem of Toronto and a favourite tourist site, rising with sleek elegance from the shores of Lake Ontario. At 1815 ft (553 m) it is one of the tallest man-made structures on Earth, offering views from its restaurant and observation decks of 100 miles (160 km) in all directions in clear weather.

Ice skating An outdoor rink in Toronto near the CN Tower.

Toronto used to be regarded as a slightly dour, very Wasp (white, Anglo-Saxon, Protestant) city – 'Toronto the Good'. But

From the 17th century onwards, missionaries, merchants and fur traders heading westwards into the North American interior set off from the Lachine Rapids near present-day Montreal and followed the Ottawa River. One of the first Europeans to use this route was the French explorer Samuel de Champlain, who travelled up the river in 1613. Where the city of Ottawa now stands, his Indian guides showed him a waterfall that hid a cave behind its curtain of water; it was a perfect hiding place where warriors would lie in wait to ambush their enemies.

Champlain named the falls the Rideau Falls, after the French word for curtain. Later, between 1826 and 1832, a canal was built linking the Ottawa River with Kingston on Lake Ontario. The man in charge was Lt-Colonel John By of the British Royal Engineers, and the settlement built to accommodate workers at the Ottawa River end came to be called Bytown. It remained a rough-and-ready sort of place

Algonquin Indians A statue of the region's original inhabitants.

until 1857, when it was plucked from obscurity to become the site of a new Canadian capital, renamed Ottawa. Rivalries between Quebec, Montreal and Toronto about which should become the seat of government of the new dominion had made this step necessary.

Modern Ottawa is an attractive city, its government ministries, embassies, two universities, museums, parks and gardens elegantly laid out. The National Arts Centre offers year-round entertainment, and the National Gallery houses important collections and regularly hosts major international exhibitions. It is a good base for outdoor pursuits, and there is even an experimental farm near the heart of the city. In spring Parliament Hill is a mass of tulips, given by the Netherlands government to express gratitude to Canada for sheltering its royal family in the Second World War.

a big influx of immigrants since the Second World War has transformed it. Nowadays, it has a distinctly cosmopolitan feel, with Portuguese, Chinese, Italian and Greek districts. In 1997, seven municipalities in the former Toronto metropolitan area were amalgamated in one city, whose metropolitan area now has a population of 4.4 million inhabitants. Contemporary Toronto is a vibrant place, an important rail, air, telecommunications, financial and industrial centre, which also boasts a lively artistic and cultural life.

The first Flatiron Toronto's own Flatiron Building, built in 1892, is now dwarfed by the gleaming modern skyscrapers of the financial district.

111

A little bit of France

The walled city of Quebec, capital of the province that bears its name, stands on a promontory above the St Lawrence. Farther west, Montreal spreads out over an island in the river. For both cities, the mighty St Lawrence is a lifeline to trade and prosperity.

Ancient and modern   Old world charm and buildings dating from the 17th and 18th centuries make Quebec City a popular tourist spot. Right, above: Montreal's attractions include this underground mall in the Place Desjardins complex of shops, offices and restaurants.

The only walled city north of Mexico, Quebec is almost arrogantly beautiful, perched astride Cape Diamond, overlooking a great sweep of the St Lawrence River 330 ft (100 m) below. In 1985, its importance as one of the oldest and most picturesque cities in the continent was confirmed when UNESCO designated it a World Heritage Site. It is also the most French of Canadian cities, where some 95 per cent of the people are native French-speakers.

The Upper and Lower Town

In the Upper Town, Quebec's 17th-century founder Samuel de Champlain stands on a pedestal on Dufferin Terrace, a superb esplanade running along the flank of Cape Diamond. Along the cape's river edge are the Plains of Abraham, where in 1759 the British under General Wolfe captured the city from the French under the Marquis de Montcalm – both generals were fatally wounded. Today, the battle site is a landscaped park. Capping the cape is the Citadel, whose cannons used to guard the river entrance to the colony of New France. Just outside the Upper Town, the Hôtel du Parlement houses the province of Quebec's National Assembly, proudly displaying the fleur-de-lys, emblem of the province and symbol of its French heritage.

Visitors to Quebec are drawn by its beauty and its historic ambience. At the base of the promontory where the Upper Town is situated lies the city's oldest district, the Lower Town, which is the site of Champlain's original 1608 settlement. Here, more than 80 heritage buildings have been restored, including the oldest, the 1684 Hazeur House.

The mosaic of Montreal

Dominated by the 763 ft (233 m) mass of Mont Royal, topped in its turn by a 100 ft (30 m) cross, Montreal lacks the elegant charm of Quebec, but makes up for it with buzz. The city offers a year-round succession of popular events, such as the matches of its professional ice hockey, baseball and football teams, and its Formula One grand prix. Cultural highlights include concerts, opera, theatre, an annual jazz festival, a Just for Laughs comedy festival, an international film festival, and the world-renowned Cirque du Soleil. Montreal's symphony orchestra is respected worldwide. The city's botanical garden is one of the largest in the world.

A dynamic, cosmopolitan city
Despite the loss of its historic role as the leading Canadian city, Montreal retains its position as a major commercial, financial and transportation centre. Moreover, its international reputation – firmly established by Expo 67 and the summer Olympics of 1976 – endures, while its importance as the home of a self-sufficient French culture in North America grows. In recent decades, the city has been enriched by an impressive array of skyscrapers, museums, galleries and theatres.

One of Montreal's appealing assets is its cosmopolitan, almost European, atmosphere. The meeting of French and English cultures, and the addition of many other ethnic influences, have created a blend unmatched in North America. Its varied and vibrant neighbourhoods, such as Old Montreal with its picturesque cobbled streets and old buildings, or the Latin Quarter of St Denis Street with its outdoor cafes, provide an exciting urban scene.

Downtown Canada   Montreal's financial and business district in the early morning.

Jazz club *Not surprisingly, when tourists come to the birthplace of jazz, they want to hear it for themselves, and there is plenty to choose from. Preservation Hall and Dixieland Hall specialise in revivals of traditional jazz.*

Vieux Carré at night *Bourbon Street's Creole-style houses with their upstairs verandahs contrast with the modern skyscrapers rising in the background.*

Swamps and jazz in New Orleans

Founded by the French, New Orleans grew rich as the chief port of the Deep South. It also gave birth to a new form of music – jazz.

For the first-time visitor, the people's way of talking can take some getting used to. In New Orleans, the Caribbean lilt, as well, perhaps, as a residual influence from the times of French Louisiana, have left their traces on the Southern drawl. French and Spanish influences also survive in the city's most picturesque district, the Vieux Carré (Old Quarter). When night falls, the Vieux Carré comes alive. The first port of call for music lovers will probably be Preservation Hall or Dixieland Hall, temples of traditional New Orleans jazz. Then they may want to wander

through the streets, cooling themselves in the sticky heat with cocktails at establishments such as Tipitina's or the Old Absinthe House.

Mud and water

New Orleans fights a constant struggle against mud and water. Many parts of the city lie as much as 5 ft (1.5 m) below sea level. To the north lies Lake Pontchartrain, crossed by one of the world's longest bridges, spanning a 24 mile (39 km) stretch of water. Flowing through the south of the city is the muddy Mississippi, and beyond the southernmost suburbs all is swamp as far as the Gulf of Mexico. For protection, the city is almost completely encircled by levees, and several huge pumping stations are constantly at the ready to deal with rises in the water level.

But New Orleans also owes its prosperity to water. The elegant French and Spanish-style houses of the Vieux Carré, and the imposing 19th-century mansions of the uptown Garden District, all bear witness to its wealth as a port through which the cotton, sugar, rice and indigo of the plantations were exported to the rest of the world.

CHAPTER 6

CULTURE AND FOLKLORE

In the North American melting pot the range of influences in the arts and entertainment is immense – African, Hispanic, Irish, Scottish, English, German, Scandinavian, Italian, Jewish, Russian, Polish. In music, North America set the world agenda for much of the 20th century, from jazz to country and western, swing to bebop, rock'n'roll to rap. Broadway gave the world the musical spectacular. Hollywood has dominated cinema, and the entertainment industry also spawned the amusement park, with extravagant concoctions such as Walt Disney World. In writing, North America has produced the black Toni Morrison, the Jewish Saul Bellow, the Southerner William Faulkner and the Canadian Margaret Atwood. Artists range from 19th-century landscapists such as the Hudson River School, through the Ashcan School in the early 20th century, to Jackson Pollock and Andy Warhol.

A giant Oscar dominates the 71st Academy Awards ceremony in Los Angeles, in March 1999.

Memphis, home of the blues

Emerging from the 'low life' district of a Mississippi river port, the blues drew on the work songs and spirituals of the old South to create a new musical language – one that told tales of hardship and doomed love, the woes of a people only recently set free.

Kinsey Report *Born in Mississippi in 1927, vocalist and guitarist Lester 'Big Daddy' Kinsey had to wait until his fifties before making it into the big time. He and his sons' band, the Kinsey Report, recorded their first album* **Bad Situation** *in 1985. Mingling traditional blues with more contemporary styles, the album was an instant hit.*

Elvis Presley: the King

Idolised while he was still alive and venerated after his death, Elvis Presley was an incarnation of the American dream. He was immortalised not only for the hundreds of songs he recorded, or the thousands of concerts he gave, but for what he represented – an attitude of rebellion, sensuality and success.

Born into a poor family in 1935, Presley's first exposure to the power of music was in the black churches of his native Memphis. He blended elements of country music, electric rock and gospel with his unique vocal talent and delivery to create a kind of music that was all his own. His effect on the popular music industry was explosive, and its repercussions were felt all round the world. His ability to electrify audiences was quite extraordinary, and his untimely death in 1977, aged just 42, left millions of desolate fans and the world of rock 'n' roll an orphan. His Memphis home, Graceland, became a shrine to his memory and is visited each year by millions of devotees.

Rock idol Elvis Presley performing Jailhouse Rock.

The steamboat was the making of Memphis. In the last decades of the 19th century increasing numbers of steamboats plied up and down the river, carrying cotton, timber and other goods. Until then a modest town, lying on the east bank of the Mississippi roughly halfway between the great cities of St Louis and New Orleans, it soon became one of the Mississippi's busiest ports.

At the same time thousands of former slaves, set free from the plantations where they had once been scattered, were drawn to Memphis by the prospect of working on the docks. Soon the district in the port area lying between Beale Street and Fourth Street became a busy night-time haunt, crowded with bars, clubs, brothels and gambling dens. It was in this 'low life' area that a new musical tradition was forged.

Entertainin' blues

The performers in these dives had to entertain customers who were rowdy and often drunk. They developed a style of dance music that had a strong rhythm and placed the emphasis on the band as a whole, rather than on individual soloists. Their instruments included the guitar, violin, mandolin, banjo and double bass, as well as some unique adaptations of their own. One was a large jug that the player hummed into, creating a booming, resonant sound. Another was the cigar-shaped kazoo, which had a piece of thin paper inside it that vibrated as the player hummed into the instrument. Against this booming backdrop of sound, the vocalists sang their melancholy lyrics, often inspired by the trials of plantation life.

Memphis has left its imprint on the blues to the extent that many of the great blues artists incorporate its name into their stage names – Memphis Willie Borum, John Williams alias Memphis Piano Red, the singer Minnie Douglas alias Memphis Minnie and the pianist Peter Chapman alias Memphis Slim.

Nashville, the cradle of country

Starting in the 1920s, Nashville's Grand Ole Opry brought together talents nurtured in the rural South and West. Rooted in the folk traditions of old Europe, a new voice was heard in American music.

The Nashville story began on November 28, 1925, on the airwaves of the city's WSM radio station. George D. Hay, one of the most famous radio presenters of the day, had arranged for the fiddler 'Uncle' Jimmy Thompson to give a concert on air. A legendary figure among a relatively small band of aficionados, the 77-year-old Thompson was much less known to the wider public. Hay's aim was to remedy this: through a series of concerts broadcast live on WSM, he introduced listeners to a range of singers and instrumentalists of rare talent.

Grand Ole Opry

For many listeners, the music was a revelation. Played on acoustic instruments such as the guitar and fiddle, it had the raw authenticity of the country areas from which it emerged. Soon crowds of people were gathering outside the radio station when a concert was due to be performed. They wanted to experience the event as members of a live audience. The radio station made a deal with the nearest thing Nashville had to a proper theatre, the Ryman Auditorium, to hold its concerts there every Saturday night. The Ryman, actually a tabernacle built for revivalist Billy Sunday, was considered Nashville's opera house, so the country musicians who played there dubbed themselves 'The Grand Old Opry'. By 1939, the Grand Ole Opry concerts were being broadcast across much of the United States.

The popularity of 'country and western' has never died – larger audiences have, if anything, demanded higher standards from the top country stars. Nashville, meanwhile, is a near-obligatory stop for young hopefuls making their name. Talents as diverse as Hank Williams, Johnny Cash, Loretta Lynn, rustic 'Grandpa' Jones, the duo Jim and Jess, Jerry Clower, Willie Nelson with his rasping voice, Bill Carlisle and his family, Dolly Parton – all in their day trod the boards in Nashville, and many of them still return.

In Nashville, an industry has grown up around the success of country music. The Grand Ole Opry still lies at its heart, together with the recording studios that now line the city's South 16th Avenue. In the early 1980s, a huge tourist complex was established to cater for the hoards of visitors. It includes luxury hotels, a museum of country and western music, extra concert halls, special radio and TV stations, film production facilities, first-aid teams – everything to ensure a smooth operation.

Bar music The Honky Tonk Bar in Memphis (above). A honky-tonk was originally a low-life nightclub. The term came to be used of ragtime piano playing and later, from the 1940s, of a style of country music, played on the fiddle and steel guitar. Below: Ernest Tubb was a pioneer of honky-tonk country music.

From jazz to rap, a century of rhythm

Jazz, swing, bebop, rhythm and blues, rock 'n' roll, soul, rock, rap – one form has succeeded another throughout the 20th century. North America has been a crucible of extraordinary musical creativity, synthesising influences from Africa and Europe.

The slave work songs of the plantations gave rise to the poignant religious lyrics of the Negro spirituals and the more secular laments of the blues. Together, they created a unique musical tradition – drawing, of course, on the African heritage, but also pulling in elements as diverse as Irish folk songs, German dances and a Hispanic beat. Mingling the sacred with the secular, echoing both the teachings of the preacher and the daily experience of survival, it was a music that gradually broke down barriers, cultural and racial alike.

Birthplace of jazz

Around the turn of the 20th century, a number of black musicians played in the dance halls and bars of New Orleans' Storyville district. Such figures as Buddy Bolden, King Oliver, Sidney Bechet and Louis Armstrong played instruments from the trumpet and trombone to the clarinet. Without realising it, they were creating a musical revolution whose repercussions would be felt for the rest of the 20th century. In 1917, when the port of New Orleans was closed after the United States' entry into the First World War, business in the bars dried up and the best musicians went north, to Memphis and St Louis and then on to Chicago and New York, introducing jazz to a wider and wider audience.

The Motown sound

It took courage, flair and sheer hard work for a black former Ford car worker to set up a record label that competed successfully with the biggest names in the music industry. But it happened in Detroit in the 1960s. Two key ingredients in Berry Gordy's success were a clear sense of the kind of music he wanted to promote and a talent for marketing it. The result was a flowering of rhythm and blues, soul and funk music. Under Gordy's guidance, strings and brass were meticulously balanced and arranged, with the rhythm section kept perfectly in place. Recording was impeccable, live shows were superbly choreographed, and the publicity machine was always ready to swing into action. The Motown label was soon world famous. Gordy's discoveries included The Supremes (including Diana Ross), Martha and the Vandellas, Smokey Robinson, The Commodores (including Lionel Richie), Stevie Wonder and The Jackson Five (including future superstar Michael Jackson).

Satchmo Louis ('Satchel Mouth') Armstrong bestrode the jazz world for nearly half a century from the 1920s. It was he who broke apart the old jazz tradition of clarinet, trumpet and trombone playing as an ensemble. This was too confining for his virtuoso skills, and a new style emerged giving prominence to solos by the different players. Left: Motown discovery, Michael Jackson. Top left: 1950s and 60s rock 'n' roller Chuck Berry.

Charlie Parker: the Yardbird

Tragedy and huge success marked the career of Charlie Parker. He was born in 1920 in Kansas City, in a black ghetto just a few streets away from the famous Club Reno, one of the jazz hotspots between the wars. He started playing the alto saxophone at the age of 13. When he reached New York in 1939, he plunged straight into the world of Harlem clubs and bars, and soon established himself as an up-and-coming star. An intoxicating improviser and virtuoso as well as an inspired composer, he helped to lay the foundations of bebop. Nicknamed 'Bird' or 'Yardbird', he played with other legendary names such as Dizzy Gillespie on trumpet, Thelonius Monk and Bud Powell on piano, Charlie Mingus on bass, and Kenny Clarke and Max Roach on drums. Problems with drugs and alcohol resulted in his untimely death in New York in 1955, aged just 34.

In the swing

During the 1920s, jazz took the Western world by storm. For a generation relieved to put the horrors of the Great War behind it, jazz with its novel and intoxicating syncopations seemed like the perfect music to dance and relax to. Then, as the world slumped into Depression following the Wall Street Crash of 1929, the mood changed, and the new big bands came into their own, led by figures such as Fletcher Henderson, Cab Calloway, Count Basie, Duke Ellington, Benny Goodman and Glenn Miller – it was the age of swing, a variant of jazz. People forgot their troubles by dancing the night away.

Voice of a generation Bob Dylan's early lyrics articulated 1960s concerns with civil rights and antiwar protest.

Swing carried jazz through the Second World War, after which a new generation of musicians emerged, ousting the traditions of their elders. Bebop or 'hot jazz' was a deliberate reaction against swing, in which musicians like Charlie Parker espoused more complex rhythms and a more virtuoso approach. For many fans who disliked the knotty sophistication of bebop another new tradition, rhythm and blues – played by black performers including Little Richard, Chuck Berry and Fats Domino – was more appealing. They were unconsciously preparing the way for yet another upheaval. Heavily influenced by the earlier black artists, a generation of white singers such as Carl Perkins, Jerry Lee Lewis and Elvis Presley electrified their audiences with a new and provocative sound – rock 'n' roll.

Heritage of rock

Like jazz, rock showed a protean ability to mould itself to succeeding generations and their moods: whether sunnily upbeat like the Beach Boys, psychedelic like Jefferson Airplane or the

Rap and country Rap star LL Cool J (above) leapt to fame in the late 1980s with albums such as **Bigger and Deffer** (1987). Right: Country singer Loretta Lynn, a Kentucky coal-miner's daughter, recorded her first single in 1960. Later hits included 'You Ain't Woman Enough To Take My Man' and 'Lyin', Cheatin', Woman Chasin', Honky Tonkin' You'.

Grateful Dead, extravagantly flamboyant like Jimi Hendrix, politically engaged like Bob Dylan, harmonic like Crosby, Stills, Nash and Young, or mesmerising like Alice Cooper, Van Halen or Nirvana. Black musicians, meanwhile – James Brown, Aretha Franklin and other artists promoted under the Motown label – fed into the rock tradition the emotional intensity of soul and the heavy beat of funk. In the late 1970s and early 80s, rap and its 'hip-hop' culture made their appearance in the urban ghettos of US cities, expressing the alienation of many young black Americans.

Hollywood, the dream factory

It had the right climate – reliable and with plenty of sunshine. There was a wide range of scenery, from lush forests to the desert, providing different backdrops. By 1910 US film-makers had spotted the advantages of southern California, and were beginning to congregate in the Los Angeles suburb of Hollywood.

Hollywood and America have been inseparably entwined for nearly a century. Almost from the start, the United States made the new art form of cinema its own. Ever since D.W. Griffith's silent epic *The Birth of a Nation* was issued in 1915, the cinema has been used to probe, explore and develop just about every aspect of US life. It was D.W. Griffith, too, who pioneered many of the technical stocks in trade of the cinema, from the flashback and crosscut to the fade-out, close-up and long shot. By his time, Hollywood in California, with its clear light and reliable climate, had already established itself as the home of US cinema.

Coming of age

In 1919, Griffith clubbed together with stars Charlie Chaplin and the husband-and-wife duo Douglas Fairbanks and Mary Pickford to found the production and distribution company United Artists. They wanted to take artistic and financial control of their own affairs. It was a sign that Hollywood was coming of age. The star system was already well established. Chaplin, Fairbanks and Pickford were household names in a way that few human beings had ever been before – their faces instantly recognisable not just in North America, but across much of the globe. They wanted and got a measure of clout that corresponded to their extraordinary pulling power.

The next revolution came with the arrival of the talkies from 1927, heralding a reshuffling of the star pack as some actors adapted to the rigours of sound better than others. Other upheavals – some of which were positive, while others were negative – included the coming of Technicolor in the 1930s, the McCarthyite anticommunist witchhunt of the 1950s that silenced or sent into exile many of Hollywood's finest actors and directors, and the competition from television, which became most acute in the 1970s. Hollywood has managed to weather them all.

Glamour goddesses
Marilyn Monroe and Jane Russell, stars of the 1950s. Above: Demi Moore.

On the Titanic *Director James Cameron with stars Kate Winslet and Leonardo DiCaprio during the filming of* Titanic. *A blockbuster success, the film won 11 Oscars.*

Self-portrait

A comprehensive portrait of America, its history and its mythology can be constructed from Hollywood movies. Images of the pioneers settling the frontier and disputing the great open spaces of the Midwest and West with the American Indians; of cowboys driving huge herds of cattle across the Rio Grande while fighting off bands of marauding Mexicans – these and others come from a clutch of classic Westerns, such as Edward Dmytryk's *Warlock* (1959), John Ford's *The Man Who Shot Liberty Valance* (1961) and Sam Peckinpah's *The Wild Bunch* (1969). The defining portrayal of the Civil War, *Gone With the Wind* (1939) was one of the first colour movies. Charlie Chaplin's *The Gold Rush* (1925) brought his special combination of humour and pathos to the Klondike gold rush of 1898, while *Modern Times* (1936) was his comment on the industrial age.

Citizen Welles Orson Welles in Citizen Kane *(above). Right: Robert De Niro in* Taxi Driver. *Left: Dennis Hopper and Peter Fonda in* Easy Rider.

Watching America

The age of the great tycoons – men such as John D. Rockefeller and William Randolf Hearst, whose power was eventually tamed by the antitrust laws – is conjured up in Orson Welles's unforgettable *Citizen Kane* (1940). The Prohibition era is evoked by *Once Upon a Time in America* (1983). The Depression and the crisis of the dust-bowl inspired John Steinbeck's novel *The Grapes of Wrath*, which John Ford made into a film (1940). In *The Longest Day* (1962), Kenn Annakin created a fresco-like commemoration of the Second World War and D-Day in particular. For the trauma of the Vietnam War, one of the most powerful evocations is Francis Ford Coppola's *Apocalypse Now* (1979), while Martin Scorsese's *Taxi Driver* (1976) records some of its effects on US society. Youth culture and some of its tensions are the themes of films such as *West Side Story* (1961) and *Saturday Night Fever* (1977). In Woody Allen's *Manhattan* (1979) the inspiration is the brittle life of arty New York. Hollywood even turns its lens upon itself in such classics as Billy Wilder's *Sunset Boulevard* (1950), Elia Kazan's *The Last Tycoon* (1976) and Robert Altman's *The Player* (1992).

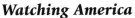

Dances with Wolves *The actor Kevin Costner making his directing debut.*

Studio wars in the dream factory

In the 1930s the five major Hollywood studios were MGM, Warner Brothers, Paramount, RKO and Fox (which merged with Twentieth Century in 1935). Their rivalry was intense, and stock exchange battles to win control of any of them received widespread press coverage. The rivalry has scarcely abated since then, and ownership of a major studio is still a valued prize. In 1989 Sony paid $4.8 billion for Columbia Pictures, which had joined the major league in the 1940s and had produced classics such as *Lawrence of Arabia* (1962).

From the start, the names of popular actors and actresses sold films and there was intense competition to grab the hottest. That is how the star system was born and still functions.

But for the movers and shakers of the Hollywood dream factory, nightmare is always a possibility. A particularly low point came around 1970: the television revolution reached its peak and cinema audiences tumbled to 20 million, from 80 million in the 1940s. In the end, sensation and science fiction saved the day for the movies, with box office hits such as *The Godfather* (1972), *The Exorcist* (1973), *Jaws* (1975) and *Star Wars* (1977) bringing back large audiences.

Studio tourism has become another money-spinner. Every year some 5 million people visit Universal Studios, for example, seeking to recapture some of the emotions they felt when watching classics ranging from *All Quiet on the Western Front* (1930) to *ET* (1982). A major attraction is Jurassic Park, where visitors can take a boat ride and enjoy their own encounters with parasaurolophus, dilophosaurus and the like. Having completed that, they can buy clothing and other souvenirs at the Jurassic Outfitters and have a dinosaur theme meal at the Cove Café.

Hollywood makes 10 per cent of the world's films and pulls in 50 per cent of global box office receipts. Increasingly, it banks on super-productions that cost hundreds of millions of dollars.

The lights of Broadway

'When a Broadway baby says good night, it's early in the morning.' So runs the song. The name alone of Broadway conjures up bright lights, high living, theatres and sparkling musicals. New York's theatreland has known its ups and downs, but it still has the power to make or break.

Hit shows A Chorus Line *was one of the most popular Broadway shows of all time (left). In the year it opened, 1975, it took nine Tony Awards (Broadway's eqivalent of the Oscars) and went on to run for a record-breaking 6137 performances until April 1990. Seven years later, its record was overtaken by* Cats *(above), which opened on Broadway in 1982 and staged its 6138th performance on June 19, 1997.*

It is one of the longest streets in the world, slicing diagonally across Manhattan from its south-eastern corner to the north-west. But Broadway's greatest claim to fame is its central section, roughly between 41st and 53rd Streets. Here, in the 1890s, the bright lights of its booming theatres earned it the nickname of The Great White Way.

Conquer Broadway, conquer the world

Today, Broadway is as much a name as a place, since most of its theatres are in side streets. It has declined since its heyday in the 1920s and 30s when, during a record season in 1927-8, 280 new productions opened. Even so, it is still a name to be conjured with, and success on Broadway with its famously picky audiences and critics can ensure success worldwide. Shows as different as Leonard Bernstein's *West Side Story* (1957), the rock musical *Hair* (1967), and Andrew Lloyd Webber's *Cats* (1982) and *The Phantom of the Opera* (1986), all had to conquer Broadway before they conquered the world.

The musical shows that Broadway has made especially its own have their roots in various European traditions, including French ballet, German melodrama and the British music hall. *The Black Crook* is generally reckoned to be the pioneer, with a plot set in the Harz Mountains of 17th-century Germany, involving an evil hunchbacked

sorcerer Hertzog (the 'Black Crook'). It opened in New York on September 12, 1866, and ran for 475 performances, appealing to lovers of both opera and music hall. By the 1920s the musical had been thoroughly Americanised in the hands of composers and lyricists of genius, including George and Ira Gershwin, Cole Porter, Jerome Kern, Richard Rodgers and Oscar Hammerstein. Rodgers and Hammerstein's string of successes in the 1940s – *Oklahoma!*, *Carousel* and *South Pacific* – confirmed the musical as a quintessentially American art form.

Nowadays, shows fall into three categories: Broadway performances have big budgets and take place in the big 'Broadway' theatres; off-Broadway productions take place in other parts of New York or the smaller theatres around Broadway; off-off-Broadway performances are low-budget and experimental.

Grace and elegance Fred Astaire and Ginger Rogers, stars of Hollywood musicals in the 1930s. Astaire first made his name dancing with his sister Adele in Broadway hits such as Funny Face (1927).

Writers of the New World

North American literature is like the landscape of the continent: many-shaped, embracing extremes, multidimensional and fabulously rich. Within a space of 200 years, North American writers, from a wide range of religious, cultural and ethnic backgrounds, have integrated a corresponding range of influences.

John Smith, one of the founders of Virginia, could also claim to be the founder of American literature. His bombastic accounts of the young colony, invariably boosting his own heroic role in events, were the first works written about North America by someone who had actually lived there. They included *The Generall Historie of Virginia, New England, and the Summer Isles*, published in 1624.

More than 150 years passed before publication of the first American novel – generally reckoned to be William Hill Brown's *The Power of Sympathy* (1789), written in the moralising style of the English writer Samuel Richardson. The Puritan founding fathers of New England had no time for the 'frivolous' forms of literature, preferring more edifying works such as books of sermons, biographies and histories. Men like the Virginia planter William Byrd wrote vivid accounts of their travels on the frontier; Benjamin Franklin, Thomas Jefferson and the other fathers of American independence used their literary talents in journalism.

Murder she writes Author Patricia Cornwell looking the part of her pathologist heroine, Kay Scarpetta (left). Right: Truman Capote, master of prose in novels such as Breakfast at Tiffany's *(1958) and* In Cold Blood *(1966).*

An American voice

It was not until after the War of 1812 that a group of writers started to produce fiction that was distinctively American. Works such as *Bracebridge Hall* (1822) by the New Yorker Washington Irving won praise even from British critics. James Fenimore Cooper wrote tales of frontier life, while Edgar Allan Poe penned his spine-chilling gothic tales and stories such as 'The Murders in the Rue Morgue' (1841), regarded as the first-ever work of detective fiction.

By the mid-century, some unique voices were beginning to be heard: Nathaniel Hawthorne, who set his greatest work *The Scarlet Letter* (1850) in Puritan Massachusetts of the 17th century and used his adulterer heroine Hester Prynne to explore the American soul; Herman Melville, with his symbolic masterpiece *Moby Dick* (1851); and the Transcendentalist philosophers Ralph Waldo Emerson and Henry David Thoreau, who believed in rugged simplicity and the power of intuitive insights into the truth. In 1855, the poet Walt Whitman published the first version of his mould-breaking *Leaves of Grass*. After the Civil War came the much-loved Mark Twain with his humorous tales of Mississippi life, such as *The Adventures of Huckleberry Finn* (1884).

Literature of multiculturalism

In the 20th century, writers such as F. Scott Fitzgerald, most famously in *The Great Gatsby* (1925), used the novel to explore the often brittle glamour of the American dream. The great waves of immigration from the late 19th century onwards inevitably left their mark. Jewish writers, including Philip Roth, Bernard Malamud, Saul Bellow and Isaac Bashevis Singer, have probed the themes of identity and how the individual fits into the wider whole of society. The world of the South has been chronicled by William Faulkner, Flannery O'Connor, Eudora Welty and the playwright Tennessee Williams. In the north, Canada has produced talents as diverse as those of Robertson Davies, Margaret Atwood and Michael Ondaatje. Black writers have explored their particular experience of North American life – including, in the 20th century, James Baldwin and Toni Morrison.

Masters of the novel Saul Bellow, winner of the Nobel prize for literature in 1976 (above). Of Russian Jewish stock, Bellow was mostly brought up in Chicago, the setting for many of his novels. Right: Toni Morrison won the Nobel prize in 1993. Many of her novels are historical, exploring the black experience of slavery.

The great collections

Museums came comparatively late to North America, but when they arrived – in the decades after the Civil War – they arrived in style. Today, often under the impetus of private foundations, the cities of North America boast some of the finest collections in the world, displaying works from around the globe as well as the best of American art. New York's Metropolitan Museum of Art has more than 2 million different works of art.

Many of North America's greatest museums and galleries were opened in the late 19th century. The Museum of Fine Arts in Boston dates from 1870, the Metropolitan Museum of Art in New York from 1871; Ottawa's National Gallery of Canada was founded in 1880, the Art Institute of Chicago in 1882. For their founders, these institutions had a key educational role to play – they would improve the taste of the general public by exposing them to some of the finest works of human creativity. They would also encourage and mould the rapidly developing culture of North America.

Funding the arts

Private philanthropy, along with revenue raised from entrance fees, remains a vital source of funding for most US museums, since

Poet of the real Summer's Night (1890), by Winslow Homer. One of the outstanding and most original North American artists of the late 19th century, Homer typically painted people in a context of majestic but indifferent nature. From 1883, he lived at the fishing village of Prouts Neck on the Maine coast, and many of his paintings were inspired by the lives of fishing people. He was also a painstaking observer of nature, making thousands of on-the-spot watercolour sketches of the effects of light and atmosphere.

Learning from the classics
An art student in the Metropolitan Museum of Art. The main building that now faces Fifth Avenue was completed in 1902.

The Metropolitan Museum of Art

It was just six years since the United States had emerged from the slaughter and destruction of the Civil War when the Metropolitan Museum of Art opened its doors. In many ways the event was symbolic of a renewed dynamism and confidence in the nation. The museum owed its existence to three men: the landscape architect and creator of Central Park Frederick Law Olmstead; the New York newspaper editor and poet William Cullen Bryant; and the Unitarian minister Henry Whitney Bellows. They had convinced New York's growing band of rich bankers and industrialists of the need for an institution of this kind, to educate the people and encourage them to raise their eyes from the mundane distractions of their everyday lives. It was an undoubted success: in 1891, after ten years of arguing the case to and fro, the New York State authorities obliged the Metropolitan Museum to open on Sundays. Some 12 000 people, of all backgrounds and levels of education, thronged the galleries on the first Sunday, and Sundays have remained the museum's busiest day. Today, around 5.5 million people visit it each year.

few receive major subsidies from local, state or federal government. Wealthy institutions such as the Ford and Rockefeller foundations regularly fork out large sums; smaller private patrons make their own contributions. The result is numerous excellent and well-funded museums all across North America. Not surprisingly, New York has a particular wealth of them. As well as the Metropolitan Museum of Art, there is the Museum of Modern Art (MoMA) with important collections of photography and film as well as painting and sculpture, the Whitney Museum of American Art, the Solomon R. Guggenheim Museum, the Frick Collection and the Brooklyn Museum.

Gallery for the modern   The East Wing of the National Gallery of Art in Washington DC, designed by the Chinese-born architect I.M. Pei, also famous for his Louvre pyramid in Paris.

American painting: realism in motion

Portraits were the staple of the first American painters in the 17th and 18th centuries. Their style was that of the English and Dutch traditions; the people who sat for the portraits were rich middle-class families, intermingled with a few more exotic models, including some American Indian chiefs. By the 18th century, artists

Indian ball game   *George Catlin recorded for posterity the vanishing way of life of the Plains Indians.*

of genuine individuality were beginning to emerge – figures such as John Singleton Copley, Gilbert Stuart, Benjamin Wade and Charles Wilson Peale. Although impregnated with Protestant values, their chief inspiration was social rather than religious: a desire to portray the social realities of the day.

In the 19th century, American painters came under the spell of nature. The artists of the Hudson River School, led by Thomas Cole, drew inspiration from the forests and lakes of the north-east. Later,

the Luminists made the land, sky and water their theme. Their leading figures were FitzHugh Lane and Martin Heade, who specialised in dramatic seascapes.

As the frontier was pushed farther west, George Catlin dedicated his art to portraying the lives of the Plains Indians, while his contemporary John James Audubon combined the precision of a naturalist with the sensibility of an artist in his paintings of the birds of North America.

Home lights

In the second half of the 19th century, artists such as James McNeill Whistler, John Singer Sargent and Mary Cassatt were drawn by the more sophisticated artistic circles of London and Paris. Others, however, preferred the light and open spaces of their native land. One was Winslow Homer, who found poetry in portraying ordinary people in natural settings.

In 1908 eight American artists led by Robert Henri held a joint exhibition in New York. They called themselves The Eight and their aim was to paint life in everyday settings – hence another nickname, the Ashcan School, for The Eight and other artists linked

to them. George Bellows and Edward Hopper, were the best-known painters to emerge from this group.

Around the same time, the photographer Alfred Stieglitz founded the magazine *Camera Work* and opened his 291 gallery in New York – taking the name from the gallery's location at 291 Fifth Avenue. Possibly his greatest achievement was promoting in the United States the modernism being pioneered in Europe. His wife, Georgia O'Keefe, was another significant figure in US art, mingling sensuality and mysticism in canvases covered

Action painting   To create works like this, Jackson Pollock poured or dripped paint onto a flat canvas.

Electric Chair *(1966)   For Andy Warhol, this instrument of execution was a symbol of American society.*

with huge flowers. Around 1930, in reaction to the international modernism of Stieglitz and his circle, the Regionalists started to affirm the values of rural America: Thomas Hart Benton and Grant Wood painted large murals of farm workers in the fields.

The Abstract Expressionists

The 1940s and 50s were the age of the Abstract Expressionists. Artists such as Jackson Pollock, Willem De Kooning, Robert Motherwell, Mark Rothko and Helen Frankenthaler explored the unconscious to create powerful images that represented a clear break with the past. In the 1960s Pop Art made its appearance, drawing inspiration from the icons of modern life, from comic-strip heroes to the face of Marilyn Monroe. With their use of screen printing, the works of Roy Lichenstein and Andy Warhol were widely distributed.

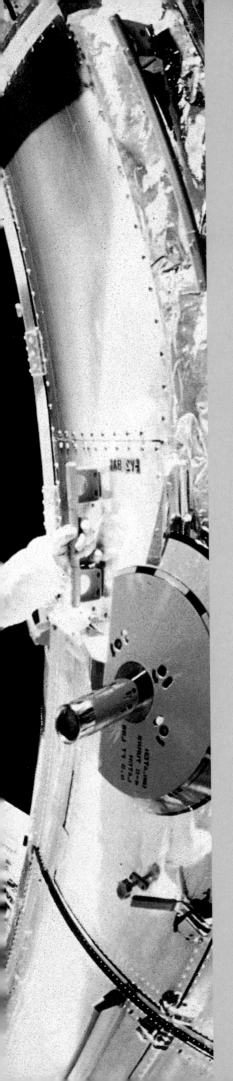

CHAPTER 7

THE NEW FRONTIERS

Levis, Coca-Cola, McDonald's, Ford, Boeing, Apple: they include some of the most widely recognised names on Earth. Not content with conquering the West, the Americans sought out new frontiers to dominate. One of the most dramatic moments in this great adventure came on July 20, 1969, when they landed the first men on the Moon. Closer to home, few areas of life have been left untouched. Jacob Davis and Levi Strauss patented their 'riveted overalls' – jeans – in 1873. A few years later, Atlanta pharmacist George S. Pemberton started selling his coca leaf and cola nut brew called Coca-Cola. In 1913 Henry Ford opened his Highland Park assembly plant – and motoring for the masses was born. Ray Kroc opened his first McDonald's at Des Plaines, Illinois, in 1955. In 1970 the jumbo jet entered service. Six years later, school friends Steven Wozniak and Steve Jobs produced their Apple I computer.

A space mechanic repairing the faulty Hubble telescope in December 1993.

The conquest of space

The Americans founded NASA (National Aeronautics and Space Administration) in 1958 and launched Explorer 1, *their first satellite. After that, it took them little more than ten years to pull off one of the extraordinary feats of the 20th century – to land the first men on the Moon. They had won the Space Race, one of the curious side effects of Cold War rivalry between the United States and the Soviet Union.*

On the red planet *The rover* Sojourner *on Mars in July 1997 (above). Left: The mission badge of Apollo 1. Virgil Grissom, Edward White and Roger Chaffee died when their space capsule caught fire during a simulation of the launch.*

Cape Canaveral has a vital place in the Florida economy. Lying about halfway down the peninsula on the Atlantic-facing shore, the NASA-run launch sites and John F. Kennedy Space Center employ some 20 000 people. They are also a major tourist attraction. Nowadays manned flights take off from the Kennedy Space Center on Merritt Island, which is linked to Cape Canaveral by a causeway, while the cape site is used only for unmanned flights.

Men in space

For the United States, the adventure of manned space flight started with Project Mercury between 1961 and 1963. On May 5, 1961, Alan B. Shepard, crammed into a tiny Mercury capsule, was propelled to the edges of outer space and then brought safely back again. He was the first American in space, but not the first person: the Soviets had got there first with Yuri Gagarin, who orbited the Earth on April 12 that year. The first American to orbit the Earth was John Glenn on February 20, 1962. He made three orbits during a space flight of nearly five hours.

In 1961 President John F. Kennedy had issued a bold challenge to the US Congress. Spurred on by Cold War rivalry with the Soviet Union, he asked them to back a commitment to put a man on the Moon by the end of the decade. This was the start of Project Apollo, and it made Project Mercury look like simplicity itself. Saturn rockets would have to launch into space a new generation of spacecraft. Once in orbit around the Moon, a lunar module would separate from the command module and land the astronauts on the Moon's surface. Then

came one of the trickiest challenges of all: getting the lunar and command modules to link up again for the journey back to Earth.

In 1965-6, during the Gemini programme, astronauts practised rendezvous and docking techniques and working outside the spacecraft. By the end of Project Gemini, US astronauts had spent 2000 hours in space. Another three preparatory flights followed using Apollo spacecraft, before NASA, true to Kennedy's promise, landed the first men on the Moon in July 1969, just before the end of the decade.

Reusable space shuttle

By the 1980s, NASA had developed a reusable craft, the space shuttle, to reduce costs. By then, a major part of the space programme was no longer strictly scientific: it was to launch civilian and military satellites into orbit. The excitement once generated by the Moon landings had long since waned. Then came the *Challenger* disaster in January 1986, when the *Challenger* shuttle exploded 73 seconds after liftoff, killing the seven crew.

During the 1980s and 90s, declining official confidence and interest in the space programme was reflected in more reluctant federal funding. When, in 1996, a NASA team

Mission control *Observing* Saturn V, *the launch vehicle that propelled the 50-ton* Apollo *spacecraft into space (right). Left: Premature smiles and cigars at NASA when* Apollo 13 *lifted off in April 1970.*

The first men on the Moon

On July 16, 1969, at 2.32 pm US Eastern Daylight Time (EDT), *Apollo 11* lifted off from Cape Canaveral. It was the start of the most memorable of all the Apollo space flights, bringing home to people across the globe just how dramatic the reach of modern technology had become.

On July 20, at 10.56 pm EDT, came the moment the world had been waiting for. Neil Armstrong stepped from the lunar module onto the Moon: the 'one small step for a man, one giant leap for mankind'. He and 'Buzz' Aldrin collected 46 lb (21 kg) of rock samples, while their colleague Michael Collins continued in orbit. On July 24 they returned to Earth: the United States had won the race to the Moon.

But it was not the end of the Moon programme. In the next mission, *Apollo 12*, the lunar module came to a rest just a few yards from its target landing spot. Astronauts Charles Conrad and Alan Bean made two long walks, spending nearly eight hours in all exploring the Moon's surface. Then in 1970, *Apollo 13* came close to disaster when an oxygen tank exploded 200 000 miles (320 000 km) out from Earth. After three nightmarish days for the three astronauts, the spacecraft was safely returned to Earth.

Apollo 15 caught the popular imagination with the first Lunar Rover, a buggy that allowed the crew to make longer excursions from the module than on previous missions and to gather a bigger clutch of samples. The last mission was *Apollo 17* in December 1972. Landing in the Sea of Tranquillity, the astronauts collected 255 lb (115 kg) of samples. From these, scientists were able to identify evidence of volcanic activity on the Moon.

Liftoff *A shuttle lifts off at the Kennedy Space Center (left). Above: Astronauts correcting faults in NASA's Hubble Space Telescope in 1993.*

announced that there was evidence that primitive life may have existed on Mars 4.5 billion years ago, some cynical observers saw it as a ploy to grab the headlines and so help to secure the agency's budget. A more solid achievement was the mission of the space probe *Pathfinder* which landed on Mars in July 1997. It offloaded a six-wheeled 'rover', *Sojourner*, which trundled across the surface of the planet gathering rocks and soil; onboard equipment analysed these and sent the results back to Earth.

Air routes over America

McDonnell Douglas, Lockheed, Northrop, Boeing – the great names of US aviation have made their mark in war and peace alike. Boeing, for example, gave the world two very different giants: the B-52 bomber and the 747 jumbo jet. Air travel, meanwhile, has become a part of the American way of life.

It is the world's largest manufacturer of both commercial and military aircraft. It employs more than 232 000 people worldwide, with operations in 27 states of the Union. Its headquarters in Seattle, Washington, are to a large extent responsible for that city's dramatic growth since the Second World War. Its revenues in 1998 stood at $56.2 billion. Boeing, the manufacturer of the jumbo jet, is a giant in every sense, dominating the aerospace industry not just in the United States, but across the globe – and all the more so since its merger in 1997 with its chief US rival, McDonnell Douglas.

Bombers and jetliners

The United States came out of the Second World War a clear leader in the manufacture of aircraft. Other countries rivalled it in aircraft design, but lacked the sheer industrial muscle of the great US corporations, often backed by generous military contracts from the government. During the war Boeing, founded in 1916 by a Yale-trained engineer and lumber magnate William E. Boeing, had developed and manufactured the two workhorses of the US bombing fleets: the B-17 Flying Fortress and the B-29 Superfortress. After the war it developed the huge eight-engined B-52 Stratofortress, which remained in operation from the mid 1950s into the 21st century. In the 1980s, the Lockheed Corporation produced the F-117A Stealth fighter, designed to be invisible to radar. Later in the decade, the Northrop Corporation produced the B-2 Stealth bomber.

In civil aviation, the Douglas Company produced the DC-7, which came into service in 1953. With a speed of 300 mph (480 km/h), the DC-7 could fly 3000 miles (4800 km) without

Presidential fly-past   The president's jet, Air Force One, over Mount Rushmore (top). There are, in fact, two Air Force Ones, both specially adapted 747-200s. In addition, the USAF operates four 747-200s as airborne emergency command and control posts. Above: Dallas-Fort Worth in Texas, one of the busiest airports in North America.

Assembly plant
Boeing 747s being assembled at Everett, Washington State. Each 747-400 has more than 170 miles (270 km) of wiring.

The Boeing revolution

The Boeing 747 was conceived on paper in 1966: the first prototype 'jumbo jet' made its maiden flight in February 1969. Boeing had overcome initial scepticism to create the world's biggest jetliner. This doubled the number of people carried on long-haul flights – thus sparking a revolution in air transport.

after 1970, when Pan Am and a few other airlines inaugurated their first commercial services using 747s, Boeing's investment appeared to some observers to be at risk. The huge aircraft felt all the more spacious because many

having to land for refuelling, making nonstop coast-to-coast flights possible. By 1957 more passengers were crossing the Atlantic by air than by sea. Then, on October 26, 1958, Pan Am put its first jetliner into service, the Boeing 707. Not only faster than the old prop planes, the 707 was also more economical because it could carry more passengers.

Pulling out of a slump

The early 1990s were hard times for the aerospace industry. With the end of the Cold War, military orders dried up and over-capacity among the world's airlines meant that few were placing orders. By mid decade the prospects were brighter, and after a shake-up among the airlines, new orders were coming in. Mergers to create larger, more efficient corporations culminated in Boeing's acquisition of McDonnell Douglas and revenues shot up to $45.8 billion in 1997.

Night flights *Some 58 million passengers passed through Dallas-Forth Worth Airport (above) in 1996.*

The plane with a hump

The very shape of the aircraft was revolutionary, with its distinctive hump, housing a second deck towards the front. Boeing assured potential customers that the 747 could easily carry 400 passengers, nearly 500 at a pinch. The new engines made by Pratt & Whitney were more powerful than those made by rival manufacturers, and they were also more economical on fuel and ten times less noisy than any other similar engine. The 747 could fly 6000 miles (9600 km) without refuelling, at a cruising speed of 640 mph (1030 km/h). Orders were soon flowing in. As early as 1968, 150 so far non-existent aircraft had been sold to eager clients.

To assemble the jumbo, Boeing built a new factory at Everett, Washington, just north of Seattle. It was the biggest building in terms of volume in the world. Boeing sank billions of dollars into the project, and for a while

of them were flying half-empty. The truth was that the jumbo jet was ahead of the market. But Boeing stuck to its guns, kept up production of the planes and the market caught up, expanding to fill the new capacity. From the 747-100 to the 747-300 and beyond, the company continued to perfect their product.

Better and better and better

The 747-400, which went into service in 1989, was more aerodynamic, lighter, safer, more powerful and up to 40 per cent more economical on fuel than the previous model. It could fly more than 7000 miles (11 000 km) without refuelling; the long-haul version could carry more than 400 passengers, the short-haul version more than 550. The 747 range was still evolving and was still competitive. Clients included all the world's major airlines. Air Force One, the US presidential jet, was a jumbo. By the late 1990s yet another version of the old warhorse was being tested – one that would carry it across the 750 passenger threshold.

PRINCIPAL US AND CANADIAN AIRPORTS – BY HOW BUSY THEY ARE

Greenland

● Principal airports

Alaska

CANADA

Hudson Bay

Vancouver

Toronto

USA

San Francisco

Chicago   Detroit

Denver   New York

Las Vegas

Los Angeles

Dallas   Atlanta

Miami

MEXICO

The giants of the car industry

The birthplace at the start of the century of the Model T Ford and the automobile assembly line, Detroit boomed with the development of motor transport. In a country of vast distances, the car soon established itself as a necessity, and the motor industry as the biggest of big business. The battle for market dominance became a true clash of giants.

Fifties classic *The Buick Century had tailfins that reached extravagant proportions in the 1960s.*

A French soldier, Antoine de la Mothe Cadillac, founded Detroit as a fortified trading post in 1701. Drawn by its strategic position on the waterway between Lake Erie and Lake St Clair, he named it Fort-Pontchartrain du Détroit ('of the strait'). Two centuries later, his own name was commandeered by the troubled Detroit Automobile Company when it was seeking to relaunch itself in time for the New York Automobile Show of January 1903. Cadillac soon became synonymous with motoring luxury, a car for movie stars and millionaires. Thus a few of the strands in Detroit's long history as a centre of trade and industry were pulled together. As well as its fame as motor capital of the world, Detroit can claim the invention of the typewriter and the soda fountain, not to mention the Motown (motor town) record label, which launched the careers of black singers from Diana Ross to Michael Jackson.

Model T revolution

The city was already a centre for engineering industry when the Detroit Automobile Company was founded in 1899, by a group of enthusiasts who included a 36-year-old former engineer with the Edison lighting company, Henry Ford. Ford did not stay with the team for long, however, and in 1903 founded his own Ford Motor Company, making his first sale that year to a Chicago dentist.

Until then cars had been rich men's toys, but Ford's vision was to produce inexpensive cars for a mass market. In 1908 he brought out the Model T or 'Tin Lizzie', which was an immediate success. Then in 1913 he opened his revolutionary Highland Park factory. Inspired partly by the overhead trolleys used in Chicago meat-packing plants and partly by the ideas of the Philadelphia engineer and management expert Frederick Winslow Taylor, Ford's new factory used assembly lines to increase productivity, as well as a working day that was divided up into three shifts of eight hours. By 1915 Ford had sold his millionth car, and by 1922 he had sold his 10 millionth. The day of mass motoring had arrived. In the United States today, there are often two to three cars for every family, and each American travels, on average, 25 000 miles (40 000 km) by road a year.

The Ford Foundation

Around 100 000 people went to Henry Ford's funeral, held at his birthplace, Dearborn, near Detroit, in April 1947. By the time of his death, aged 83, Ford had become one of the most famous men in the world, and not just because of his industrial success. He had set up the Ford Foundation in 1936 with four aims: to strengthen democratic values worldwide, to reduce poverty and injustice, to promote international cooperation and to advance human achievement.

Since 1936, the foundation has given more than US$8 billion in grants to countless charitable organisations across the United States. The fight against urban poverty is one of its priorities, and it finances many housing renewal programmes. Since the 1950s, it has also been involved in the fight against rural poverty in a number of countries in Asia, Africa and Latin America. Population control has been one of its chief concerns. It is active, too, in promoting the arts, and in the field of communications, notably public television.

Since the fall of the Berlin Wall, the Ford Foundation has taken an interest in the problems of Eastern Europe. The foundation, which is no longer linked either to the Ford family or the Ford Motor Company, does not receive donations. It draws its funds from a portfolio of stocks and shares.

Success story *The son of farm workers, Henry Ford built up a global empire. He never lost his love of things mechanical, and would occasionally join his workers on the assembly line.*

The Big Three

The development of the car industry led to the growth of huge conglomerates. By the end of the 1920s, the 'Big Three' were Ford, General Motors and Chrysler. All were based in the state of Michigan with their headquarters in Detroit, making the city one of the powerhouses of the US economy. Auto workers were among the most privileged in the United States, represented by one of the most powerful unions, the UAW (United Automobile Workers).

By the 1970s, however, trouble was looming. The Second World War had brought boom times for Michigan's motor industry, and large numbers of blacks had moved there from the South. Race riots had erupted in Detroit during the war itself, in June 1943, leaving 35 people dead, 29 of them blacks. More trouble flared in July 1967, leaving 43 dead and causing $2 billion worth of damage. Inner city Detroit was becoming a wasteland of crumbling housing and polluted air and water; the middle class had fled to the suburbs. To make matters worse, by the 1970s the Big Three were under increasing pressure as Japanese motor manufacturers launched an assault on the US market. The Japanese set up factories locally, employed new production methods, and offered a high-quality product.

New generations of drivers had new priorities, and the US giants were not fast enough in responding to them. In 1979 Chrysler had to be bailed out with a $1.5 billion federal loan. But it took up the challenge of technical innovation and was at the forefront in introducing electric windows, air conditioning and curved windscreens to improve the car's aerodynamics. Chrysler won back its market share, and in 1983 paid off the federal loan seven years early.

On-screen design   A designer at Chrysler's headquarters in Auburn Hills, Michigan, works on a new prototype. Chrysler, the third of the Big Three motor corporations, has placed special emphasis on state-of-the-art technology.

General Motors, the giant

General Motors is used to setting records. Not just the world's biggest vehicle manufacturer, it is also the world's biggest industrial corporation. The General Motors stable includes Buick, Cadillac, Chevrolet, GMC, Isuzu, Oldsmobile, Opel, Pontiac, Saab, Saturn and Vauxhall. One of its subsidiaries, Delphi, is an important player in the aeronautical and defence industries, as well as information technology. In many ways General Motors stays true to the philosophy of its founder, William C. Durant, who saw the advantages of offering a variety of models, each with its own brand identity and following, while benefiting from factors such as the control over suppliers that comes with size.

Fit for a millionaire   Unlike their British counterpart, the stately Rolls-Royce, Cadillacs such as this 1950s Eldorado proclaimed their owners' wealth with brash aplomb.

Coca-Cola, McDonald's: symbols of America

In both cases, the product started as a simple idea; within a few decades it was being sold from one end of the world to the other. In soft drinks and fast food respectively, Coca-Cola and McDonald's are global giants, dominating their markets, the very emblems of 'go get it' American-style capitalism.

One of the most famous brands on Earth, and among the most instantly recognisable symbols of US cultural and economic dominance, was born in Atlanta, Georgia, in 1886. In its original formulation, it was a syrup with two base ingredients: a trace of cocaine from coca leaves (removed in 1906 after the federal Pure Food and Drug Act was passed) and caffeine-rich extracts from the kola nut. Its inventor, Atlanta pharmacist John S. Pemberton, initially marketed it as a pick-me-up and tonic for treating minor ailments. It was his bookkeeper Frank Robinson who hit upon the name Coca-Cola, and wrote it out in the flowery hand that is now the world-famous logo. Sold as a syrup to be mixed with soda water, it was soon one of the best-selling drinks in the South.

Expanding business

In 1891 Pemberton sold the business to a fellow Atlanta pharmacist, Asa Griggs Candler. Within a decade Candler had improved sales fortyfold. Coca-Cola was first sold in the distinctive contoured bottle in 1916. In 1919 Candler sold out for $25 million to a group of Atlanta businessmen, headed by the Woodruff family, who ran the company until the 1950s.

The Prohibition years from 1919 to 1933 gave a massive boost to non-alcoholic drinks, and Coca-Cola duly profited. By 1928, when it despatched 1000 cases with the US team to the Amsterdam Olympics, it was beginning to project itself worldwide. But it was not until the Second World War that it started to make a truly global impact. In June 1944, just after D-Day, the Allied supremo General Eisenhower sent a cable asking for 3 million bottles to be shipped to Europe, along with the equipment to wash, refill and cap them twice monthly. A bottle of Coke became a standard item in the GI's kit.

Postwar expansion was based on the principle of the three 'A's: Availability, Affordability, Acceptability. A pleasant drink, available cheaply, would quench the world's thirst. The boast was by no means vain. By the 1990s, 80 per cent of Coca-Cola's revenues came from foreign sales in nearly 200 countries, excluding Iraq, Libya, North Korea and Cuba.

Sign of the Golden Arch
McDonald's in New York's Times Square (right). German immigrants in the 19th century are believed to have introduced the hamburger to North America. It soon came to be regarded as a typical all-American food. Nowadays, McDonald's, the pioneer of the fast-food hamburger chain, faces competition worldwide from other companies such as Burger King.

Worldwide growth
McDonald's international expansion began in 1967 when they opened a restaurant in Canada; Japan, Germany, France, Australia and Britain followed in the 1970s. McDonald's operating principle is QSC & V – Quality, Service, Cleanliness and Value.

McDonald's

More than 24 500 restaurants in 115 countries, including around 13 000 in the USA, 1000 in Canada and 700 in Britain

Every day McDonald's serves around 38 million customers worldwide

McDonald's employs more than a million people worldwide at any one time

Letting out the fizz *Courtesy of Coca-Cola, a refreshing spray of water for a girl in Atlanta (above). Right, below: A bottling factory in India. Bottling companies are locally owned, but the syrup comes from Coca-Cola.*

Every day more than a billion servings of Coca-Cola and Coca-Cola-owned products such as Fanta and Sprite are sold in nearly 200 countries

Coca-Cola and its subsidiaries employ nearly 30 000 people worldwide

Fast-food formula

In San Bernardino, California, brothers Maurice and Richard McDonald applied assembly-line techniques to preparing and selling hamburgers, French fries and milk shakes. But it was a former paper-cup salesman, Ray Kroc, who took their name and their formula and made it into a global 'fast food' empire.

Kroc opened his first McDonald's restaurant at Des Plaines, Illinois, in April 1955, agreeing to pay the brothers 0.5 per cent of gross receipts. By 1961, when he bought them out for $2.7 million, he had set up 228 restaurants: his chief method of expansion was to sell franchises. The three 'F's – Food, Folks and Fun – were a key marketing message; the golden double arch, shaped like an 'M' for McDonald's, became the chain's universally recognisable emblem. By the 1990s McDonald's had established itself in every corner of the globe.

Silicon Valley, home of the chip

California's 'technopolis' is a proliferation of high-tech businesses, based on a remarkable blending of research and entrepreneurial dynamism. Nobel prizewinners, academics, financiers and hard-headed business tycoons, all play their part in the astonishing success of Silicon Valley, a place where companies started in a backroom or garage can sprout into multinational megacorporations within the space of a decade or two.

Orchards of apricot and plum trees once covered the valley that stretches between Palo Alto, near the southernmost tip of San Francisco Bay, and San Jose some 25 miles (40 km) to the south-east. Today, most of these orchards have gone. Instead, electronics assembly workshops, microprocessor factories and computer research and marketing centres are the big business of California's Santa Clara County, better known to the world as Silicon Valley. Towns and cities such as Santa Clara, Sunnyvale, Los Altos and Mountain View are the hub of a computer industry worth billions of dollars every year.

Stay West

The story started in the 1920s and 30s with Frederick Terman, a professor of electrical engineering at Stanford University in Palo Alto. He had a special concern that he plugged constantly with his students: when they graduated, rather than go 'back east' to safe jobs with established firms, they should work for local companies or, even better, found their own. Two who heeded his advice were William Hewlett and David Packard, who in 1938 set up a company producing and marketing oscillators used to test sound equipment. This was the foundation stone on which the computer giant Hewlett-Packard was built; its headquarters are still in Palo Alto.

After the Second World War, a number of big electronics companies, including General Electric and Westinghouse, set up research and manufacturing bases in the valley. In 1955 William Shockley founded the Shockley Semiconductor Laboratory in Palo Alto. The next year, he and fellow research scientists John Bardeen and Walter H. Brattain won the Nobel prize for physics for their development of the transistor. The Shockley laboratory was a seedbed for talent, and played a key role in the continued development of 'Silicon Valley' – a term coined by the writer Don Hoeffler in 1972.

Pinhead chips

In 1958 Robert Noyce, a Shockley alumnus, founded Fairchild Semiconductor, based in Mountain View. This was the company that first successfully mass-produced the pinhead-sized device that became the true business of the region – the integrated circuit or silicon chip. Later Noyce became one of the founders of Intel; by the early 1970s, Intel and a growing number of other companies were producing tinier and tinier chips capable of storing more and more information.

Around the same time, two friends, working in a garage in Los Altos, had a vision of creating an affordable, user-friendly personal computer. Steven Wozniak and Steve Jobs revealed their Apple I computer in 1976; the next year, they launched the more compact Apple II. Over the following decades Apple, despite a roller-coaster ride which on occasion brought it close to disaster, would establish itself as one of the most innovative players in Silicon Valley, particularly after the introduction of its Macintosh computers in 1982.

By the 1990s the emphasis in Silicon Valley was shifting from manufacturing to research and development in a range of fields including laser technology, the further miniaturisation of microchips, genetics, intelligent software and satellites.

Bill Gates, king of software

The world's richest man (born in 1955) was still a 20-year-old student at Harvard when he cofounded the Seattle-based computer software business, Microsoft. The big break, in 1981, was to provide the operating system for IBM's personal computers. More an astute businessman than a computer genius, Gates expanded Microsoft's hold on the software market until in 1998 it became the world's largest corporation – valued at $179 billion on the New York Stock Exchange.

The valley *Silicon Valley (left). Above left: Apple's founders, Steve Jobs (left) and Steven Wozniak, in the 1970s.*

LEVI'S

A legend in blue jeans

The hard-wearing trousers known as 'riveted overalls' were ideal for pioneers of the West. Later, jeans became a near-universal uniform of relaxation.

Jacob Davis was a tailor in Reno, Nevada; he regularly bought bolts of cloth from Levi Strauss & Co, a wholesale house in San Francisco, set up by a Bavarian immigrant, Levi Strauss, in 1853. Among Davis's customers was one who was constantly ripping the pockets of his trousers. This posed the tailor with a problem, until one day he had the inspired idea of putting metal rivets in the client's trousers at the points of strain, such as the pocket corners. His customer was delighted, and so many other people showed an interest in the riveted trousers that Davis became worried in case someone stole his idea. He wanted to patent it, but had difficulty raising the funds, and so wrote to Levi Strauss, asking him to go in with him as an equal partner. Strauss, seeing a business opportunity, accepted. The patent was granted on May 20, 1873.

Waist overalls

Very soon, Strauss and Davis had two factories in San Francisco making riveted 'waist overalls' – the word 'jeans' did not come into vogue until the 1960s; they used the tough fabric known as denim. Within a few years, the overalls had become standard working wear across the West for farmers, ranchers, cowboys, railroad workers and gold prospectors. In 1890, Levi Strauss & Co started giving their products lot numbers; the copper-riveted overalls were designated 501s. When riveting clothing came

Universal appeal
A Levis ad from the 1970s uses President Nixon's rapprochement with Mao Zedong's Communist China to make its selling point. During the previous decade, jeans established themselves as the uniform of rebellious youth.

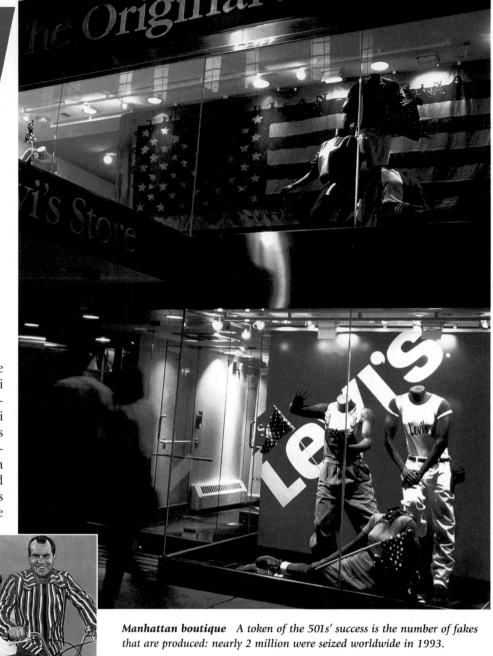

Manhattan boutique   A token of the 501s' success is the number of fakes that are produced: nearly 2 million were seized worldwide in 1993.

out of patent in 1908, other manufacturers jumped on the bandwagon. During the Second World War, US servicemen abroad wore their denim overalls while on leave, introducing them to the world at large. In the less formal age after the war, the overalls became more and more popular. By the late 1970s, a billion pairs of jeans from different manufacturers were sold across the globe each year.

In 1985, Peter Haas, a great-great-nephew of Levi Strauss, along with other descendants, organised a family buyout to return the company to private ownership. Today the company has a reputation for compassion and social caring and has won awards for its positive portrayal of disabled people in TV adverts.

Jeans from Genoa

The cloth used to make the original riveted overalls came from the Amoskeag Mill in Manchester, New Hampshire. The hard-wearing material was known as denim – *serge* de Nîmes – after the French city where an early version of the cloth was manufactured. The word jeans comes from a similar hard-wearing fabric, 'Jene', that was made in Genoa, Italy, in the Middle Ages.

137

Maps, Facts and Figures

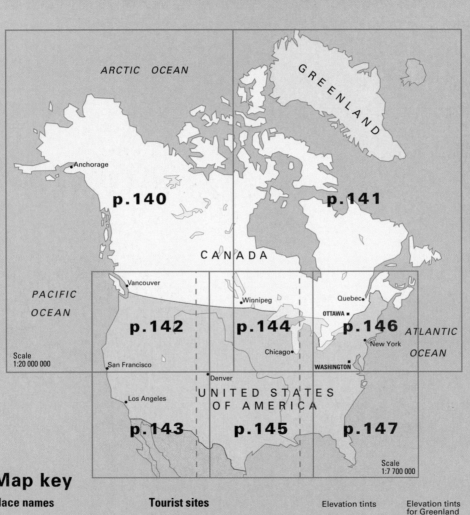

ARCTIC OCEAN

GREENLAND

Anchorage

p.140

p.141

CANADA

PACIFIC
OCEAN

Vancouver

Winnipeg

Quebec

OTTAWA ■

p.142

p.144

p.146

ATLANTIC
OCEAN

Scale
1:20 000 000

San Francisco

Chicago

New York

WASHINGTON ■

Denver

Los Angeles

UNITED STATES
OF AMERICA

p.143

p.145

p.147

Scale
1:7 700 000

Map key

Place names

■ **CAPITAL**

● Major city

• City

• Town

Borders

⎯⎯⎯ International borders

⎯ ⎯ ⎯ Maritime national borders

⎯⎯ State or province borders

Tourist sites

★ *YELLOWSTONE* Park, reserve or
national monument

Topography

▲ Mt Caribou
1 036 m Peak

ROCKY MTS Mountain range

Elevation tints

Metres

| 4000 |
| 3000 |
| 2000 |
| 1500 |
| 1000 |
| 500 |
| 200 |
| 0 |

Elevation tints for Greenland

Metres

| 500 |
| 200 |
| 0 |

Depth tints

Metres

| 0 |
| -200 |
| -2000 |

Canada • Greenland • Alaska

RUSSIA

CHUKCHI SEA

ARCTIC OCEAN

BEAUFORT SEA

BERING SEA

Providenija
Mys Dezhneva
Cape Prince of Wales
Bering Strait
Wales
Arctic Circle

PRINCE-PATRICK I.
QUEEN ELIZABETH ISLANDS
PARRY ISLAND
BATHUR
BELCH
MELVILLE I.

Barrow
Prudhoe Bay
Cape Prince Alfred
McClure Strait
BANKS I.
Sachs Harbour
Prince of Wales Strait
Viscount Melville Sound
McClintock Channel
PRINCE OF WAL ISLAND

ST LAWRENCE ISLAND

Nome
Kotzebue Sound
St Michael
Norton Sound
Yukon
Kusko kwim

ALASKA
BROOKS RANGE
Mt Doonerak 2 320 m
Co ille
Mt Michelson 2 816 m
Tanana
College Fairbanks
Porcupine

Mackenzie Bay
Tuktoyaktuk
Liverpool Bay
Cape Bathurst
Amundsen Gulf
Holman
VICTORIA ISLAND

Inuvik
Fort McPherson
Fort Good Hope
Prince Albert Sound
Coronation Gulf
Kugluktuk (Coppermine)
Dease Strait
Cambridge Bay
Queen Maud Gulf
KING WILLIAM ISLAND

2 109 m
2 857 m
2 857 m
Bristol Bay
Mt Katmai 2 047 m
Iliamna Lake
Mt McKinley 6 194 m
ALASKA RANGE
Mt Hayes 4 216 m

Anchorage
Mt Sanford 4 939 m
Mt Wrangell 4 268 m
Mt Blackburn 4 918 m
Seward
Prince William Sound
Mt Logan 5 959 m
Mt St Elias 5 489 m
KLUANE
Malaspina Glacier

Dawson
Mayo
Whitehorse
YUKON TERRITORY
Pelly
Yukon
Richardson Mts
MACKENZIE MTS

Norman Wells
Ft Norman
Wrigley
Great Bear Lake
Port Radium
Bathurst Inlet
NU

Shelikof Strait
Kodiak
KODIAK ISLAND

ALEUTIAN ISLANDS

PACIFIC OCEAN

Gulf of Alaska

Mt Fairweather 4 663 m
CHICHAGOF I.
Atlin Lake
Juneau
Sitka
BARANOF
ALEXANDER ARCHIPELAGO
PRINCE OF WALES I.
Stikine
Mt Ratz 3 136 m

Mt Sir James McBrien 2 762 m
NAHANNI
Liard
Fort Liard
Fort Simpson
Fort Providence
Rae
Yellowknife
Lac la Martre
NORTHWEST TERRITORIES

Mt Roosevelt 2 898 m
Fort Nelson
Churchill Peak 2 743 m
Finlay
Parsnip
Peace

Great Slave Lake
Hay River
Fort Resolution
Pine Point
Fort Smith
1 036 m CARIBOU MOUNTAINS
WOOD BUFFALO
Uranium City

Back
Thelon
Garry Lake
Baker Lake
Dubawnt Lake
Nuel Lak

Prince Rupert
QUEEN CHARLOTTE ISLANDS
Hecate Strait
Skeena
Prince George
BRITISH COLUMBIA
Mt Crysdale 2 423 m
COAST MOUNTAINS

Fort Vermillion
Lake Athabasca
Wollaston Lake
Reindeer Lake
Southe Indian L

Queen Charlotte Strait
FRASER PLATEAU
Mt Waddington 3 994 m
Fraser
Mt Robson 3 954 m
Mt Columbia 3 747 m

Lesser Slave Lake
ALBERTA
BANFF
Edmonton
North Saskatchewan
SASKATCHEWAN
PRINCE ALBERT
Saskatoon
Saskatchewan

PACIFIC RIM
Vancouver
Juan de Fuca Strait
Cape Flattery
Mt Baker 3 285 m
Mt Olympus 2 428 m
Seattle
WASHINGTON
Mt Rainier 4 392 m
Portland
Mt Hood 3 426 m
Salem

Mt Assiniboine 3 618 m
Calgary
South Saskatchewan
ROCKY MOUNTAINS
Columbia

Lake Winnipegosis
Lake Winnipe
Regina
RIDING MTN.
Assiniboine
Winnipeg
Lake Manito

Spokane
BLUE MTS
OREGON
Snake
Mt Shasta 4 317 m
Lassen Peak 3 187 m
CASCADE RANGE
CALIFORNIA
SIERRA NEVADA
NEVADA

Mt Aldo 3 372 m
Butte
Borah Peak 3 859 m
Bitterroot Range
IDAHO
Cloud Peak 4 013 m
Gannett Peak 4 207 m
MONTANA
WYOMING
BLACK HILLS

San Francisco
Cape Blanco
Cape Mendocino

Great Salt Lake
Salt Lake City
Laramie Peak 3 131 m
UNITED
UTAH
COLORADO
Souris
Missouri
James
NORTH DAKOTA
SOUTH DAKOTA
Bismarck
NEBRASKA
KANSAS

United States of America • The West Coast

E

D

C

B

A

PACIFIC OCEAN

CANADA

ALBERTA

SASKATCHEWAN

BRITISH COLUMBIA

WASHINGTON

OREGON

IDAHO

MONTANA

WYOMING

NEVADA

UTAH

CALIFORNIA

COLORADO

ROCKY MOUNTAINS

LEWIS RANGE

BITTERROOT RANGE

SALMON RIVER MTS

BLUE MOUNTAINS

ABSAROKA RANGE

BIGHORN MTS

WIND RIVER RANGE

LARAMIE MTS

FRONT RANGE

PARK RANGE

UINTA MTS

WASATCH RANGE

GREAT SALT LAKE DESERT

EGAN RANGE

SHOSHONE MTS

SIERRA NEVADA

KLAMATH MTS

WARNER MOUNTAINS

BLACK ROCK DESERT

STEENS MTN.

COLUMBIA PLATEAU

GREAT BASIN

NORTH CASCADES

OLYMPIC

VANCOUVER ISLAND

Strait of Georgia

Strait of Juan de Fuca

Cape Flattery

Cape Blanco

Cape Mendocino

GLACIER

CRATER LAKE

LASSEN VOLCANIC

YOSEMITE

KINGS CANYON

SEQUOIA

REDWOOD

ARCHES

CANYONLANDS

CAPITOL REEF

Great Salt Lake

Yellowstone Lake

Honey Lake

Pyramid Lake

Mono Lake

Lake Tahoe

Goose Lake

Upper Klamath Lake

Harney Lake

Malheur Lake

Flathead Lake

Pend Oreille Lake

Utah Lake

Bear Lake

Vancouver
New Westminster
Victoria
Calgary
Medicine Hat
Lethbridge
Kelowna

Seattle
Tacoma
Olympia
Everett
Bellingham
Mount Vernon
Port Angeles
Port Townsend
Bremerton
Aberdeen
Hoquiam
Centralia
Longview
Astoria
Spokane
Wenatchee
Yakima
Ellensburg
Richland
Kennewick
Pasco
Walla Walla
Pullman
Moscow
Lewiston
Clarkston

Portland
Salem
Albany
Corvallis
Eugene
Springfield
Cottage Grove
Roseburg
Grants Pass
Medford
Newport
Coos Bay
Bend
Redmond
Maupin
The Dalles
Pendleton
La Grande
Baker
John Day
Burns
Seneca
Lakeview
Klamath Falls
Chemult
Crescent City
Eureka
Fort Bragg
Ukiah

Boise
Nampa
Caldwell
Payette
Ontario
Jordan Valley
McDermitt
Twin Falls
Gooding
Mountain Home
Burley
Rupert
Arco
Idaho Falls
Pocatello
Rexburg
Salmon
Grangeville
Orofino
Kellogg
Coeur d'Alene
Sandpoint
Bonners Ferry
Colville
Omak
Okanogan
Grand Coulee

Helena
Missoula
Butte
Bozeman
Livingston
Anaconda
Hamilton
Dillon
Lima
Great Falls
Browning
Cut Bank
Shelby
Townsend
Polson
Whitefish
Kalispell
Libby
St-Regis
Havre
Chinook
Malta
Glasgow
Opheim
Jordan
Miles City
Forsyth
Billings
Hardin
Roundup
Lewistown
Harlowton
Big Timber
Sheridan
Buffalo
Gillette

Casper
Douglas
Lander
Riverton
Shoshoni
Thermopolis
Worland
Powell
Cody
Jackson
West Yellowstone
Dubois
Rawlins
Rock Springs
Green River
Kemmerer
Evanston
Montpelier
Soda Springs
Logan
Bear
Malad City
Ogden
Salt Lake City
Tooele
Provo
Orem
Delta
Nephi
Richfield
Milford
Cedar City

Ely
Eureka
Wells
Elko
Winnemucca
Battle Mountain
Austin
Tonopah
Goldfield
Beatty
Lovelock
Fallon
Reno
Sparks
Carson City
Minden
Hawthorne
Walker Lake

Fort Collins
Greeley
Longmont
Boulder
Lakewood
Denver
Englewood
Littleton
Colorado Springs
Salida
Grand Junction
Rifle
Glenwood Springs
Craig
Price
Vernal
Moab
Monticello
Gunnison

Sacramento
Stockton
Modesto
Merced
Fresno
Oakland
Berkeley
San Francisco
San Jose
Santa Cruz
Salinas
Monterey
Napa
Vallejo
Santa Rosa
San Rafael
Sonoma
Woodland
Yuba City
Marysville
Roseville
Oroville
Chico
Red Bluff
Redding
Weed
Yreka
Dunsmuir
Klamath
King City
Hanford
Watsonville
Lodi
San Joaquin

Mt Baker 3285 m
Glacier Peak 3221 m
Mt Rainier 4392 m
Mt St Helens 2950 m
Mt Adams 3742 m
Mt Hood 3426 m
Mt Jefferson 3199 m
Mt Olympus 2428 m
Mt Thielsen 2799 m
Mt Scott 2724 m
Mt Shasta 4317 m
2530 m
Lassen Peak 3187 m
White Mt Peak 4341 m
Mt Whitney 4418 m
San Benito Mt 1598 m
Eagle Peak 3015 m
Granite Peak 2961 m
Steens Mtn. 2967 m
Wagontire Mtn. 2291 m
Borah Peak 3859 m
Big Baldy 2791 m
Bears Paw Mts 2108 m
Cloud Peak 4013 m
Gannett Peak 4207 m
Fremont Peak 4189 m
Grand Teton 4198 m
Wheeler Peak 3982 m
Delano Peak 3709 m
Kings Peak 4123 m
Mt Peale 3877 m
Mt Ellen 3512 m
Mt Elbert 4399 m
Pikes Peak 4301 m
Longs Peak 4345 m
Medicine Bow Peak 3662 m
Laramie Peak 3131 m
Mt Jefferson 3640 m
3471 m

Missouri
Milk
Marias
Yellowstone
Musselshell
Big Horn
Powder
Tongue
Clark Fork
Snake
Columbia
Salmon
Bitterroot
Jefferson
Madison
Big Hole
Owyhee
South Fork Owyhee
Humboldt
Green
North Platte
South Platte
Arkansas
Colorado
Sweetwater
Yampa
Bear
Sevier
Deschutes
John Day
Williamette
Umpqua
Rogue
Klamath
Eel
Fraser
Koatenay
Pend-Oreille
Okanogan
Snake
Fort Peck Lake

Columbia

Cypress Hills

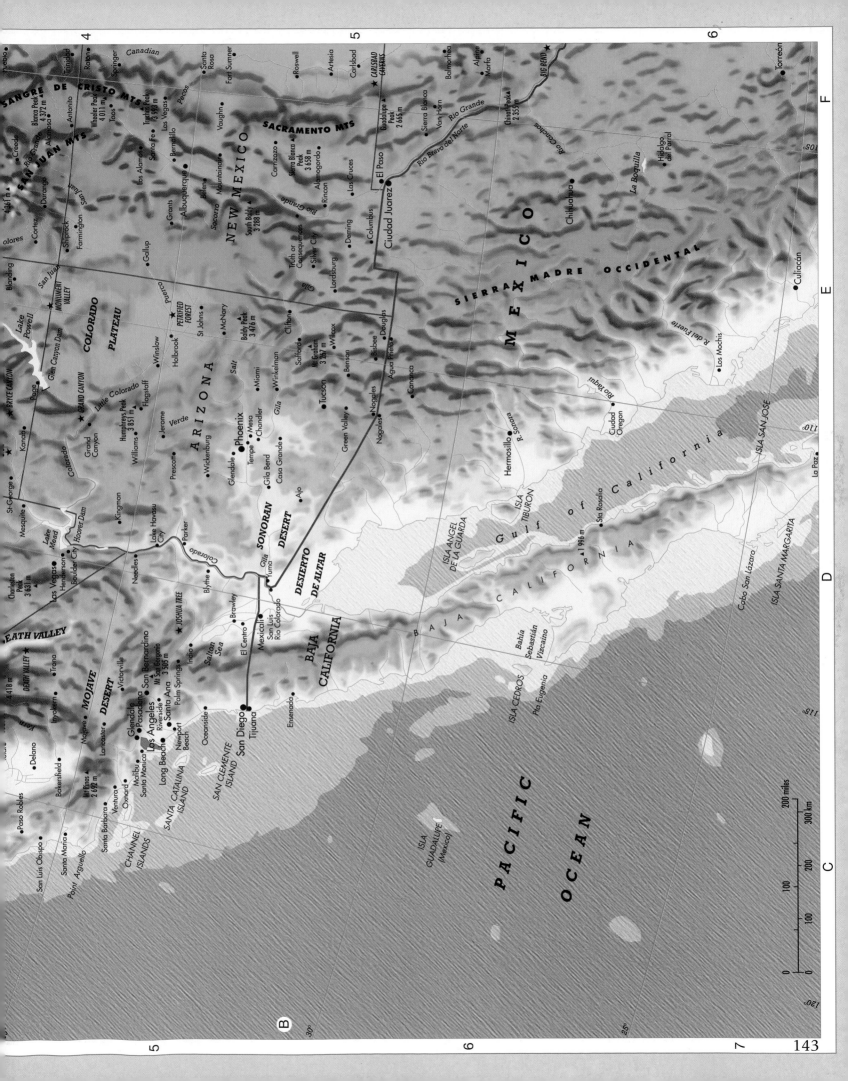

F

Canadian
Pueblo • Raton
Blanca Peak • Trinidad • Springer • Santa Rosa • Roswell • Artesia • Carlsbad • Balmorhea • Alpine • Marfa • Big Bend • Torreón
4 372 m • Alamosa • Antonito • Taos • Fort Sumner • CARLSBAD CAVERNS
SANGRE DE CRISTO MTS Wheeler Peak • Vaughn • Guadalupe • Sierra Blanca • Van Horn • Chinati Peak
Creede 4 011 m Truchas Peak SACRAMENTO MTS Peak • 2 355 m
• Taos 3 993 m 2 667 m
Durango • San Juan • Santa Fe • Las Vegas • Rio Grande • Chinati Peak
4 361 m • Los Alamos • Carrizozo • Río Conchos
SAN JUAN MTS Bernalillo • Sierra Blanca
Colores • Cortez • San Juan • Albuquerque • Belen • Peak • Alamogordo • Río Bravo del Norte • 105
• Shiprock • Farmington • Socorro 3 658 m • Rincon • El Paso • La Boquilla
• Grants • Mountainair • Truth or • Ciudad Juárez • Chihuahua • Hidalgo
Blanding • San Juan NEW MEXICO Consequences • Silver City • Deming • Columbus • del Parral
MONUMENT • Gallup Rio Grande • Lordsburg
VALLEY • Puerco SIERRA MADRE OCCIDENTAL
Lake COLORADO • St Johns • Clifton M E X I C O E
Powell PLATEAU PETRIFIED • McNary • Safford
BRYCE CANYON • Page FOREST • Baldy Peak • Mt Graham • Douglas • R. del Fuerte • Culiacán
• Kanab Little Colorado • Winslow 3 476 m 3 267 m • Bisbee • Agua Prieta • Los Mochis
GRAND CANYON • Holbrook • Winkelman • Benson Cananea
St George Humphreys Peak • Flagstaff • Miami • Nogales Río Sonora
• Mesquite GRAND 3 851 m • Verde • Gila • Tucson • Nogales • Hermosillo • Ciudad
CANYON • Jerome Obregón
Lake Mead • Williams • Prescott ARIZONA Salt • Green Valley ISLA • Sta Rosalía D
Charleston • Kingman • Phoenix TIBURÓN • 1 996 m
Peak Hoover Dam • Wickenburg • Glendale • Tempe Chandler ISLA ANGEL
3 631 m • Boulder City • Lake Havasu • Mesa DE LA GUARDA Gulf of California
Las Vegas • Henderson City • Gila Bend • Casa Grande
• Parker SONORAN • Ajo
DEATH VALLEY Colorado • Needles DESERT Gila • La Paz
• Blythe Gila • Yuma DESIERTO B A J A ISLA SAN JOSÉ
4 418 m JOSHUA TREE • Brawley DE ALTAR C A L I F O R N I A
DEATH VALLEY • Indio Salton • El Centro • San Luis Río Colorado Bahía ISLA SANTA MARGARITA D
• Trona Sea • Mexicali Sebastián
MOJAVE • Victorville • Palm Springs BAJA Vizcaíno Cabo San Lázaro
• Mojave San Bernardino Mt San Gorgonio CALIFORNIA
DESERT • Lancaster Riverside 3 505 m Pta Eugenia 115
• Bakersfield Glendale • Pasadena ISLA CEDROS
Mt Pinos Los Angeles • Santa Ana • Oceanside Bahía
2 692 m Malibu • Long Beach • Newport Beach • San Diego ISLA
• Delano Santa Monica • Tijuana GUADALUPE
• Paso Robles SANTA CATALINA • Ensenada (Mexico)
ISLAND
• San Luis Obispo SAN CLEMENTE
• Santa Maria ISLAND
• Ventura • Oxnard
Point Arguello • Santa Barbara CHANNEL
ISLANDS
P A C I F I C C

O C E A N

0 100 200 miles
0 100 200 300 km

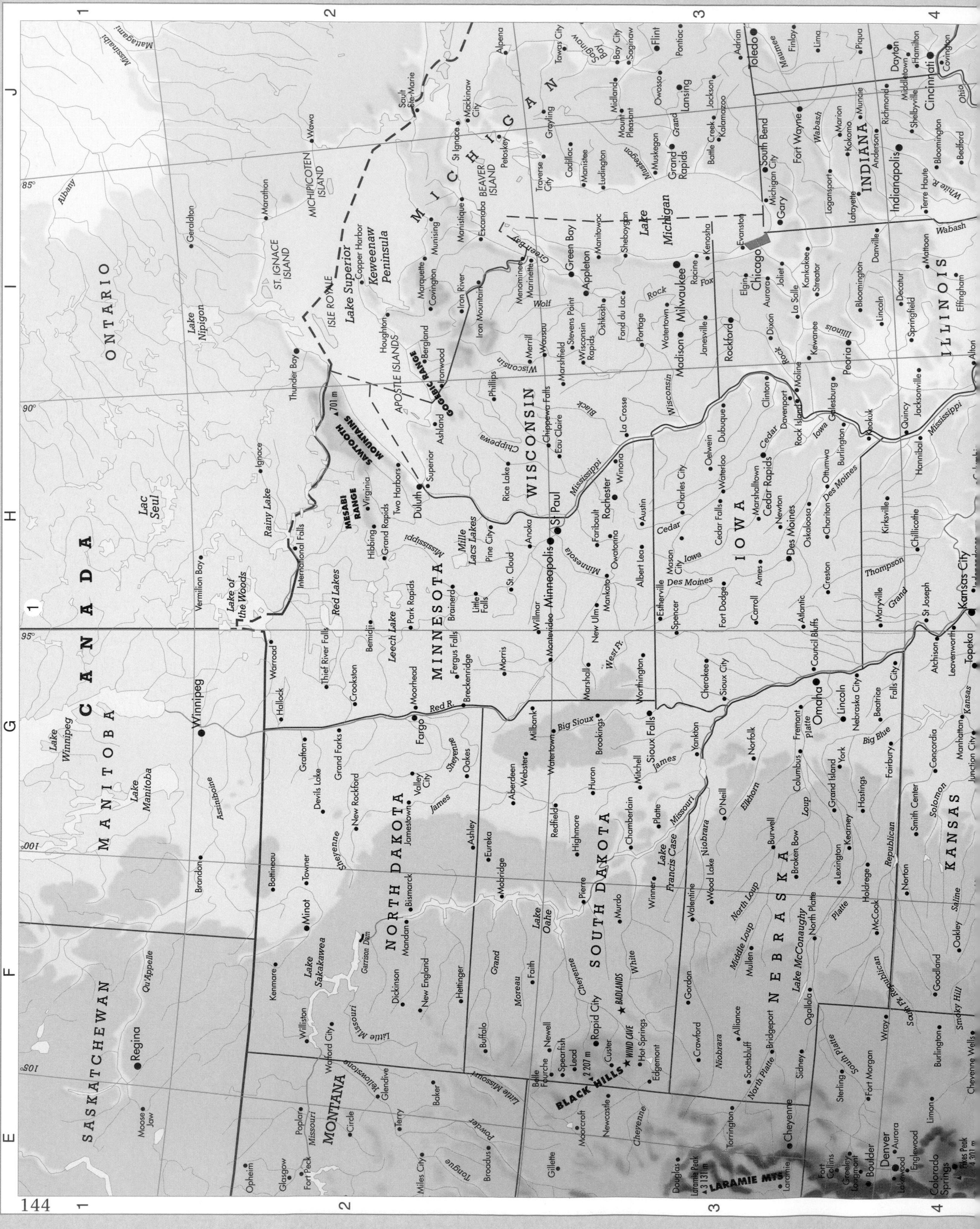

Grid references: 1 2 3 4 (top), J I H G F E (left)

Countries/Provinces/States:
SASKATCHEWAN · MANITOBA · ONTARIO · CANADA
MONTANA · NORTH DAKOTA · SOUTH DAKOTA · NEBRASKA · KANSAS
MINNESOTA · IOWA · WISCONSIN · MICHIGAN · ILLINOIS · INDIANA

Water bodies & features:
Lake Winnipeg · Lake Manitoba · Lac Seul · Lake Nipigon · Lake of the Woods · Rainy Lake · Red Lakes · Leech Lake · Mille Lacs Lakes · Lake Superior · Lake Michigan · Lake Sakakawea · Lake Oahe · Lake Francis Case · Lake McConaughy

Missouri · Mississippi · Little Missouri · Yellowstone · Red R. · Cheyenne · James · Wisconsin · Chippewa · Black · Iowa · Cedar · Des Moines · Platte · North Loup · Middle Loup · South Platte · North Platte · Republican · Smoky Hill · Saline · Solomon · Big Blue · Niobrara · White · Grand · Moreau · Sheyenne · Wabash · White R. · Ohio · Fox · Rock · Wolf · Thompson

MESABI RANGE · GOGEBIC RANGE · SAWTOOTH MOUNTAINS · BLACK HILLS · BADLANDS · WIND CAVE · LARAMIE MTS · Keweenaw Peninsula · Apostle Islands · Isle Royale · St. Ignace Island · Michipicoten Island · Beaver Island

▲701 m · ▲2 207 m · ▲3 131 m · ▲4 301 m

Latitude/Longitude: 85° · 90° · 95° · 100° · 105°

Cities (selection):
Regina · Moose Jaw · Winnipeg · Brandon · Thunder Bay · Geraldton · Marathon · Albany · Ignace · International Falls · Fort Peck · Glasgow · Opheim · Poplar · Miles City · Glendive · Baker · Gillette · Newcastle · Rapid City · Spearfish · Lead · Custer · Hot Springs · Edgemont · Belle Fourche · Newell · Moorcroft · Williston · Kenmare · Minot · Bottineau · Towner · New Rockford · Devils Lake · Grafton · Grand Forks · Dickinson · Mandan · Bismarck · New England · Hettinger · Jamestown · Valley City · Ashley · Eureka · Mobridge · Faith · Buffalo · Pierre · Murdo · Winner · Chamberlain · Redfield · Highmore · Aberdeen · Webster · Watertown · Milbank · Huron · Mitchell · Brookings · Sioux Falls · Yankton · Gordon · Crawford · Alliance · Scottsbluff · Bridgeport · Sidney · Ogallala · North Platte · McCook · Valentine · O'Neill · Norfolk · Elkhorn · Omaha · Lincoln · Columbus · Fremont · Grand Island · Kearney · Lexington · Broken Bow · Burwell · Holdrege · Hastings · York · Beatrice · Fairbury · Nebraska City · Falls City · Wood Lake · Mullen

Fort Collins · Greeley · Longmont · Boulder · Denver · Aurora · Lakewood · Englewood · Colorado Springs · Limon · Goodland · Oakley · Oberlin · Norton · Smith Center · Concordia · Salina · Junction City · Manhattan · Topeka · Atchison · Leavenworth · Kansas City · St Joseph · Maryville · Council Bluffs · Atlantic · Creston · Chariton · Osceola · Ottumwa · Oskaloosa · Des Moines · Newton · Marshalltown · Ames · Fort Dodge · Carroll · Spencer · Estherville · Sheldon · Cherokee · Sioux City · Mason City · Charles City · Waterloo · Cedar Rapids · Iowa City · Cedar Falls · Oelwein · Dubuque · Davenport · Clinton · Rock Island · Moline · Burlington · Keokuk · Hannibal · Quincy · Kirksville · Chillicothe

Duluth · Superior · Two Harbors · Virginia · Hibbing · Grand Rapids · Bemidji · Park Rapids · Brainerd · Little Falls · St. Cloud · Willmar · Montevideo · Marshall · Worthington · New Ulm · Mankato · Owatonna · Faribault · Albert Lea · Austin · Rochester · Winona · La Crosse · Eau Claire · Chippewa Falls · Rice Lake · Ashland · Bergland · Ironwood · Phillips · Wausau · Merrill · Marshfield · Wisconsin Rapids · Stevens Point · Green Bay · Appleton · Oshkosh · Fond du Lac · Portage · Watertown · Madison · Janesville · Beloit · Rockford · Freeport · Dixon · Kenosha · Racine · Milwaukee · Sheboygan · Manitowoc · Marinette · Menominee · Escanaba · Iron Mountain · Iron River · Covington · Marquette · Munising · Manistique · Houghton · Copper Harbor · Sault Ste. Marie · St Ignace · Mackinaw City · Petoskey · Cheboygan · Alpena · Traverse City · Cadillac · Manistee · Ludington · Grayling · Mount Pleasant · Midland · Bay City · Saginaw · Flint · Pontiac · Lansing · Grand Rapids · Muskegon · Owosso · Battle Creek · Kalamazoo · Jackson · Adrian · Toledo · Maumee · Finlay · Lima · Piqua · Covington · Cincinnati · Hamilton · Middletown · Dayton · Shelbyville · Bedford · Bloomington · Richmond · Muncie · Anderson · Indianapolis · Terre Haute · Lafayette · Logansport · Kokomo · Marion · Wabash · Fort Wayne · South Bend · Michigan City · Gary · Chicago · Evanston · Elgin · Aurora · Joliet · Kankakee · La Salle · Streator · Peru · Ottawa · Kewanee · Galesburg · Peoria · Bloomington · Decatur · Springfield · Lincoln · Jacksonville · Alton · Effingham · Mattoon · Danville

Winnipeg · Warroad · Hallock · Thief River Falls · Crookston · Fargo · Moorhead · Breckenridge · Fergus Falls · Morris · Wadena · Vermilion Bay · Crofton · Red Lake Falls

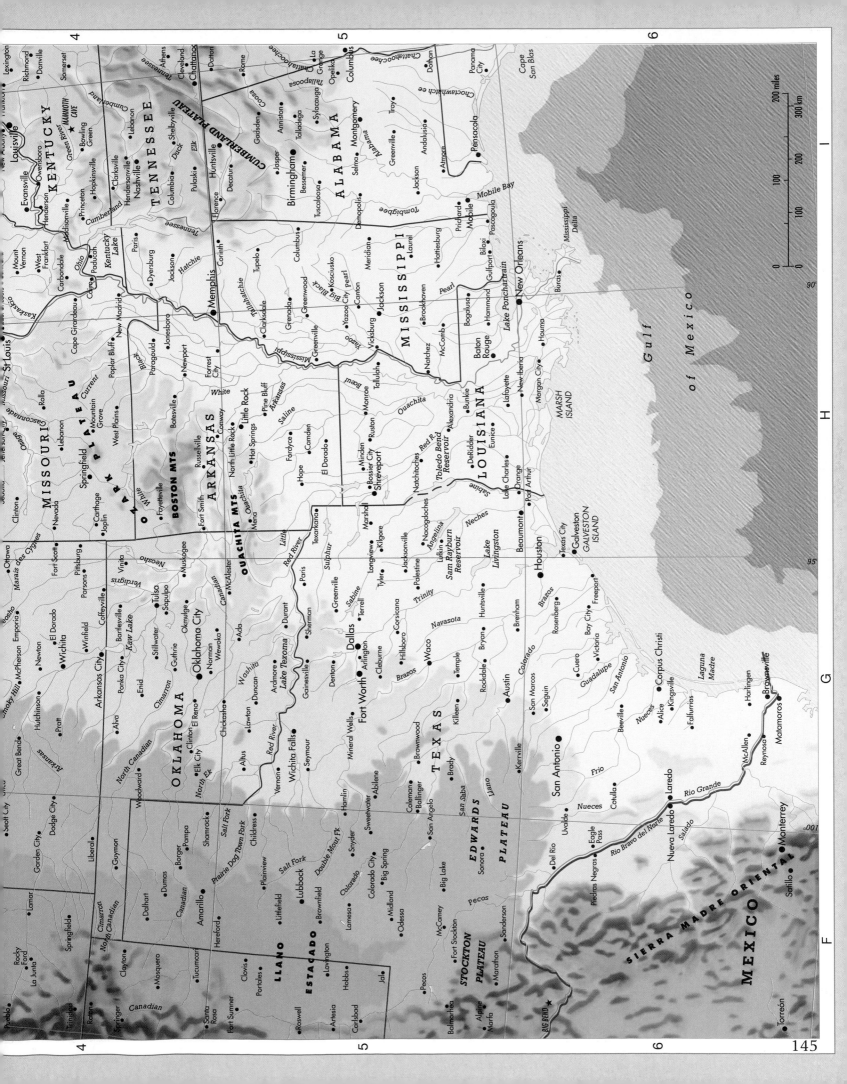

CANADA

QUEBEC

ONTARIO

NEW BRUNSWICK

NOVA SCOTIA

PRINCE EDWARD ISLAND

MAGDALENE ISLANDS (Quebec)

Gulf of St Lawrence

CAPE BRETON ISLAND

Cabot Strait

Cape Breton

Sydney

New Glasgow

Charlottetown

Halifax

Northumberland Strait

Cape Sable

Gulf of Maine

Yarmouth

Bay of Fundy

St John

Cape de Gaspé

Cape Gaspé

Gaspé

Gaspé Peninsula

NOTRE DAME MTS

Matane

Chaleur Bay

Bathurst

Moncton

Grand Lake

Fredericton

Calais

Monmagny

Rimouski

Rivière-du-Loup

St John

Eagle Lake

Caribou

Presque Isle

Houlton

Millinocket

Penobscot

Bangor

Belfast

Augusta

Brunswick

Portland

Biddeford

Saco

Kennebec

Waterville

Lewiston

MAINE

Moosehead Lake

Portsmouth

Cape Ann

Cape Cod

NANTUCKET ISLAND

MARTHA'S VINEYARD

New Bedford

Fall River

Brockton

Boston

Cambridge

Lynn

Lowell

Manchester

Concord

Laconia

Berlin

Mt Washington 1 917 m

NEW HAMPSHIRE

VERMONT

Montpelier

Barre

Burlington

Lake Champlain

Rutland

Worcester

Springfield

Pittsfield

Greenfield

Hartford

MASSACHUSETTS

RHODE ISLAND

Providence

CONNECTICUT

Waterbury

New Haven

New London

Bridgeport

LONG ISLAND

New York

Long Branch

Atlantic City

NEW JERSEY

DELAWARE

Dover

Delaware Bay

Salisbury

Delmarva Peninsula

Chesapeake Bay

Potomac

York

Wilmington

Camden

Trenton

Philadelphia

Lancaster

Reading

Allentown

Wilkes Barre

Scranton

Paterson

Jersey City

Newark

West Point

Newburgh

Hudson

Kingston

Poughkeepsie

Albany

Schenectady

Troy

Slide Mt 1 281 m

ADIRONDACK MTS

Mt Marcy 1 628 m

Glens Falls

Saratoga

Mohawk

Rome

Utica

Syracuse

Auburn

Ithaca

Binghamton

Elmira

Williamsport

Harrisburg

Hagerstown

MARYLAND

WASHINGTON

Annapolis

Baltimore

Arlington

Winchester

Cumberland

Fredericksburg

Charlottesville

Harrisonburg

Staunton

VIRGINIA

WEST VIRGINIA

Charleston

Kanawha

Ohio

Ashland

Huntington

Covington

Cincinnati

Hamilton

Middletown

Dayton

Springfield

Columbus

OHIO

Chillicothe

Portsmouth

Marion

Mansfield

Zanesville

Marietta

Parkersburg

Clarksburg

Morgantown

Wheeling

Steubenville

Canton

Massillon

Akron

Youngstown

New Castle

Oil City

Du Bois

Johnstown

Altoona

ALLEGHENY MTS

PENNSYLVANIA

Pittsburgh

McKeesport

Morgantown

Lima

Finlay

Lorain

Cleveland

Sandusky

Toledo

Maumee

Adrian

Lake Erie

Erie

Dunkirk

Ashtabula

Jamestown

Olean

Buffalo

Niagara Falls

St-Catharines

Hamilton

NEW YORK

Rochester

Lake Ontario

Oswego

Watertown

Ogdensburg

Potsdam

Massena

Plattsburg

St Lawrence

OTTAWA

Hull

Montreal

Cornwall

Kingston

Peterborough

Toronto

Oshawa

London

Kitchener

Georgian Bay

Lake Simcoe

MANITOULIN ISLAND

North Bay

Lake Nipissing

Pembroke

Riv. des Outaouais (Ottawa)

Lac Kipawa

Réservoir Cabonga

Réservoir Baskatong

Réservoir Gouin

Lac Kempt

Lac St-Jean

Chicoutimi

Jonquière

Chibougamau

Lac Mistassini

Lac Evans

Réservoir Pipmuacan

Baie Comeau

Saguenay

LAURENTIDES

Quebec

Trois-Rivières

Sherbrooke

Périhonka

Matagami

Harricana

Abitibi

Lake Abitibi

Timmins

Sudbury

Sault

Lake Huron

Detroit

Windsor

Dearborn

Port Huron

Port Austin

Bay City

Saginaw

Alpena

Towas City

Flint

Pontiac

Lake St-Claire

Lake Erie

Sandusky

SUSQUEHANNA MTS

Susquehanna

65°

30°

ATLANTIC

OCEAN

M

25°

70°

200 miles

300 km

200

100

100

0

0

75°

KENTUCKY

Lexington

Richmond

Danville

Somerset

Williamson

Beckley

Bluefield

Bristol

Johnson City

Knoxville

Oak Ridge

Athens

Cleveland

Chattanooga

Dalton

Hazard

CUMBERLAND PLATEAU

Cumberland

Holston

Clinch

Tennessee

GREAT SMOKY MTS

Asheville

Mt Mitchell
2 037 m

BLUE RIDGE

New R.

Covington

VIRGINIA

Petersburg

Lynchburg

Roanoke

Martinsville

Danville

James

Roanoke

Suffolk

Newport News

Norfolk

Portsmouth

Elizabeth City

Albemarle Strait

Chowan

Roanoke

Roanoke Rapids

Pamlico Sound

NORTH CAROLINA

Greensboro

Winston-Salem

Durham

Raleigh

Rocky Mount

Tar

Neuse

Washington

Greenville

Goldsboro

New Bern

Morehead City

Cape Lookout

Onslow
Bay

Salisbury

Kannapolis

Hickory

Gastonia

Charlotte

Jordan

Rock Hill

Monroe

Fayetteville

Lumberton

Cape Fear

Wilmington

Cape Fear

Myrtle Beach

Long Bay

Spartanburg

Greenville

Anderson

Catawba

Broad R.

SOUTH CAROLINA

Greenwood

Columbia

Sumter

Florence

Conway

Georgetown

Pee Dee

Pee Dee

L. Marion

Santee

L. Moultrie

Charleston

Elberton

Athens

Clarks
Hill Lake

Aiken

Augusta

Orangeburg

Edisto

Port Royal

Savannah

Rome

Athens

Cleveland

Marietta

Atlanta

Griffin

La Grange

Opelika

Columbus

Chattahoochee

Etowah

GEORGIA

Milledgeville

Macon

Oconee

Ocmulgee

Flint

Cordele

Moultrie

Albany

Dublin

Statesboro

Ogeechee

Altamaha

Jesup

Fitzgerald

Waycross

Folkston

Brunswick

Savannah

Ocmulgee

Valdosta

Suwannee

Lake City

Gainesville

Tallahassee

Apalachee
Bay

Chattahoochee

Dothan

Panama
City

Apalachicola

Apalachicola

Cape
San Blas

Flint

Gulf of

Mexico

FLORIDA

Ocala

St Johns

Jacksonville

St Augustine

Palatka

L. George

Daytona Beach

Sanford

Orlando

Cape Canaveral

Lake Kissimmee

Lakeland

Vero Beach

Fort Pierce

Lake
Okeechobee

West Palm
Beach

Clearwater

Tampa

St Petersburg

Tampa Bay

Sarasota

Sebring

Fort Myers

Naples

Everglades
City

Everglades

Fort Lauderdale

Hialeah

Miami

EVERGLADES
NAT. PARK

Florida Bay

Cap Sable

Key West

FLORIDA KEYS

Straits of Florida

80°

BAHAMAS

GRAND
BAHAMA

Freeport

LITTLE ABACO

GREAT
ABACO

NEW
PROVIDENCE

NASSAU

ANDROS

ELEUTHERA

Exuma Sound

GREAT
EXUMA

CAT ISLAND

SAN SALVADOR

RUM CAY

LONG ISLAND

85°

I   J   K   L

USA

Political system Federal republic
Capital Washington DC

Area 3 787 319 sq miles (9 809 155 km²)
Languages English; Spanish widely spoken
Population 270 311 756 (1998)
Population density 75 per sq mile (29 per km²)
Currency 1 US dollar = 100 cents
GDP per head US $30 200 (1997)

CANADA

Political system Federal parliamentary monarchy
Capital Ottawa

Area 3 844 928 sq miles (9 958 319 km²)
Languages English and French
Population 30 675 398 (1998)
Population density 8 per sq mile (3 per km²)
Currency 1 Canadian dollar = 100 cents
GDP per head US $21 700 (1997)

GREENLAND

Political system Self-governing division of Denmark
Capital Nuuk (Godthaab)

Area 840 000 sq miles (2 175 600 km²)
Languages Greenlandic and Danish
Population 59 309 (1998)
Population density 0.07 per sq mile (0.03 per km²)
Currency 1 Danish krone = 100 øre
GDP per head US $16 100 (1997)

Aspects of North America

With mighty peaks topping 15 000 ft (4600 m), deserts stretching for hundreds of miles, temperatures that rise higher than 50°C (120°F) and sink lower than –60°C (–75°F), North America can justifiably call itself a continent of extremes.

THE NATIONAL FLAGS

The star-spangled banner

The rebellious American colonies hoisted their first, unofficial, flag on New Year's Day, 1776. It consisted of 13 horizontal stripes – seven red ones and six white ones – to represent each of the 13 colonies. This was before they declared their independence, and their flag still displayed the British Union

Old Glory *Parading the Stars and Stripes.*

Flag in its top left-hand corner. The next year, the Continental Congress approved the first version of the 'Stars and Stripes', in which the Union Flag was replaced with 13 stars. Since then, stars have been added as new states joined the Union, but the number of stripes has remained the same, in honour of the original 13 colonies. The last star was added in 1960, after Hawaii was admitted as the 50th state.

Under US law, it was a crime to damage or destroy the Stars and Stripes. When the explorer Robert Peary reached what he believed to be the North Pole in 1909, he cut out a piece of the flag and left it there in commemoration. This apparently patriotic gesture was criticised by some commentators when he returned home.

The flag that floated over the US base at Pearl Harbor when the Japanese attacked in December 1941 was carefully preserved. Nearly four years later, on August 14, 1945, the same flag was hoisted over the White House when news came through of the Japanese surrender.

The maple leaf flag

The present Canadian flag has floated over Parliament Hill in Ottawa since 1965. Before then, the Canadian Red Ensign was the national flag; it had a red background with the Union Jack in the top left corner and the arms of Canada.

Canadians have used the maple leaf symbol since the 18th century. The maple is one of the most common species in their land's immense forests, and one of the most useful. Its sap makes maple syrup;

'I remember' *Quebec's motto on a licence plate.*

the wood is good for furniture and floors. The maple leaf appears on Canadian one cent, five cent and two dollar coins. The beaver – another

important national symbol – also appears on the five cent coin.

Each of Canada's provinces and territories also has its own flag. Quebec's white cross on an azure background recalls the military flags of pre-Revolutionary France, while the four fleurs-de-lys symbolise the French monarchy – the French heritage that Quebec never forgets.

THE LAND, THE PLANTS, THE ANIMALS

The United States

Rocky Mountains: They stretch from Alaska in the north to the Mexican frontier in the south, reaching their highest point in Alaska's Mount McKinley (20 320 ft/6194 m). Their highest peak in the United States excluding Alaska is Mount Elbert in Colorado rising to 14 433 ft (4399 m). They are home to grizzly and brown bears, elk (wapiti), Rocky Mountain goats, bighorn sheep and puma (cougar).

Grand Canyon and deserts: In the south-west, the Colorado River carved the Grand Canyon through layers of multicoloured rock. It is more than 250 miles (400 km) long, and in places up to 1 mile (1.6 km) deep. Deserts cover 17 000 sq miles (44 000 km²) of the south-west, including places such as Death Valley, where the temperature regularly rises over 50°C (120°F). These are the realms of cacti, yucca plants and the Joshua tree; animals include various species of rattlesnake, the venomous Gila monster (a lizard) and a kind of cuckoo, the roadrunner.

Interior lowlands: The Great Plains and central lowlands spread out between the Rockies in the west and the Appalachians in the east. In the north, they have fertile black soil. The Mississippi meanders through the south, flooding the plains and forming bayous and swamps in its huge delta, leading to the Gulf of Mexico.

The north-east: The Great Lakes and a part of the St Lawrence River form a natural frontier with Canada. Between Lake Ontario and Lake Erie, the flow of water over the Niagara Falls is 750 000 gallons (3.4 million litres) per second. In New England, the northern outcrops of the Appalachian chain create a rugged and picturesque landscape.

The south-east: The Appalachian chain reaches its highest point in Mount Mitchell (6684 ft/2037 m) in North Carolina. At their southern end, the mountains are covered with the world's largest broad-leaved deciduous forests, including beech, maple, lime and walnut trees. In the far south-east, the Florida peninsula is low-lying and dotted with lakes and the vast swamplands of the Everglades, home to alligators, crocodiles, turtles, pelicans and bald eagles.

NORTH AMERICA: THE TERRAIN

▼

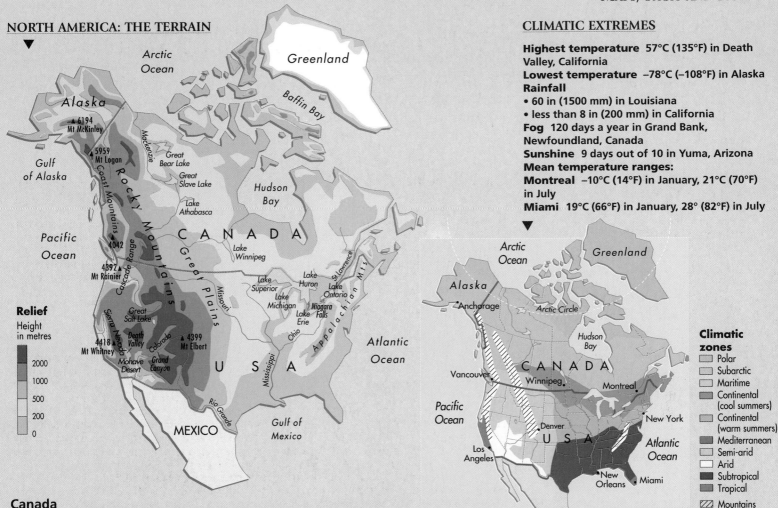

Relief

Height
in metres

2000
1000
500
200
0

CLIMATIC EXTREMES

Highest temperature 57°C (135°F) in Death
Valley, California
Lowest temperature –78°C (–108°F) in Alaska
Rainfall
• 60 in (1500 mm) in Louisiana
• less than 8 in (200 mm) in California
Fog 120 days a year in Grand Bank,
Newfoundland, Canada
Sunshine 9 days out of 10 in Yuma, Arizona
Mean temperature ranges:
Montreal –10°C (14°F) in January, 21°C (70°F)
in July
Miami 19°C (66°F) in January, 28° (82°F) in July

▼

**Climatic
zones**
☐ Polar
☐ Subarctic
☐ Maritime
☐ Continental
(cool summers)
☐ Continental
(warm summers)
☐ Mediterranean
☐ Semi-arid
☐ Arid
☐ Subtropical
☐ Tropical
▨ Mountains

Canada

The far north: Glaciers, mountains, rock deserts
and snow are features of Canada's Arctic islands
and northernmost mainland fringe. Farther
south lies the band of tundra with permanently
frozen subsoil where only lichens, mosses,
dwarf shrubs and stunted birch trees can grow.
Prairies and Shield: Spreading out across the
provinces of Alberta, Saskatchewan and
Manitoba, Canada's prairies are its largest farming area. To the north, the Canadian Shield is a
vast zone of forests, lakes and rocks, that
stretches west from Labrador as far as the
northern Rockies.
Great rivers: In the east, the St Lawrence flows
for 800 miles (1287 km) from Lake Ontario to
the North Atlantic. In the Northwest Territories,
the Mackenzie River rises in the Great Slave
Lake and flows for 2640 miles (4250 km) into
the Arctic Ocean.

Greenland

Around 80 per cent of the world's largest island
after Australia lies under an ice cap. The only
habitable part of Greenland is the coastal strip,
little more than 15 miles (24 km) wide. Almost
no crops can grow here; the only livestock are a
few flocks of sheep. Cod and shrimps are the
chief exports. The average depth of the ice is
nearly 1 mile (1.6 km), though research by
NASA published in March 1999 showed that the
Greenland ice cap is currently thinning by up to
3 ft (1 m) a year. Partly this may be a result of
global warming; if it continues, it poses a threat
to coastal communities worldwide.

THE HIGHEST PEAKS

USA

Mount McKinley (Alaska)	20 320 ft/6194 m
Mount Foraker (Alaska)	17 401 ft/5304 m
Mount Bona (Alaska)	16 421 ft/5005 m
Mount Blackburn (Alaska)	16 390 ft/4990 m
Mount Whitney (California)	14 494 ft/4418 m
Mount Elbert (Colorado)	14 433 ft/4399 m
Longs Peak (Colorado)	14 255 ft/4345 m

CANADA

Mount Logan (Yukon)	19 550 ft/5959 m
Mount St Elias (Yukon)	18 008 ft/5489 m
Mount Lucania (Yukon)	17 145 ft/5226 m
King Peak (Yukon)	16 972 ft/5173 m
Mount Steele (Yukon)	16 624 ft/5067 m
Mount Wood (Yukon)	15 873 ft/4838 m
Mount Vancouver (Yukon)	15 699 ft/4785 m

GREENLAND

Gunnbjørns Fjeld	12 139 ft/3700 m
Mont Forel	11 024 ft/3360 m
Borgtinderne	10 984 ft/3348 m
Ejnar Mikkelsens Fjeld	10 699 ft/3261 m

Canadian cold

Winters are always severe in Canada. The only
parts of the country where the average winter
temperatures are not below zero and accompa-
nied by continuous snow cover are Vancouver
and the surrounding region of the west coast.
The lowest temperature ever recorded was at
Snag in the Yukon: –63°C (–81°F). In a climate
like this, people are geared up to the cold, and
this includes burrowing into the ground. To provide protection against the cold, some Canadian
cities have created networks of subterranean
passageways. Downtown Montreal boasts inter-
linked underground shopping and commercial
complexes, where people can go about their
business without having to emerge into the
cold. Huge skylights let daylight into the open
areas between the shops and other premises.

THE GREENLAND ICE CAP

AREA	666 390 sq miles/ 1 725 900 km² *– more than three times the size of France, the second-largest ice cap after the Antarctic one*
VOLUME	480 000 cu miles/ 2 000 000 km³
AVERAGE THICKNESS	5000 ft/1500 m
MAXIMUM THICKNESS	11 200 ft/3400 m

Patterns of living

North America's population is spread irregularly across the continent, creating more a patchwork of communities than the melting pot envisaged by many politicians in the 19th century and at the start of the 20th.

THE WORK NORTH AMERICANS DO ▼

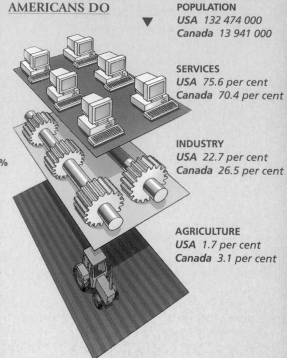

TOTAL ACTIVE POPULATION
USA 132 474 000
Canada 13 941 000

SERVICES
USA 75.6 per cent
Canada 70.4 per cent

INDUSTRY
USA 22.7 per cent
Canada 26.5 per cent

AGRICULTURE
USA 1.7 per cent
Canada 3.1 per cent

THE AGE PYRAMID ▼

The bulge in the North American population aged over 50 is linked to the postwar baby boom and immigration. Birth rates have since tumbled to 1.8 children for every woman.

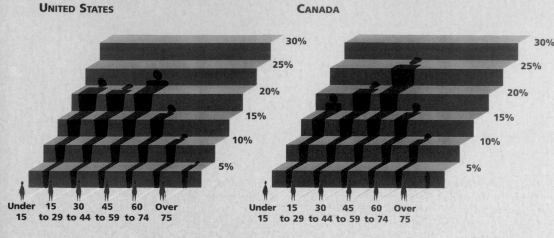

UNITED STATES

Under 15	15 to 29	30 to 44	45 to 59	60 to 74	Over 75

CANADA

Under 15	15 to 29	30 to 44	45 to 59	60 to 74	Over 75

LIFE EXPECTANCY AT BIRTH

	MEN	WOMEN
Canada	76	81
United States	73	80
Greenland	65	74

THE CANADIAN MOSAIC

The descendants of Canada's Aboriginal inhabitants now constitute about 3 per cent of the population. They include a little over 550 000 North American Indians and 51 000 Inuit. Among the descendants of European settlers, two groups predominate: those of French stock and those of British (English, Irish, Scottish) stock. In the late 19th century, immigrants began arriving from eastern and southern Europe. This influx peaked in 1913, when more than 400 000 people entered Canada. The Depression of the 1930s led the government to introduce tighter immigration controls, but these were relaxed after the Second World War. Canada became a favourite destination for political refugees, who accounted for around 10 per cent of immigration into the country in the postwar years. It welcomed refugees from communist Europe in the 1950s, from North Africa and Haiti in the 1960s, from Asia in the 1970s, from Lebanon, Guatemala and El Salvador in the 1980s. Nowadays, more than 50 per cent of immigrants to Canada come from Asia, though not necessarily as political refugees.

VARYING POPULATION DENSITY ▶

The average population density across the United States is 75 people per sq mile (29 per km²). But within the country the range is considerable: under 5 per sq mile (2 per km²) in Wyoming, nearly 1000 per sq mile (400 per km²) in New Jersey. Only about 10 per cent of Canada is inhabited at all. Most sparsely populated are the Yukon and Northwest Territories with just over 5 people for every 100 sq miles (2 people for 100 km²).

Population density
Inhabitants per sq km
- More than 100
- 50 - 100
- 10 - 50
- 1 - 10
- Fewer than 1

ETHNIC DISTRIBUTION
Minorities within local populations ▼

Minority rights
The original inhabitants, American Indians, Inuit and Aleuts, account for less than 1 per cent of the US population. Hispanics make up 8 per cent, African-Americans 12 per cent.

Indian, Aleutian and Eskimo 1%
- More than 50%
- 15 - 50%

Hispanic 9%
- More than 50%
- 9 - 50%

Black 12%
- More than 50%
- 12 - 50%

Continental riches

Between them, the United States and Canada make up the richest industrial region in the world. The continent's wealth includes abundant mineral resources as well as the riches of its fertile soils.

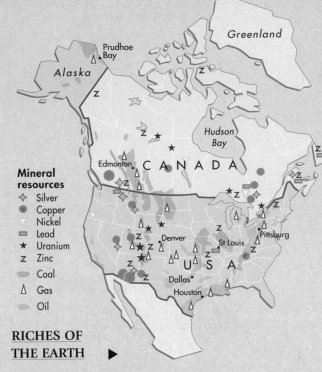

Mineral resources

⬦ Silver
● Copper
▽ Nickel
▭ Lead
★ Uranium
z Zinc
◗ Coal
△ Gas
◖ Oil

RICHES OF THE EARTH ▶

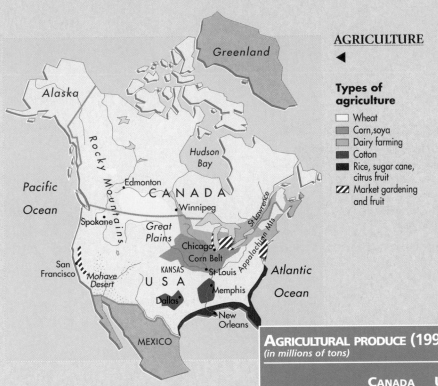

AGRICULTURE ◀

Types of agriculture

◻ Wheat
◼ Corn, soya
◻ Dairy farming
◼ Cotton
◼ Rice, sugar cane, citrus fruit
▨ Market gardening and fruit

EXTERNAL TRADE ▼

For both the USA and Canada, most imports and exports are in industry and transport.

IN THE USA
Figures in millions of US dollars

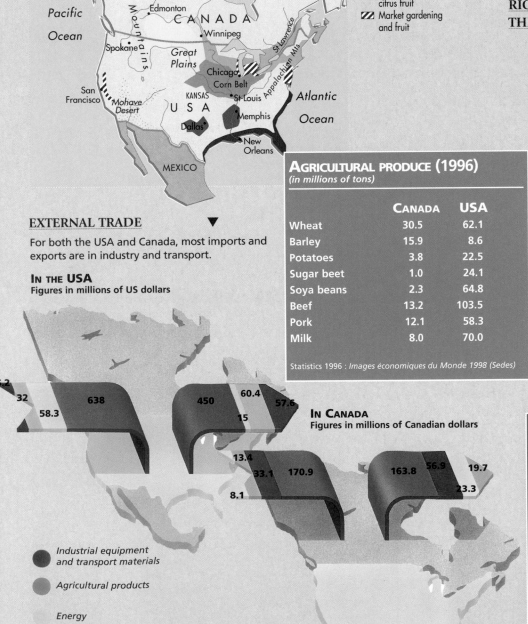

15.2
32
58.3
638
450
60.4
57.6
15

IN CANADA
Figures in millions of Canadian dollars

13.4
33.1
170.9
8.1
163.8
56.9
19.7
23.3

● Industrial equipment and transport materials

● Agricultural products

Energy

● Others

AGRICULTURAL PRODUCE (1996)
(in millions of tons)

	CANADA	USA
Wheat	30.5	62.1
Barley	15.9	8.6
Potatoes	3.8	22.5
Sugar beet	1.0	24.1
Soya beans	2.3	64.8
Beef	13.2	103.5
Pork	12.1	58.3
Milk	8.0	70.0

Statistics 1996 : *Images économiques du Monde 1998 (Sedes)*

MEANS OF TRANSPORT ▼

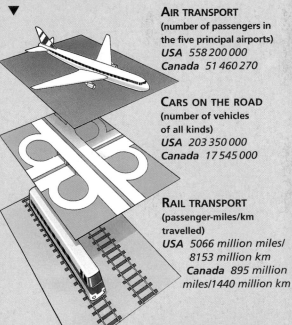

AIR TRANSPORT
(number of passengers in the five principal airports)
USA 558 200 000
Canada 51 460 270

CARS ON THE ROAD
(number of vehicles of all kinds)
USA 203 350 000
Canada 17 545 000

RAIL TRANSPORT
(passenger-miles/km travelled)
USA 5066 million miles/ 8153 million km
Canada 895 million miles/1440 million km

THE LARGEST PORTS

	TONNAGE HANDLED (imports and exports, by millions of tons)
Long Beach (USA)	87.1
Houston (USA)	72.1
Corpus Christi (USA)	70.4
Vancouver (Canada)	67.6
Los Angeles (USA)	65.0
Philadelphia (USA)	56.8
New Orleans (USA)	53.6
Hampton Roads (USA)	53.2
New York (USA)	51.4

Statistics 1994 (except Houston, 1993) : *Images économiques du monde 1998 (Sedes)*

Snapshots of society

Freedom of expression, high average standards of living and military might – even with advantages like these, North America still suffers from a full range of social ills. Washington DC has more than its share.

RELIGIOUS ALLEGIANCES
▼

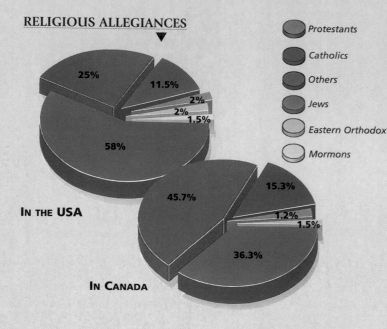

- Protestants
- Catholics
- Others
- Jews
- Eastern Orthodox
- Mormons

In the USA

25%
11.5%
2%
2%
1.5%
58%

In Canada

15.3%
45.7%
1.2%
1.5%
36.3%

HEALTH: SERVICES AND COSTS
▼

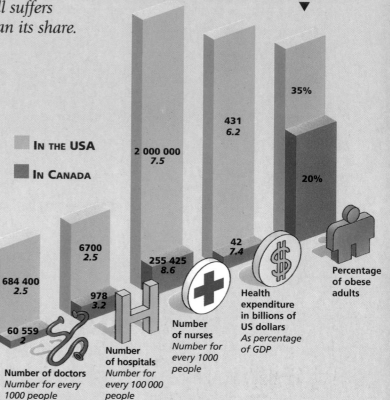

In the USA

In Canada

684 400 2.5	6700 2.5	255 425 8.6	2 000 000 7.5	431 6.2	35%
60 559 2	978 3.2		42 7.4		20%

Number of doctors Number for every 1000 people

Number of hospitals Number for every 100 000 people

Number of nurses Number for every 1000 people

Health expenditure in billions of US dollars As percentage of GDP

Percentage of obese adults

AVERAGE EXPENDITURE BY HOUSEHOLD
▼

In the USA

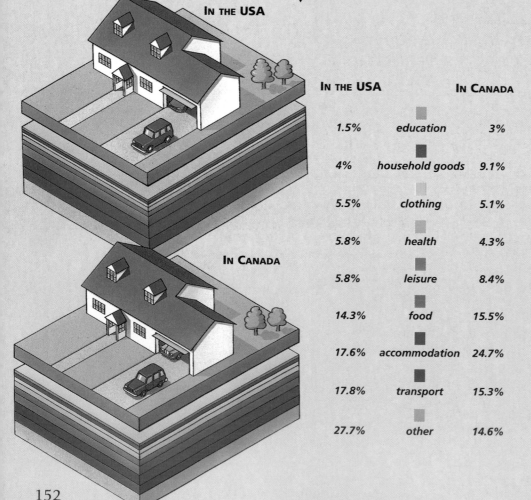

In Canada

In the USA		In Canada
1.5%	education	3%
4%	household goods	9.1%
5.5%	clothing	5.1%
5.8%	health	4.3%
5.8%	leisure	8.4%
14.3%	food	15.5%
17.6%	accommodation	24.7%
17.8%	transport	15.3%
27.7%	other	14.6%

HEALTH INSURANCE COVERAGE

In 1997, around 20 per cent of US citizens had no kind of health insurance. They included not only people who fell just below the poverty line, but also self-employed workers and employees of small businesses.

Contrasting standards of living

The overall figures for the United States' black and white populations reveal significant contrasts. Around 33 per cent of blacks live below the poverty line, as opposed to just 12 per cent of whites. Unemployment runs at 12 per cent among the black population, more than twice the level among whites who have a relatively modest 5 per cent unemployment. The average annual income among blacks is only 60 per cent that of whites.

The good life in Canada

For quality of life, Canada regularly comes top of the table – according to the United Nations Human Development Index. This was devised by the UN Development Programme and uses statistics for adult literacy, average years of schooling and life expectancy, as well as income levels, to show how 'developed' countries are. In 1995, the United States came third equal with Norway, and after France.

US EDUCATION: RACIAL INEQUALITY ▼

- ■ Whites
- ■ Blacks
- ■ Hispanics

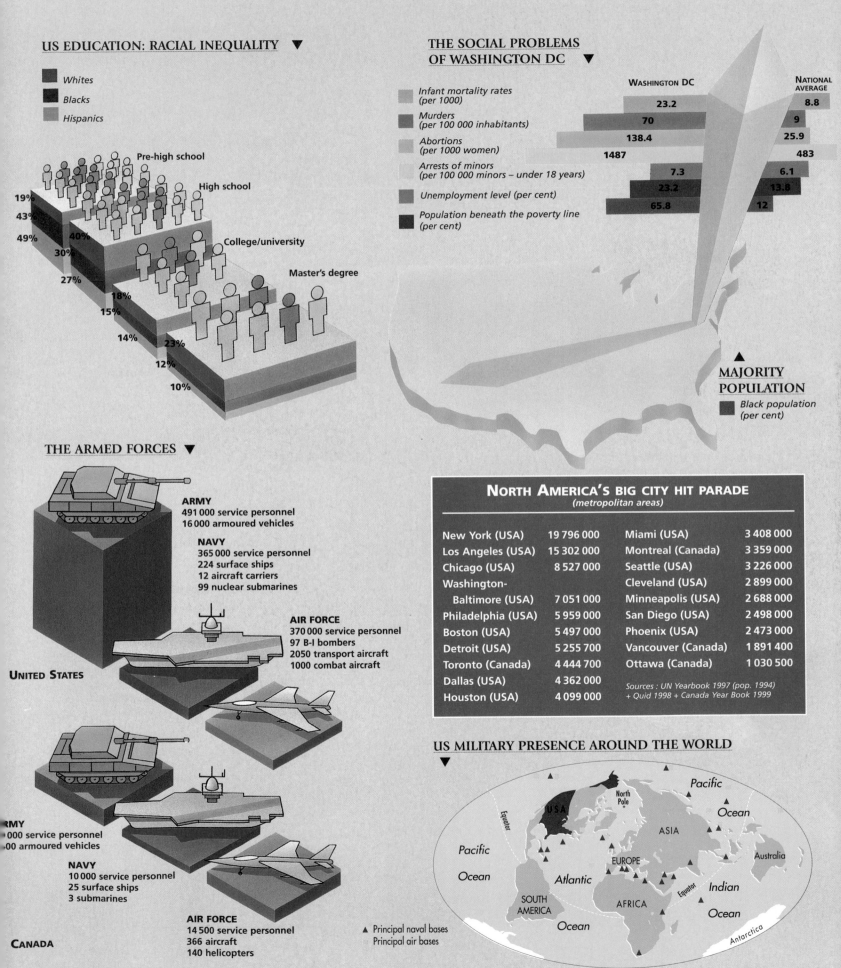

Pre-high school
19%
43%
49%   40%
30%
27%

High school
18%
15%
14%   23%
12%
10%

College/university

Master's degree

THE SOCIAL PROBLEMS OF WASHINGTON DC ▼

	WASHINGTON DC	NATIONAL AVERAGE
Infant mortality rates (per 1000)	23.2	8.8
Murders (per 100 000 inhabitants)	70	9
Abortions (per 1000 women)	138.4	25.9
Arrests of minors (per 100 000 minors – under 18 years)	1487	483
Unemployment level (per cent)	7.3	6.1
Population beneath the poverty line (per cent)	23.2	13.8
	65.8	12

▲ MAJORITY POPULATION

■ Black population (per cent)

THE ARMED FORCES ▼

UNITED STATES

ARMY
491 000 service personnel
16 000 armoured vehicles

NAVY
365 000 service personnel
224 surface ships
12 aircraft carriers
99 nuclear submarines

AIR FORCE
370 000 service personnel
97 B-I bombers
2050 transport aircraft
1000 combat aircraft

CANADA

ARMY
...000 service personnel
...00 armoured vehicles

NAVY
10 000 service personnel
25 surface ships
3 submarines

AIR FORCE
14 500 service personnel
366 aircraft
140 helicopters

NORTH AMERICA'S BIG CITY HIT PARADE
(metropolitan areas)

New York (USA)	19 796 000	Miami (USA)	3 408 000
Los Angeles (USA)	15 302 000	Montreal (Canada)	3 359 000
Chicago (USA)	8 527 000	Seattle (USA)	3 226 000
Washington-Baltimore (USA)	7 051 000	Cleveland (USA)	2 899 000
Philadelphia (USA)	5 959 000	Minneapolis (USA)	2 688 000
Boston (USA)	5 497 000	San Diego (USA)	2 498 000
Detroit (USA)	5 255 700	Phoenix (USA)	2 473 000
Toronto (Canada)	4 444 700	Vancouver (Canada)	1 891 400
Dallas (USA)	4 362 000	Ottawa (Canada)	1 030 500
Houston (USA)	4 099 000		

Sources : UN Yearbook 1997 (pop. 1994)
+ Quid 1998 + Canada Year Book 1999

US MILITARY PRESENCE AROUND THE WORLD

▼

▲ Principal naval bases
  Principal air bases

Tourist highlights

There is something for everyone in this continent of diversity. For lovers of nature, the great national parks offer a wealth of scenery, exotic natural phenomena and wildlife. Florida has Walt Disney World, Las Vegas its casinos, Milwaukee its annual Harley-Davidson rally. For the buzz of the big city, the choices range from Quebec to New York, San Francisco to Boston. Sites of historic interest include the Viking settlement at L'Anse-aux-Meadows in Newfoundland.

Niagara Falls *Visitors are dressed in waterproofs, to protect them from the spray, as they view the mighty spectacle.*

UNITED STATES

Cape Cod, Boston, Salem: where the *Mayflower* pilgrims landed; the city they founded; where the infamous witch hunts took place.

Salt Lake City, Utah: where the Mormons built a new city by the Great Salt Lake, a city of wide streets around an imposing Temple block.

Las Vegas: for its casinos, bright lights, fantastical architecture.

Grand Canyon: for the dizzying splendour of this great gash made by the Colorado River across the Arizona desert.

San Francisco: a city of hills; for its buzzing cosmopolitan atmosphere and its glorious Golden Gate Bridge.

Boston *The Charles River Basin, with the Beacon Hill district on the left and the skyscrapers of the financial district behind.*

New York: for the Manhattan skyline, the Empire State Building, the Statue of Liberty, its exuberant delight in being 'over the top'.

Washington DC: with all its splendours and contradictions, home of the world's mightiest 'movers and shakers'.

Florida: for Mickey Mouse and the rest of the Disney pantheon at Orlando; for the space centres at Cape Canaveral; for Miami and Miami Beach; for the Everglades.

Niagara Falls: traditionally popular with honeymoon couples and stuntmen such as tightrope walkers.

Memphis, Tennessee: to pay tribute to Elvis Presley 'the King' at his former home, Graceland.

Mississippi *Casino paddlesteamers take gamblers on river jaunts.*

Yellowstone National Park: for its geysers and its bears and other wildlife.

Hollywood: for the magic of celluloid illusion.

Alaska: for Denali National Park, with North America's highest peak, Mount McKinley.

Milwaukee, Wisconsin: for the Harley-Davidson factory and Harley-Davidson rally each June. In 1998, more than 300 000 bikers came for the 95th anniversary of the founding of the company.

Tinseltown *Movie capital of the world.*

CANADA

L'Anse-aux-Meadows: national historic site near the northernmost tip of Newfoundland. Its Viking remains are evidence of the earliest known settlement by Europeans in the Americas.

Mingan and Anticosti: an archipelago and an island in the Gulf of St Lawrence. The Mingan Archipelago for its fantastical monolithic rock formations and for whale-watching in the surrounding waters. Anticosti island was once the private sports preserve of the French chocolate manufacturer Henri Menier. It is rich in wildlife and renowned for deer hunting and salmon fishing.

Louisbourg, Nova Scotia: for North America's largest historic reconstruction, re-creating a fortified French town, built in 1720-60.

L'Anse-aux-Meadows.

Grand Pré, Nova Scotia: for its national historic site, which commemorates the French-speaking Acadians, expelled by the British in 1755; for its statue of Evangeline, the Acadian poetic heroine immortalised by Henry Wadsworth Longfellow.

Quebec: the only walled city north of Mexico, declared a world heritage site by UNESCO.

Ellesmere National Park Reserve: at Canada's northern extremity, the closest park to the North Pole, a wilderness of glaciers, mountains and Peary's caribou and musk-oxen.

Banff National Park, Alberta: Canada's first national park (1887), in the heart of the Canadian Rockies, home to black and grizzly bears, elk, caribou, bighorn sheep and Rocky Mountain goats.

Dawson City, Yukon: for its relics of the Klondike Gold Rush (1897-8).

Drumheller, Alberta: for its dinosaur fossil remains, with a Dinosaur Fossil Museum and 31 mile (50 km) Dinosaur Trail, and the nearby Royal Tyrrell Museum of Palaeontology, containing the world's largest displays of dinosaur skeletons.

Pacific Rim National Park, British Columbia: a ruggedly dramatic coastline, thickly overgrown and with a rich variety of land and sea wildlife.

Maligne Lake *Jasper National Park, Alberta, includes more than 4000 sq miles (10 000 km²) of Rocky Mountain landscape.*

Index

159

Acknowledgments

Abbreviations: t = top, m = middle, b = bottom, l = left, r = right.

Front cover: ALTITUDE/Y. Arthus-Bertrand.
Back cover: EXPLORER/S. Cordier

4-5: O. Grunewald. 6-7: COSMOS/S.P.L-Worldsat. 8: GAMMA/ P. Halley. 8-9: RAPHO/G. Sioen. 9tr: COSMOS/G. Russel; b: COSMOS/K. Kasmauski-Marix. 10-11r: RAPHO/G. Sioen. 12-13: COSMOS/R. Watts-Wesilight. 12b: O. Grunewald. 13tr: PHONE/J.P. Ferrero; br: RAPHO/Le Diascorn. 14t: EXPLORER/ S. Cordier; tr: G. Chenuet; bl: O. Grunewald. 15: RAPHO/G. Sioen. 16-17tr: R.M.N/Château de Versailles (*Jacques Cartier discovers and travels up the St Lawrence River in 1535*, dated 1847, by T. Gudin). 16ml: HOA QUI/C. Sappa; mr: ARTEPHOT/Oronoz. Museum of the Americas. Madrid. 17t: J.L. CHARMET/Ministry for Foreign Affairs (*Atlas Hondius*. Amsterdam); b: EXPLORER/M. Evans. Schoolcratt's Indian Tribes (*Henry Hudson meets the natives*, S. Eastman, 1609). 18t: G. DAGLI ORTI/Museum of the New World. La Rochelle (*Indians chasing bison*, school of G. Catlin); bl: ARTEPHOT (C. Bodmer, *Women dancing*, 1844); m: EXPLORER/S. Grandadam. 18-19b: JOSSE (Anonymous, 19th century, Private collection, 1876). 19tr: RAPHO/J.E. Pasquier; box border: JOSSE; br: EXPLORER/ A. Thomas – OK Corral Museum, Tombstone. 20mr: JOSSE/Museum of the New World, La Rochelle (*Trapper bartering with American Indians*, Le Loir, 19th century, lithograph, detail); bl: ARTEPHOT/ Bridgeman Art Library. Private collection (*First Thanksgiving*, J. Léon Jérôme Ferris, 1863-1930); br: J.L. CHARMET/B.N. Paris (Engraving by Nangis, 18th century. 20-21t: S.R.D/Bettman Archives. 20 box border, 21mr: GAMMA LIAISON/Ibourki; b: EXPLORER/M. Evans. 22ml, tr: JOSSE/B.N. Paris; b: ARTEPHOT/Bridgeman Art Library. Metropolitan Museum of Art, New York (*Washington crossing Delaware River*, G. Leutze, 1816-1868). 23m: ARTEPHOT/Bridgeman Art Library. Private collection (*Independence Day*, J. Léon Jérôme Ferris 1863-1930); ml: G. DAGLI ORTI/Château de Versailles (*Siege of Yorktown*, H. Van Blarenberghe, 1734-1812); br: ARTEPHOT/ A.D.P.C. 24t: PPCM; mb: ARTEPHOT/Bridgeman Art Library. Private collection (*Let us Have Peace*, J. Léon Jérôme Ferris, 1863-1930); br: EXPLORER/M.Evans. 25tr, box border: HOA QUI/B. Pérousse; m: EXPLORER/Coll. Béranger, *The Pilgrim*, 1923; tr: Archives S.R.D/ Photo X, D.R.; box border: S.R.D/Archives; bl: EXPLORER/Coll. Lausat. 26-27 THE STOCK MARKET. 28-29 O. Grunewald. 30bl: EXPLORER/G.Rowell-Light; bl, tr: O. Grunewald. 30-31t: GAMMA LIAISON/Mingasson. 31tl: EXPLORER/J.M. Loubat; tr: EXPLORER/ C. Lenars. 31: drawing from a photograph by PHONE/F. Gohier. 32ml: EXPLORER/S. Cordier; bl: G. Chenuet; mr: E. Sander. 32-33t: PHONE/F. Gohier. 33bl: O. Grunewald; tl: EXPLORER/ F. Gohier; tr: STUDIO/P. Desclos; b: FOTOGRAM-STONE IMAGES/ P. Pearson. 33tl: EXPLORER/P. Brylak. 34-35m: EXPLORER/G. Boutin. 35tl: EXPLORER/S. Cordier; mr: EXPLORER/A. Thomas; br: ADVENTURE PHOTO/A.E.F/T.I.B/J. Nelson. 36ml: GAMMA/ C. Hires. 36-37b: STOCK IMAGE/E. Brissaud. 36br: EXPLORER/ K. Straiton; tr: PHONE/F. Gohier. 37mr: EXPLORER/S. Grandadam. 37: drawing after a photograph by O. Grunewald. 38tr: O. Grunewald; tl: EXPLORER/F. Forget; br: EXPLORER/F. Jourdan. 39tl: EXPLORER/ E. Sampers; bl: RAPHO/G. Sioen; tr: GAMMA/Gould; mr: GAMMA/ F. Darmigny. 40-41 SYGMA/O. Sentinel. 42tl, m: G. Chenuet; bl: PHONE/F Gohier; br: PPCM/KOBAL, *Stagecoach*, J. Ford, 1938. 42-43t: O. Grunewald. 43tr, mr, br: PHONE/F. Gohier. mr: ALTITUDE/J. Wark; bl, mb: O. Grunewald. 44tr: GAMMA/ P. Halley; bl: ADVENTURE PHOTO/A.E.F/T.I.B/D. Schultz; mr: HOA QUI/G. Bosio. 45tl: SYGMA/Watertown Times; mr: SYGMA/J.P Poulin. 46 ml: COSMOS/W. Faidley-Picture Group; bl: SYGMA/ A. Tannenbaum. 46-47t: STUDIO/NASA's Goddard Space Flight Center. 47tr: SYGMA/J. Lopinot; mr: COSMOS/W. Faidley-Picture Group. 48ml: SYGMA/S. Takushi-St-Paul Pioneer Prees; tr: GAMMA LIAISON/D. Koeck; br: GAMMA LIAISON/L. Mayer. 49tl: EXPLORER/S. Grandadam; m: GAMMA LIAISON/The Modesto Bee; b: A.E.F/T.I.B./A. Beinat. 50b: PPCM. 51tl: EXPLORER/ Weintraub-Photo Researcher. 51 bl: RAPHO. Yager. 51mr, tr: ADVENTURE PHOTO/A.E.F/T.I.B/Macduff; br: HOA QUI/Kraft-Images and volcanoes. 52-53 HOA QUI/Ph. Bourseiller 54mb: A.E.F./T.I.B./S. Attal. 54-55t: GAMMA/ Fisher. 55tr: GAMMA LIAISON/S. Kagan; br: GAMMA LIAISON/Giboux. 56ml: RAPHO/ M. Yamashita. 56-57t: SYGMA/Laffont. 56br: SCOPE/P. Gould.

57bl: RAPHO/H. Donnezan; m: RAPHO/G. Sioen. 58m: STUDIO B/R. Olsenius-Black Star. 58-59b: SYGMA/J.B. Russel. 59tl: SYGMA/J.B. Russel; tr: STUDIO B/K. Ruohomaa-Black Star. 60tl: GAMMA/Mingasson; bl: EXPLORER/G. Boutin; t: GAMMA LIAISON/S. Katz; m: GAMMA LIAISON/Rotolo. 61m: GAMMA LIAISON/Laude; br: EXPLORER/Photo Researcher-Library of Congress, Washington. 62tr: GAMMA/G. Mingasson; m: RAPHO/ J.E. Pasquier; mr: GAMMA LIAISON/Ferry. 63tr: RAPHO/ J.E. Pasquier; bl: GAMMA LIAISON/Ferry. 64tl: STUDIO B/J. Launois-Black Star; tr: STUDIO B/O. Bierwagen-Black Star; br: Coll. G. Sirot. 65tr: RAPHO/C. Pick; br: RAPHO/P. Koch; l: STUDIO B/J. Rychetnik-Black Star. 66t: GAMMA/C. Poulet; m: GAMMA LIAISON/B. Willcox; b: GAMMA LIAISON/Brylak. 67ml: G. Chenuet; tr: EXPLORER/ A. Evrard; br: STUDIO B/K. Vandiver-Black Star. 68b: STUDIO B/C. Karp-Black Star; tr: STUDIO B/R. Ferro-Black Star. 69tr: GAMMA LIAISON/Rolle; m: E. Sander; br: EXPLORER/ F. Gohier. 70-71 GAMMA LIAISON/R. Sandler. 72t: A.E.F/T.I.B./ P. Curtet; b: VANDYSTADT/P. Salvaire. 73tr: Coll. KIPA, *Duel*, S. Spielberg, 1971; br: VANDYSTADT/R. Brice. 74tr: GAMMA LIAISON/Chiasson; tr: GAMMA/Ch. Vioujard; b: GAMMA LIAISON/E. Adams. 75tl: RAPHO/N. Leider-Time Magazine; tr: GAMMA LIAISON/Bresse; mb: RAPHO/R. Ohanian; 76tl: VANDYSTADT/B. Taylor-AllSport; mr: VANDYSTADT/B. Nunez-AllSport; mb: VANDYSTADT/S. Dunn-AllSport. 76-77tm: GAMMA LIAISON/Rose. 77bl: RAPHO/J. Leighton-Network; tr: HOA QUI/ C. Boisvieux; br: GAMMA LIAISON/Halebian-Novovitch. 78t: GAMMA LIAISON/R. Rotolo; b: EXPLORER/R. Baumgartner. 79t: GAMMA LIAISON/O. Koniewski; ml: GAMMA LIAISON/ T.Zimberoff; mb: RAPHO/G. Sioen; br: GAMMA LIAISON/Ferry. 80tl: STUDIO B/W.Volz-Bilderberg; tr: STUDIO B/S. Fellerman-Black Star; m: GAMMA LIAISON/J.L. Bulcao. 81tl: GAMMA/Weiner; bl: GAMMA/B. Copin; br: RAPHO/G. Sioen. 82tl: GAMMA/ Chiasson; mr: EXPLORER/G. Boutin; b: RAPHO/Spiegel. 83tl: STUDIO B/D.Brack-Black Star; mr: EXPLORER/I. Bertrand; m: GAMMA LIAISON/Breese. 84tr: RAPHO/G. Sioen; b: GAMMA LIAISON/Halebian; tl: EXPLORER/L. Fleury. 85tl, tr: b: GAMMA/ E. Sander; 85mb: COLL. KIPA/Sunset, *Gone with the Wind*, V. Flemming, 1932. 86t: HOA QUI/ P. Bourseiller; mr: EXPLORER/ M. Dumas. 87tl: HOA QUI/C. Moreno-N.F; br: VANDYSTADT/ D. Givois; mb: VANDYSTADT/R. Martin. 88tl: EXPLORER/ J. P. Nacivet; bl: GAMMA/X. Testelin; mt: EXPLORER/J. Brun; m: RAPHO/M. Yamashita; br: G. Chenuet. 88-89t: EXPLORER/T. Adina. 89b: GAMMA LIAISON/E. Sander. 90t: VANDYSTADT/S. Cazenave; mr: GAMMA/A. Seitz; b: EXPLORER/J.P. Nacivet. 91tl: RAPHO/ H. Donnezan – DISNEY. By special authorisation of TWDCF; r: HOA QUI/S. Grandadam; b: HOA QUI/M. Denis-Huot. 92-93 DIAF/ G. Simeone. 94tl: GAMMA LIAISON/S. Kagan. 94-95b: STOCK IMAGE; m: T.I.B/M. Loiseau-A.E.F. 95tr: GAMMA LIAISON/Giboux (Statue of Michael Jordan by Julie and Onri Anrany). 96tl: GAMMA LIAISON/Abron; m: EXPLORER/R. Nowitz; tr: EXPLORER/ A. Woolfitt; mt: GAMMA/F. Lochon. 97tl: STUDIO B/J. Rodriguez-Black Star; tr: GAMMA LIAISON/Moyer; ml: EXPLORER/I. Bertrand; b: GAMMA LIAISON/T. Vogel. 98-103: ALTITUDE/Y. Arthus Bertrand. 98br: R. Leslie; bl: STUDIO B/C. Carlton-Black Star. 99tl: G. Chenuet; ml: EXPLORER/L. Giraudou; bl: RAPHO/ L. Goldman; mb: GAMMA LIAISON/Moyer; br: STUDIO B/N. Okamoto-Black Star. 100tl: RAPHO/M. Yamashita 'An Interior View of the Guggenheim Museum, New York' by Frank Lloyd Wright. Adagp, Paris, 1998; bl: GAMMA LIAISON/Agostini; bl, mb, tr: G. Chenuet; br: R. Leslie. 101tl, m: G. Chenuet; bl: GAMMA/ Lannuzel; tr: STUDIO B/H. Matsumoto-Black Star. 102tl: GAMMA LIAISON/Charles; ml, mr: G. Chenuet; bl: R. Leslie; mt: ARCHIPRESS/F. Eustache (Flatiron Building, 1902. Archi: Daniel H. Burnham); tr: R. Leslie; m: GAMMA LIAISON/Benali; br: EXPLORER/L. Giraudou. 103tl: GAMMA LIAISON/Moyer; bl: RAPHO/L. Goldman; tr, br: G. Chenuet. 104t: EXPLORER/ G. Boutin. 105t: FOTOGRAM STONES IMAGES/J. Lawrence; ml: ARCHIPRESS/G. Halary (Sears Tower, 1974. Archi: Skidmore-Owings-Merril); b: ARCHIVE-PHOTO/*King Kong*, Merian E. Cooper, 1933; br: FOTOGRAM-STONES IMAGES/S. Grandadam. 106 ml: EXPLORER/S. Frances; bl: GAMMA LIAISON/E. Sander; 106tr, mr: G. Chenuet; br: EXPLORER/J. Raga. 107t: GAMMA/Figaro

Magazine; bl: RAPHO/G. Sioen; tr: A.E.F/T.I.B./Weinberg-Clark. 108tl: ARCHIVE PHOTO/FIA; ml: RAPHO/G. Sioen; b: FOTOGRAM STONES IMAGES/M. Busselle; tr: EXPLORER/H. Matsumoto. 109tl: A.E./T.I.B./F-G. Lhôte; bl: GAMMA LIAISON/E. Sander; tr: SYGMA/Taylor; mr: GAMMA/B. Alistaire-Spooner. 110t: HOA QUI/G. Boutin; mr: HOA QUI/G. Guittard; b: GAMMA/ G. Berthoud. 111tr: RAPHO/Staquet. 111tl, bl: STUDIO X/E. Grames-Bilderberg. 112tl: HOA QUI/P. De Wilde; tr: G. Chenuet; br: STUDIO X/T. Soriano-Bilderberg. 113tl: EXPLORER/J. Raga; mr: EXPLORER/E. Sampers; b: GAMMA/P. Gould 114-15 SYGMA/ D. Crane. 116tl: EXPLORER/D. Lefranc; bl: EXPLORER/D. Lefranc; tr: STILLS/Coll. A. Pelé. 117t: EXPLORER/D. Lefranc; br: C. Gassian. 118tl: STILLS/Pictorial; mr: STILLS/D. Redferns-Redferns; b: STILLS/Emerson-Onyx. 119tl, mr: STILLS/Gottlieb-Redferns; bl: STILLS/Letto; br: STILLS/Curtis-Omi. 120tl: SYGMA/F. Trapper; bl: ARCHIVE-PHOTO; br: SYGMA/*Titanic*, J. Cameron, 1998, UFD Twentieth Century Fox. 121tr: Coll. KIPA/*Citizen Kane*, O. Welles, 1941; ml: Coll. KIPA/*Easy Rider*, D. Hopper, 1969; mr: Coll. KIPA/ *Taxi Driver*, M. Scorsese, 1976; b: Coll. KIPA/*Dances with Wolves*, K. Costner, 1990. 122ml: ENGUERRAND/C. Masson-*Chorus Line* de M. Bennett, B. Avian, Lyrics de E. Kleban, Mus. M. Hamlish; tr: GAMMA LIAISON/F. Charles; b: ARCHIVE-PHOTOS/Everett. 123tr: STUDIO B/P. Berg-Black Star; m: GAMMA LIAISON; b: STUDIO B/F. Schnell-Black Star; br: GAMMA/U. Andersen. 124ml: G. DAGLI ORTI/Musée d'Orsay, Paris (*Summer Night*, 1890, W. Homer, 1836-1910); br: STUDIO B/N. Okamoto-Black Star. Museum of Art NY. 124-5t: EXPLORER/G. Boutin. National Gallery of Art, Washington. Arch. I.M.Pei, Pei Cobb Freed & Partners Architects LLP. 125 ml: G. DAGLI ORTI/Château de Blérancourt (*Indian Ball Games*, Catlin, 1794-1872); mr: G. DAGLI ORTI/Centre Pompidou (*The Electric Chair*, 1966, A. Warhol) Adagp, Paris 1998; b: G. DAGLI ORTI/Museum of Modern Art. Rome (*Watery Paths*, J. Pollock, 1947) Adagp, Paris 1998. 126-7 SYGMA. 128tr: SYGMA/ A. Koester; m: GAMMA LIAISON/M. Salaber; bl: GAMMA LIAISON/ Nasa. 128-9b: GAMMA LIAISON/Gifford. 129tr: GAMMA LIAISON/ Howell; m: GAMMA LIAISON/M. Brown. 130t: GAMMA LIAISON/ Markel; mr: STUDIO B/H. Kokojan-Black Star. 131tl: GAMMA LIAISON; tr: A.E.F./T.I.B./M. Loiseau. 132tr: A.E.F./T.I.B./P. Bolusset; bl: A.E.F./T.I.B./Dingo; mr: STUDIO B/Goro-Black Star. 133t: GAMMA LIAISON; b: A.E.F./T.I.B./A. Ernoult. 134ml: COCA-COLA France. 134-5: G. Chenuet. 135tr: GAMMA; mr: GAMMA/ N. Bers. 136tr: SYGMA/D. Giry; ml: GAMMA LIAISON; bl: GAMMA LIAISON/Mimouni. 137tr: GAMMA LIAISON/C. Schaefer; mt: LEVI'S. 138-9 ALTITUDE/S. Grandadam. 148t: GAMMA LIAISON/Giboux; b: HOA QUI/B. Naegelen. 154tl: STOCK IMAGE; tr: EXPLORER/A. Thomas; m: EXPLORER/E. Sampers; ml: EXPLORER/ F. Gohier; mr: O. Grunewald; b: HOA QUI/C. Sappa.

Printing and binding: Printer Industria Gráfica S.A., Barcelona
Colour Separations: Station Graphique, Ivry-sur-Seine
Paper: Perigord-Condat, France